EXPLORING
PSYCHOLOGY AND
CHRISTIAN FAITH

Exploring Psychology and Christian Faith

An Introductory Guide

Paul Moes and
Donald J. Tellinghuisen

B
Baker Academic
a division of Baker Publishing Group
Grand Rapids, Michigan

© 2014 by Paul Moes and Donald J. Tellinghuisen

Published by Baker Academic
a division of Baker Publishing Group
P.O. Box 6287, Grand Rapids, MI 49516-6287
www.bakeracademic.com

Printed in the United States of America

Library of Congress Cataloging-in-Publication Data is on file at the Library of Congress, Washington, DC.

ISBN 978-0-8010-4926-2

In keeping with biblical principles of creation stewardship, Baker Publishing Group advocates the responsible use of our natural resources. As a member of the Green Press Initiative, our company uses recycled paper when possible. The text paper of this book is composed in part of post-consumer waste.

14 15 16 17 18 19 20   7 6 5 4 3 2 1

This book is dedicated to our families,
and to all students exploring the reconciliation
of faith and psychology.

Contents

Five Themes of a Biblical View of Human Nature

The following five themes of how the Bible depicts humans serve as the backbone of this book, and will be referred to throughout as we explore the relationship between Christian faith and psychology's perspectives on persons. These themes are described more fully in chapter 1. The Bible shows humans to be:

1. **Relational persons:**
   We are made in the image of God, meant for relationship with him and meant to steward his creation.

2. **Broken, in need of redemption:**
   We are sinners in need of salvation through Christ, living in and part of creation that suffers the consequences of all humanity's sin.

3. **Embodied:**
   We bear God's image in real bodies in a real world.

4. **Responsible limited agents:**
   We make choices (within constraints) that result in actions for which we are both individually and corporately responsible.

5. **Meaning seekers:**
   We seek to make sense of our surroundings, our experience, and our purpose through perceiving patterns, creative meaning making, and desire for a deity.

Preface

There are many good books that integrate psychology and Christian faith—so why add one more? Many recent and very valuable books on this topic focus on important specialized topics, but most are not accessible to introductory students. We hope this book will become a useful companion to introductory psychology textbooks for students who are interested in the intersection of Christian faith and psychology.

Scientific psychology and religious faith differ in how they explain the nature of humans and their goals in doing so. However, they both carry assumptions about human nature. These assumptions, which are sometimes implicit and sometimes explicit, serve as the common threads that are woven throughout the chapters of this book. The questions raised about human nature in this book are not unique to Christians, since people from very diverse perspectives have sought to understand our basic nature. And while the principles provided to answer these questions are drawn from Christian theology, people from differing backgrounds will likely find agreement with at least some of these principles.

In chapter 1 of this book, we develop five themes about persons that we believe are evident throughout the pages of Scripture and that should resonate with many diverse Christian groups. While many of these themes appear to be compatible with a variety of approaches in psychology, conflicts also exist. Although there are no simple answers to the real or apparent conflicts between biblical assumptions and psychological theories, we attempt to help students critically analyze various theories from a biblical perspective. Through the remainder of this book we relate these themes to the many subfields in psychology in a structure similar to that of college-level introductory psychology textbooks. We have designed this book so that, after reading the introduction and chapter 1, the remaining chapters could be read in any order, allowing flexibility in studying topics as they come up in an introductory psychology course.

This thematic approach is perhaps another unique feature of this book. By relating many disparate findings within psychological science to common themes, we hope to develop a more cohesive Christian approach to the field. We are certainly not proposing any profound or completely new interpretations to the field of psychology, since many ideas presented in this book have been discussed in other writings. However, our hope is that by distilling many themes and findings into a more cohesive approach, we will provide a fresh way of examining past, present, and future ideas within psychology.

Readers who are familiar with faith and psychology integration issues will quickly notice that we have not included an extended discussion of the various models of integration outlined in other books and articles. While we value these ideas and have gained a great deal from these discussions, our experience as instructors of introductory psychology courses is that it can be difficult to appreciate the distinctions in these approaches when first encountering the discipline in its entirety. So we encourage instructors or individual students to engage the many excellent additional readings on integration models.[1] As for us, we find that we do not easily identify exclusively with one particular model. We can say that we do hold scientific methods in high regard and believe that Christians have an obligation to identify truth regardless of the source. We also hold steadfastly to the Truth of Scripture and the power of the Word to convict us of our need for, and way to, salvation. We also believe that Christians should, as Nicholas Wolterstorff has suggested, "develop theories in psychology which do comport with, or are consistent with, the belief-content of our authentic commitment. Only when the belief-content of the Christian scholar's authentic Christian commitment enters into his or her devising and weighing of psychological theories in this way can it be said that he or she is fully serious both as scholar and as Christian."[2]

---

1. Johnson (*Psychology and Christianity: Five Views*) provides an excellent overview of major models of integration.
2. Wolterstorff, *Reason within the Bounds of Religion*, 77.

Acknowledgments

This book would not have been possible without the incredibly helpful comments of our colleagues in the psychology department at Calvin College: John Brink, Laura DeHaan, Marjorie Gunnoe, Emily Helder, Blake Riek, Alan Shoemaker, Scott Stehouwer, Glenn Weaver, and Julie Yonker. Our departmental colleagues joined us in two intensive gatherings (sponsored by the Calvin Center for Christian Scholarship) where we all discussed the ideas of our book, reviewed chapter drafts, and discussed the broader topic of how to teach psychology's relationship to Christian faith. William Struthers and Scott VanderStoep joined one of these two-day discussions and also provided invaluable feedback on chapters. In addition, several other reviewers provided insight in shaping earlier drafts of specific chapters, including Laird Edman, Elizabeth Lewis Hall, Christopher Koch, and Angela Sabates. Thanks also to Cathy Parks for her work in editing footnotes and references.

We also thank the Calvin College Board of Trustees for funding sabbatical leaves for both of us and for the funding from the Calvin Center for Christian Scholarship. We also wish to thank our wives, Phyllis Moes and Becca Tellinghuisen, for supporting us through this project and for Becca's proofreading of earlier drafts.

Introduction

Why Did I Do That?

Chapter Summary: We all have questions about our own actions. This chapter introduces the basic questions that psychologists, persons of faith, and all of us ask about our everyday behavior. It also addresses the fundamental ideas that we have about human nature that influence how we answer questions about our own behavior.

> I have the desire to do what is good, but I cannot carry it out. For I do not do the good I want to do.
>
> Romans 7:18b–19a

> Psychology keeps trying to vindicate human nature. History keeps undermining the effort.
>
> Mason Cooley, *City Aphorisms*

> I also would not know how I am supposed to feel about many stories if not for the fact that the TV news personalities make sad faces for sad stories and happy faces for happy stories.
>
> Humorist Dave Barry, *Miami Herald*

Jasmine had no fear of flying, and she thought people who did were completely irrational. Then two events changed her attitude. The first involved flying through a terrible storm in a twenty-passenger jet. The storm was so violent that, even with her seat belt buckled, Jasmine hit her head on the ceiling several times. The second event was when Jasmine flew out of an airport where there had been a plane crash just a few weeks earlier. The national news had repeatedly shown horrific scenes of a DC-10 crashing in a ball of fire on this same runway. The wreckage of that aircraft was still visible to Jasmine as the plane ascended. She felt very anxious and uneasy the rest of that flight, and afterward she grew increasingly anxious about flying. At one point she considered taking a train on one of her trips to avoid flying. Even though she could identify the events that had changed her thoughts, she still wondered exactly why she couldn't just overcome these feelings. After all, she still felt that it was irrational to have a fear of flying. She was also a Christian and wondered why her faith had not sustained her more through these events—wasn't her trust in God enough to overcome these feelings?

Likely you have had similar questions about something you have done or felt, asking questions such as, Why did I do that? or Why do I keep doing that? You may recognize that the questions we ask about our own behavior or the behavior of others often have both psychological and religious overtones. That is because both psychology and religion have a lot to say about why we do what we do and about our basic human nature.

As Christian psychologists, our purpose for this book is to approach questions about human behavior from a biblical point of view and then apply the answers to issues addressed by contemporary psychology. Some people believe that this mixing of psychology with Christian faith or any other religion is not very useful or even possible. Their approach has religion and psychology operating in "parallel," with religion answering questions about the next life and morality, and psychology addressing scientific questions about everyday behavior.[1] Others feel that religion is of far greater importance in asking basic questions about human beings and feel that psychological science is of little value.[2] Still others value psychological explanations and feel that religious faith has little to say about our behavior.[3]

While difficult issues can arise when we try to relate a faith perspective to psychological science, we believe that a Christian worldview or faith perspective can and should inform our understanding of psychology. This approach is not simply about overruling psychological science with religious ideas whenever research findings appear to contradict religious teachings. Rather, we will

1. Carter and Narramore, *Integration of Psychology and Theology*, 91–101.
2. See Farber, *Unholy Madness*.
3. See Pinker, *Blank Slate*.

examine basic beliefs or assumptions about human nature and show how
these beliefs can influence a deeper understanding of research and practice
in psychology. Most psychologists rarely raise deep questions about human
nature in their research or practice, but they typically have unspoken assumptions about our "essence" and how this influences the way we act. In fact,
psychologist Noel Smith suggested that "psychology may be the sorriest of
all disciplines from the point of view of hidden biases"[4] because psychologists rarely state or even acknowledge their presuppositions. So religion and
psychology address different aspects of life and operate at different levels
of analysis, but both come with insights about the basic human condition
that sometimes contradict and other times show considerable agreement. For
example, religion and psychology include spoken and unspoken ideas about
whether we are basically good or evil, whether or not we can make free choices
and act responsibly, and how we relate to God (or some "cosmic" idea), to
one another, and to the natural world.[5]

To see how these basic assumptions might influence our explanations for
human behavior, consider this story. Ethan was a bright kid in elementary
school (e.g., creative, good in math) but he often ran out of time or lost
interest in his work. By fourth grade, his grades started to go down. Ethan
brought his work home but often forgot to take it out, and when he did get
assignments completed, they were often wrong because he didn't follow directions. His ability to tell funny but "inappropriate" jokes helped his popularity
with other students but also made him a regular in the principal's office. His
pediatrician diagnosed him as having ADHD (attention-deficit/hyperactivity
disorder) and prescribed medication to help with his attention. The school
psychologist set up a plan where the teacher gave specific rewards for positive
actions like finishing assignments on time and remaining in his seat at school,
and mild punishments (e.g., time-out) for misbehaviors like interrupting others when speaking. Ethan also received tutoring in reading, math, and homework completion. The medication, the behavior-improvement plan, and the
tutoring all helped, but he still struggled with social behavior and academic
issues. After more testing by the school psychologist, Ethan was diagnosed as
having a learning disability in addition to ADHD. The school social worker
interviewed his parents and discovered that Ethan's dad probably had some
of the same academic and emotional problems as a child.

Although these interventions helped Ethan improve in school, by the time
he was in high school he began to have more social difficulties. His circle of

---

4. Smith, *Current Systems in Psychology*, xiv.
5. See Jeeves, *Human Nature at the Millennium*, 156–57.

friends started to shrink, and he spent most of his free time playing video games. He seemed to lose interest in a variety of common activities. For example, he rarely went with his parents to their church, even though he said that he still believed basically the same things. His parents began having marital problems, and Ethan struggled emotionally following their divorce. A private counselor helped Ethan cope with his personal and social issues, but by the time he got out of high school, he continued to struggle with mild depression and eventually started abusing alcohol. Now in his late twenties, Ethan has become a relatively responsible person, with his alcohol-abuse problem under control and working at a full-time job. However, many aspects of his life continue to be a struggle for him. Looking forward, he wonders if the rest of his life will be such a struggle and if there might be something more for him than just holding down a job.

Many of you may find Ethan's circumstances familiar, either because you know someone like Ethan or you yourself have experienced some of these difficulties. You probably have your own ideas about why Ethan has problems, but let's consider some common explanations that friends, family, and professionals may suggest (key thoughts are emphasized). You may find yourself agreeing with at least some of these explanations.

1. Shawna, a friend of Ethan's family, feels that Ethan did not need medication or therapy. She believes Ethan was a spoiled only child and that his parents should have disciplined him more. He is just *making bad choices* and it is time to grow up and *take on adult responsibility*. Shawna also feels that this is a good example of *"the apple not falling far from the tree"* since Ethan's dad had similar issues. Finally, and most importantly, Shawna feels that the main issue in anyone's life is the *condition of their heart and soul*. If Ethan's family had more faithfully given their problems over to Jesus through prayer, working on their spiritual lives instead of spending a lot of time and money on counselors and doctors, they would have all been a lot better off.

2. Ethan's counselor feels that Ethan's problems are the result of him having *low self-esteem*. He never learned to *accept himself* because other people set expectations that were impossible to meet. Deep down *he is a good person* just waiting to come out—all he needs is more love and acceptance. Ethan has also struggled to find some greater meaning for his life, so he lacks direction and drifts from one problem to another. While the main cause lies with how other people treated him, only he can *freely choose* to be the person he would like to be in the future.

3. The school psychologist believes Ethan is *neither good nor bad* (deep down); his *brain just works differently* than other people. This problem

was likely *passed on genetically* from his dad. His *environment* is also part of the problem because he has received a lot of "rewards" from others for misbehaving (e.g., attention for his inappropriate jokes), which leads to more misbehavior in the future. He needs to *take his medication*; receive better "*feedback*" (e.g., rewards and punishments) from family, friends, and professionals; and practice better (e.g., more logical) *thinking patterns*.

4. The social worker believes the problems result from a *bad social environment and damaged relationships*. Ethan *can't be blamed entirely for his problems*; his problems are the result of the way the whole *social "system"* works (or doesn't work). It's obvious from his parents' divorce and his lack of friends that *his relationships had become "toxic."* In other words, each person in the situation was fine individually, but the relationships themselves had become distorted.

5. Ethan's friend Ryan (who recently took two psychology classes) thinks that Ethan is *unconsciously driven to satisfy his instinctive motives that we all inherit*. This is not an immoral tendency, but it does mean that Ethan *ultimately cares more about himself than about others*. However, because social and moral rules conflict with these motivations, he has become anxious and "conflicted." This conflict just "comes to the surface" without his awareness and results in troubled behavior. He needs to dig deep inside himself to find all the inner demons and release them by just letting it all out and cleansing himself from all these unconscious influences *that determine his actions*.

Take a minute to ask yourself how you would explain Ethan's problems. Do you think that one of these five responses, some combination of them, or something completely different accounts for Ethan's difficulties?

If you are familiar with the field of psychology, you may recognize that some of these ideas match various psychological theories. Your choice for the best theories or explanations of human behavior may depend on research evidence, but it is also likely to be influenced by the way you view human nature. Most of us, including most psychologists, don't talk very often about the essence of human nature, but these ideas often operate at an implicit level. In other words, we have beliefs that we act on, but we often don't realize that we have the belief in the first place (i.e., the beliefs are unconscious). In other cases we "sort of know" that we believe something, but we rarely give it much thought, and we are not sure why we believe this. Sometimes we may actually hold two beliefs that are exact opposites, but we don't notice that we use both beliefs—at different times of course. For example, Shawna believes that Ethan is very much responsible for his actions, yet she also attributes his problems to his dad (i.e., "the apple doesn't fall far from the tree").

Let's examine the explanations given about Ethan's behavior to get a better idea of what this looks like. If you focus on the italicized phrases in the explanations given above, you may notice a set of themes, dilemmas, or questions that arise. While we present these as opposing views, keep in mind that they represent a continuum of beliefs for most people, where their beliefs fall on neither one extreme nor the other. We believe the dilemmas can be summarized this way:

Dilemma 1: Are we complete as individuals, or are we dependent on others? This may be one of the least common questions that we ponder, but it still influences how we think about people. The individualistic view stresses that each person is a unique personality and that each person is individually accountable and responsible for his or her actions. On the other side of the coin, being dependent on others suggests that we are not simply individuals acting in the world but that we are defined relationally, as part of a social "system," and are embedded in community or cultures.

Dilemma 2: Are we good or bad? We all have implicit ideas about whether people are basically good (i.e., deep down they desire to do the right thing—whatever that is), basically bad (i.e., mostly interested in themselves and not really caring too much about others), or essentially neutral (i.e., not really self-centered or caring—just trying to get by).

Dilemma 3: Are we simply part of the natural world, or are we something more? The vast majority of people in the world believe that our mind—and perhaps a related thing, our soul—is what makes us a human beings. Most often this mind or soul is thought of as a separate "thing" from the physical body—and that it is the thing that ultimately controls our behavior. Others believe that human beings are nothing but highly "intelligent animals," shaped by their physical and social experiences.[6]

Dilemma 4: Do we have free will (and responsibility) or are we determined? Determinism suggests that many different forces could act on us to create who we are and what we do.[7] Some combination of genetics, brain function, evolution, the social environment, the physical environment, and/or our unconscious minds could all destine us to think or behave in certain ways. The "free will" idea suggests that we can freely choose

6. Crick, *Astonishing Hypothesis*, 4.
7. Farnsworth, *Whole-Hearted Integration*, 86–88.

our own destiny and set our own path in spite of the internal or external forces that act on us.

Dilemma 5: Are we motivated by survival, or do we seek something higher? Most people will certainly acknowledge that we are motivated to survive, but is that the only motivation we have? Some psychologists believe that we are products of our genes, our environment, and our learned patterns, so we are simply responding to the conditions that we experience and nothing more.[8] Others believe that we are also motivated to find meaning at a basic level (i.e., to explain why things happen) and at a deeper level (i.e., to find a bigger purpose or deeper meaning).[9]

Most of us tend to be somewhere in between these competing positions, or we alternate at times between various views. However, going back to the various responses to Ethan's problems, if you emphasize our individuality over our relationality and believe that people are more evil than good, you are likely to agree more with Shawna and Ryan, who both stress Ethan's individual responsibility and his tendency to be self-centered. If you emphasize group membership, believe that people are basically good, stress "free will," and feel that we are motivated to find meaning, then you might agree more with the counselor and social worker, who stress these aspects of human nature. If you feel that people are basically neutral (i.e., neither good nor bad), stress our physical existence, and believe that humans are only motivated for survival, then you might agree more with the school psychologist, who believes that Ethan is just responding to his genetic inheritance and his environment.

Of course, it's possible to agree with the school psychologist or any other response without accepting all of the underlying ideas about human nature. You may feel that one approach is good simply because it offers a practical solution, or you only partially agree with some of the basic perspectives. However, the main point is still that our views of human nature push us to favor certain approaches more than others.

So hopefully you can see that everyone has views about human nature, determinism, the mind, individuality, and so on. All introductory psychology textbooks proclaim that psychology is an "empirical" (i.e., observational) science—and indeed it is. But because the subject matter is human behavior, we can also see a lot of philosophies, worldviews, and personal interpretations influencing the larger theory. Sometimes these worldviews are implicit

8. Crick, *Astonishing Hypothesis*, 3–12.
9. Smith, *Current Systems in Psychology*, 113–44.

and well below the surface; other times they are very explicit and promoted strongly. Either way, it's hard to be completely neutral in psychology given that psychologists make statements about human behavior that cut to the core of who we are.

Most major religions and many philosophical movements also address or have ideas about these fundamental questions.[10] This is why we believe that the best starting point to understand how faith relates to something like psychology—or even to everyday life—is to focus on these fundamental questions. Some Christians in psychology focus on interesting applications of faith to practice, but we feel that in order for Christians to start addressing questions of psychology, foundational questions need to be addressed first. For example, over the years Christian therapists have addressed interesting questions related to the Holy Spirit in therapy, therapy as evangelism, the use of prayer in therapy, and so on.[11] These are certainly interesting and important questions, but we feel that we should first answer questions like, To what extent does a faith perspective promote a more individualistic or relational view? or If we use a scientific approach to studying human beings, does that mean that we necessarily accept the notion of determinism? Addressing these questions of human nature first allows us to build a foundation for answering practical issues as we move to applications and practice.

In chapter 1, we articulate basic biblical principles of human nature that address the dilemmas posed in this chapter. These principles do not settle all questions in psychology or explain completely why people do what they do, but they can guide us in grappling with complex theories and research in psychology and life. The remaining chapters in this book expand on these principles and are an attempt to apply them to many of the specialty areas in the study of human behavior.

======================== DISCUSSION QUESTIONS ========================

1. If you are familiar with various movements or schools of thought in psychology (i.e., psychoanalytic, behavioristic, humanistic, cognitive), can you match these ideas with the explanations given by: number 2 (counselor), number 3 (school psychologist), and number 5 (friend Ryan)?

10. See discussion in Miller and Delaney, *Judeo-Christian Perspectives on Psychology.*
11. For examples, see McLemore and Brokaw, "Psychotherapy as a Spiritual Enterprise," 178–95.

2. Do you think that psychology can be, or should be, a science?

3. Do you agree that religious faith should be used in understanding questions in psychological science? What are some of the dangers or benefits to psychology of trying to relate these areas? What are some of the dangers or benefits to religion?

Who Am I?

Themes of Human Nature

Chapter Summary: This chapter describes major themes that address the basic questions and dilemmas raised in the introduction. We have based these themes on scriptural principles about human nature that are relevant for addressing pressing issues in psychology. In the remaining chapters in this book we seek to apply each of these themes to various areas of study within the field of psychology. Our approach with this chapter is to assume that doing psychology from a Christian perspective requires that we start with a biblical foundation to answer the question, Who am I?

> What is mankind that you are mindful of them,
>   human beings that you care for them?
> You have made them a little lower than the angels
>   and crowned them with glory and honor.
> You made them rulers over the works of your hands;
>   you put everything under their feet.
>
> Psalm 8:4 6

If you're a college student, you are used to being asked, Where do you go to school? or What's your major? These questions are attempts to get a sense of your identity—who you are and who you want to be.[1] While these are common questions, it's interesting that the Bible focuses on who *God* thinks you are rather than who *you* or *other people* think you are. Starting with the first words of Scripture, "In the beginning, God created,"[2] we can see that the Bible describes humans as *creatures*, made "in his own image." Through the early chapters of Genesis, we can also see that humans are called to bear God's image by acting on his behalf and being his agents in the world he made.

Although the Bible says we are creatures, humans have a unique status in God's creation and are placed into a unique relationship with him. The quotation from Psalm 8 opening this chapter asks and answers why God cares so much for us. While Psalm 8 makes obvious that we're not God, nevertheless God "cares for" and is "mindful of" us. We are "crowned" with "glory and honor." So we are creatures, but creatures with whom God chooses to have a particular relationship. In addition, humans have unique work to do as responsible "rulers" over God's creation.

The introduction to this book presented many of the dilemmas we face when trying to explain behavior. Various psychological theories, religions, and worldviews provide different answers to these questions, so we believe persons of faith need to start by exploring basic themes about human nature found in Scripture. While even Christians do not agree completely on how to understand these basic themes, there are consistent principles about our nature and our condition that can help us address many of our dilemmas.

Throughout the rest of this book, we will come back to these themes to explore the relationship between Christian faith and psychology's perspectives on persons, including addressing the basic dilemmas outlined in the introduction. These themes suggest that humans are (1) relational persons; (2) broken, in need of redemption; (3) embodied; (4) responsible limited agents (our free will is limited); and (5) meaning seekers. While not every aspect of human nature is captured by these five themes, they cover many of the key aspects of human nature that are relevant to psychology. Keep in mind that each of these characteristics is distinct, but they are also interrelated, as we will discuss later. The remainder of this chapter is devoted to describing these five characteristics with brief discussions of how each is addressed in psychology. The rest of the book explores in greater depth how these characteristics are addressed in the major topic areas of psychology.

1. Kroger, *Identity Development*, 34.
2. Gen. 1:26.

Theme 1: Humans Are Relational Persons

While Scripture clearly speaks of our individual nature, uniqueness, and responsibilities, it also makes clear that we cannot be understood apart from our relationships. In the book of Genesis, God says, "Let us make mankind in our image, in our likeness. . . . It is not good for the man to be alone. I will make a helper suitable for him."[3] The phrase, "Let us make mankind in our image" reveals the relationality within the very nature of God. God's essence is relational, shown in the interrelatedness of the Father, Son, and Holy Spirit. That quality has also been imprinted on humans. God extends this relatedness to humans as seen in the Genesis story. God created Eve for Adam because "it is not good for the man to be alone." In addition, just as God creates things, humans are called to the task of being fruitful and caring for God's handiwork.[4] Humanity has creative work to do within and as a part of creation. As one theologian puts it, humanity is tasked by God to be his "authorized representatives on earth,"[5] bearing God's image as a collection of people, not just individually. Humans were given God's approval to do the work God intended to be done on earth, as the crown of creation. In so doing, humans would have a thoroughly interrelated existence with God and others (Adam with Eve, and all who would follow).

Being made in God's image has traditionally implied that we are made for at least three kinds of relationships.[6] These relationships are described by Christian psychologists David Myers and Malcolm Jeeves, who write, "The biblical account is a God-centered view and is preoccupied with relationships—first and foremost the relationship of God to humanity, but also of person to person, and of humankind to the created order, of which it is both a part and a steward."[7] Let's explore the implications of each of these three relationships.

First, we are made to be in relationship with God, not as equals but dependent on God as his treasured creation. God made us for himself, out of his love and for his glory, to be in fellowship with him.[8] Our very existence depends on God's ongoing activity.[9] As theologian Philip Hefner states, "God does not

---

3. Gen. 1:26; 2:18.
4. Gen. 1:28.
5. Middleton, *Liberating Image*, 289.
6. Hoekema, *Created in God's Image*, 81; Roberts, "Christian Psychology," 77.
7. Myers and Jeeves, *Psychology through the Eyes of Faith*, 33.
8. Isa. 43:7.
9. See Heb. 1:3. This is a notion strongly held in Christian theologies, including the *Catechism of the Catholic Church*, part 1, sec. 2, chap. 1, art. 1, par. 4.5.302 (http://www.vatican .va/archive/ccc_css/archive/catechism/p1s2c1p4.htm) and by Protestants, such as the Lutheran Philip Hefner (see his "Imago Dei").

deal with us only impersonally through deterministic processes, or treat us as things, but rather carriers on a history with us."[10]

Second, rather than focusing on individual differences between persons, the Bible strongly emphasizes that humans are part of something much larger—the human family[11]—and, for Christians, the body of Christ, which is the church.[12] This church is much bigger than an individual congregation, as it includes all Christians, both now and throughout all history—the "holy catholic" ("universal") church.[13]

The apostle Paul uses the analogy of a body to describe how Christians are to live and work within creation: "Just as a body, though one, has many parts, but all its many parts form one body, so it is with Christ."[14] He goes on to say that one part of the body cannot live without the other parts. Being just a head or just a foot is useless. Paul implies that our fundamental relationality leaves us unable to go it alone. Those parts need to work together, and when they do, the body of Christ (the church) can function as it was meant to do. Being in relationship with each other as well as with God is fundamental to being a full person—what theologians and Christian psychologists call *personhood*.[15] The Christian position is that fully being what God intended for each human to be only comes in the context of the body of Christ where we collectively bear God's image and fully love each other in each other's personal uniqueness.[16]

The Bible, chronicling the interactions between God and his people, also shows that God's relationship with humans is both personal and communal. There are times in Scripture when God blesses families, tribes, or nations. For example, God establishes a promise or covenant with Abraham *and* all of his descendants, to make them a "great nation."[17] God says of that group, which later becomes known as Israel, "all peoples on earth will be blessed through

10. Hefner, "Imago Dei," 86.
11. Gen. 5:1.
12. By "the church" here, we are not referring to just the nearest one down the street or even particular denominations or branches such as Protestant, Catholic, or Eastern Orthodox.
13. Note that "catholic" is not capitalized as it refers to being universal. This notion goes back to ancient statements of faith such as the Apostles' Creed written in the first centuries of Christianity (and can be found here: http://www.ccel.org/creeds/apostles.creed.html). There is a very similar line in the Nicene Creed, which is used by Catholics, Protestants, Anglicans, and Eastern Orthodox churches (and can be found here: http://www.ccel.org/creeds/nicene.creed .html). Given the conflicts that happen among Christians, it may seem impossible that this is a "group," but through God's Holy Spirit, the church is a fellowship that extends through time and across the diversity of races and countries.
14. 1 Cor. 12:12.
15. Hefner, "Imago Dei," 71.
16. Yannaras, *Freedom of Morality*, 23.
17. Gen. 12:2.

you."[18] There are also times when people are condemned as groups or nations. In the case of Israel once again, the prophet Ezekiel proclaims, "Now this was the sin of your sister Sodom: She and her daughters were arrogant, overfed and unconcerned; they did not help the poor and needy."[19] Although the city of Sodom may be most associated with its sexual sins,[20] it is the collective indifference to the poor and needy that is condemned here. Likewise in the New Testament, members of the early church are treated as a unified body. Even though the apostle Paul names specific persons when writing to the churches,[21] his letters are addressed to groups of Christians: he praises the Philippians as a group (e.g., "I thank my God every time I remember you")[22] and condemns the Corinthian church as a group (e.g., "Brothers and sisters, I could not address you as people who live by the Spirit").[23] God calls out particular persons to fill specific roles, but God's interactions with humans emphasize the fundamental interrelatedness of humanity.

The third core relationship implies that just as God created and sustains the creation, people are also to be creative and care for creation.[24] Humans are created creatures with a particular role to rule over creation as creative caretakers, which includes each person as well as the environment. This caretaking includes our development of science and social institutions that allow us to better care for each other and the world. To sum up, being made in God's image "represents God as commanding us to love him with all our heart, our neighbor as ourselves, and to be faithful stewards of the creation."[25]

Relationality and Psychology

Relationality is also a central topic of psychology. Ethan from the introduction to this book is in a series of relationships with others, including friends and family, and all of these relationships doubtless influence him as he has influenced them. Many areas of psychology explore how we interact with, influence, and are influenced by our environment (people as well as things). The way we learn from others, the ways our brain recognizes another person's face, why we laugh, and why individuals suffering from anxiety may fear others all reveal an interest in relationships. The biblical emphasis on relationships is

18. Gen. 12:3.
19. Ezek. 16:49.
20. Sodom is the basis of the word sodomy.
21. Paul pleads with Euodia and Syntyche to agree with each other in the Lord in Phil. 4:2.
22. Phil. 1:3.
23. 1 Cor. 3:1.
24. Gen. 1:28.
25. Roberts, "Christian Psychology," 77.

very compatible with many ideas and research findings in psychology. There are, however, at least two emphases of relationality that differ between psychology and the Bible. First, by allowing only natural explanations of behavior (supernatural explanations are not allowed in science), psychology does not directly study how God relates to people. Psychologists sometimes study religious behaviors and thoughts of people, but they do not explore the behaviors and thoughts of God toward us. Second, psychology places a great deal of emphasis on a type of relationality barely mentioned in the Bible: relationship to oneself. The fact that the Bible says little about how we relate to ourselves may surprise you—it surprised us when we were doing our research for this book. Terms like *self-concept* and *self-esteem* are common in psychology, and therapy emphasizes self-awareness and self-fulfillment. The Bible seems far less concerned about these notions than is psychology, and although some think the phrase "know thyself" is found in the Bible, it's not.[26]

Despite an increased emphasis on relationality in recent years, research has shown that psychological science that has come out of Western cultures has tended to emphasize individuality over relationality.[27] The Bible, however, encourages us to recognize that people cannot be understood outside of the context of their relationships. As one theologian remarked, "If an individual has no relationships, then he also has no characteristics and no name. He is unrecognizable, and does not even know himself."[28] Does this Christian emphasis on interrelatedness have any impact on how one approaches psychology? Knowing that we hold a unique place within creation as collective image bearers of God might influence how we study group behavior, worker motivation, gender differences, and how to conduct therapy—to name just a few.

Theme 2: Humans Are Broken, in Need of Redemption

God designed us to thrive in the three core relationships we just described.[29] God calls his people to (1) love him, (2) love their neighbors as themselves,[30] and (3) lovingly care for creation.[31] Those are the right plans to most successfully live out the image of God. What would it look like if humans lived out God's image in God-intended relationships (as described above), living the

26. One place it appears is in Shakespeare's *Hamlet*.
27. Nisbett et al. "Culture and Systems of Thought," 307.
28. Jürgen Moltmann, cited in Brown, "Conclusion," 225.
29. James 4:7.
30. Lev. 19:18.
31. Gen. 1:28.

Eden of Genesis 1 and 2? Every day would involve a guilt-free, harmonious relationship with God and people, tending God's flawless creation, totally at peace with each other, creation, and God. Our situation would still merit the designation given at the end of the Genesis 1 creation narrative: "God saw all that he had made, and it was very good."[32]

Of course, that's not our situation. We live in a world of war, selfishness, and disease. Why? Christian theology and the Bible teach that rather than trusting God's plan, humans chose instead to trust their own. Putting *our* will and *our* plans before God's is the essence of *sin*. God created us, but we rebelled against our "creaturehood" and our Creator, declaring ourselves the "creators" of our own lives, choosing self-determination instead of living in creaturely obedience as God's representatives on earth. This rebellion is known as the fall—humanity going from its state of goodness and obedience to one of disobedience. God called humanity to be in relationship (communion) with him. In the fall, rather than embracing personhood (creatures fully in relationship with God and others), we chose an individuality that creates a gulf between God and each person. As one Greek Orthodox Christian writer puts it, "From the moment when the human person rejects this call and this communion in which he himself is grounded . . . he becomes alienated from himself."[33] Theologian Miroslav Volf writes that humans "affirm themselves in contrast to others (other human beings, other creatures, and God), necessarily creating distance between themselves and all others."[34] As a result of this fallenness, "The natural needs of the individual being, such as nourishment, self-perpetuation and self-preservation, become an end in themselves."[35] We lose the deep, relational interconnections of "God, humans, and all creation in justice, fulfillment, and delight"[36] mentioned by theologian Cornelius Plantinga and instead focus on ourselves and fulfilling our immediate needs. In our sinfulness we try to go it alone, and we are not up to the task. Because of sin, "we live anxiously, restlessly, always trying to secure and extend ourselves with finite goods that can't take the weight we put on them."[37]

The pervasiveness of sin is absolute: everyone sins—everyone gives priority to someone or something other than God. "If we claim to be without sin, we deceive ourselves," says 1 John 1:8. Even really "good" people do some bad

---

32. Gen. 1:31.
33. Yannaras, *Freedom of Morality*, 30.
34. Volf, *After Our Likeness*, 81.
35. Yannaras, *Freedom of Morality*, 31.
36. Plantinga, *Not the Way*, 10.
37. Ibid., 61.

things.[38] Sinfulness shows up in external behavior but also in internal thoughts; while one may not steal, one may envy. The Bible states that the only sinless person—the only one not totally self-centered—was Jesus Christ.

Sin's cumulative consequences, however, are even larger than the fallout of individual choices and attitudes. Sin not only affects each person's life but also the lives of others and the lives of people in the future,[39] so that sin leaves us in a creation that is "not the way it's supposed to be," as Plantinga writes in his book of the same title.[40] Plantinga writes that sin is "a polluted river that keeps branching and rebranching into tributaries," a parasite that keeps tapping its host (humans and all of creation) for survival, and "breaks down great institutions and whole societies."[41] Roman Catholic theology similarly concludes that the fruit of sins in social structures and relationships can affect people,[42] as "every sin has repercussions on . . . the whole human family."[43]

The outcome of this tendency has been nothing short of disastrous. The self-focus of people in the past, whether for personal gain, emotional power, or a host of other desires, has damaged relationships. The child of a convicted felon suffers from the parent's crime by being without that parent. But the troubles are deeper: society's inequalities impact becoming a criminal. But the troubles are also wider: greed brings wars fought for money and prestige, with countries pillaged of goods and natural resources, leaving lasting animosities that pave the way for future wars. In a sin-free world, desires to follow God would be pure; in a sinful world, things get pretty messed up. The result of being in a sinful world—even if we ourselves could live righteous lives—is to distort our relationships and thereby distort how we think (more on this later). Each of us has suffered the consequences of being in a world with sin.

Although we are damaged by sin and live in a broken, fallen world, the relational core of the image of God is still there. The good news of the *gospel* is that the story does not end with our sin. God has provided a way out of this mess through the death and resurrection of God's Son, Jesus Christ.

38. Some examples: David, God's chosen king of Israel killed out of lust in 2 Sam.; Moses, God's chosen leader to free the Israelites from Egyptian slavery, did not reach the Promised Land due to his own disobedience as described in Num. 20; the apostle Paul when talking about sinners described himself as "the worst" in 1 Tim. 1:15.

39. Sins can affect future generations. In Exod. 20:5 (part of the Ten Commandments), worshiping other gods in place of God is unfaithfulness toward God, and this results in breaking the covenant with God. If a father rejects God's promises and takes his family into sin, the children will suffer the consequences.

40. Plantinga, *Not the Way*.

41. Ibid., 55.

42. Catholic Church, *Catechism of the Catholic Church*, 103.

43. Catholic Church, *Reconciliation and Penance*, 52.

Although our current condition is one of brokenness in sin, it is not one of hopelessness. Romans 3:23–24 clearly indicates that "all have sinned and fall short of the glory of God, and all are justified freely by his grace through the redemption that came by Christ Jesus." As C. Stephen Evans wrote, it is God who "created us in his image, who sorrowfully allowed us to reject him and break fellowship, and who sacrificially became one of us and suffered the effects of our rebellion so as to bring about a triumphant reconciliation."[44] The relationship with God is made right for people who accept Christ's death on their behalf. This is *salvation*, and the Bible says that everyone is in need of it. All of creation is also damaged and in need of renewal.

Despite this gracious reconciliation, sin's consequences remain in creation— it is still "not the way it's supposed to be." On a personal level, old habits die hard and better ones are not always easily acquired. On a community level, structural sin infects all of the institutions and groups of which people are a part. God desires better of us and for us than continuing to sin; he wants us to lead more Christlike lives. For the Christian, becoming Christlike is a lifelong process—a process typically called *sanctification*. As Paul writes, a "good work" was begun in believers by God, and that will be carried on "to completion until the day of Christ Jesus"[45]—that is, when Christ returns. Writing to Christians, the writer of Hebrews encouraged fellow believers to "run with perseverance the race marked out for us"[46] and to battle against sinful desires, making "every effort to live in peace with everyone and to be holy."[47]

God calls his people back to the task of transforming all of his creation by being God's representatives. Christians begin this by taking on Christian virtues and behaviors,[48] as part of the body of believers (the church). We are not alone in this: God has given believers the guidance and help of the Holy Spirit.[49] The earthly life of the Christian is one of long-term transformation by God, not instantaneous change. The task does not end with personal transformation, nor does it stop with individual action, but continues with collective efforts to restore justice, love mercy, and transform a broken society.

Can we really do this? Even those who claim Christ and live by the power of the Holy Spirit still struggle with sin, being part of a broken creation. And what of those who don't claim Christ's goodness but still do "good" things?

44. Evans, "Concept of the Self," 4.
45. Phil. 1:6.
46. Heb. 12:1.
47. Heb. 12:14.
48. Col. 3:12–13.
49. Rom. 8.

Humans cannot bring about their own salvation, despite actions that they do that may be very helpful to others. As we said above, salvation is a gift from God that cannot be earned by human efforts.

Human Brokenness and Psychology

What does all of this talk of sin and salvation have to do with psychology? Biblical truths about sin profoundly influence how Christians think about a host of issues such as how predictable we are; how we perceive, learn, and think; how our personalities are formed; how we relate to others around us; and even how we conduct therapy. Human brokenness brings in some tricky questions about human behavior. For example, when children misbehave at age three and then gradually learn to be more obedient, is this sin followed by sanctification, or is it normal learning? Does Ethan—as described in the introduction—simply need to pray more and be more devout, as family friend Shawna suggests, or are his problems the result of genetics and environment? Pressing the issue even deeper, is sin an "extra ingredient" added to the source of his problems, or is sin woven into the fabric of his relationships, his mental processes, or even his physical being?

To be perfectly honest, as Christian psychologists we have struggled to understand how our sinful tendencies are to be understood in the context of psychological theories, and so we do not have simple answers for these complex questions. However, we are fairly certain that those psychological approaches that strongly emphasize ultimate human goodness or complete neutrality of human nature are going to fall short when trying to provide a comprehensive explanation of human behavior. We will provide specific examples of these shortcomings in many of the chapters that follow.

Theme 3: Humans Are Embodied

If you were an alien visiting Earth for the first time, perhaps the most obvious thing to notice about humans (perhaps more obvious than our relationality or sinfulness) is that we have physical substance that we use to interact with other physical substances. We are *embodied*. Scripture uses many words and ideas to describe body, mind, soul, and spirit—but how do we put all this together as "me"? Whatever the meaning of these terms, the Bible clearly confirms that our physical being is a central characteristic of who we are—and perhaps much more important than contemporary Christians have generally assumed. Genesis says that God breathed life into dust, and Adam became a living, physical being.[50] All of our relationships have a physical dimension. Like Jesus, we live in a physical world and interact with it physically: we touch, change our gaze to look someone in the eye, or even throw things when we're angry.[51] People physically interact with God—kneeling to pray or audibly speaking praise, just as Christ did.[52] Physical existence impacts our way of interacting, making our relationality shaped by being embodied. A comforting touch is pleasing, while a harsh look hurts. We are made in God's image and have a unique relationship with him, so we occupy a special place in his creation, yet we are made from the "dust of the earth"[53] and have much in common with the rest of creation (e.g., hunger, pain, emotions, etc.). God created us to be physical in order to care for a physical creation—to tend the garden.

The Bible teaches that some physical activities may bring people closer to God (e.g., prayer, giving food to the hungry), while other activities may widen the gulf between people and God (e.g., withholding care for others, failing to offer God what is his).[54] In the Lord's Supper (or Eucharist or Communion, depending on church tradition), believers physically eat and drink as Christ commanded his disciples,[55] and Christ said that by doing so, one "remains in me, and I in them."[56] There appear to be important spiritual consequences of physical behavior, in addition to the more obvious physical outcomes. Many of Jesus's interactions were with people who were born with physical disabilities like blindness[57] or who had contracted diseases like leprosy.[58] And of course people in the Bible became old, suffered illness, and died—just as we do.

Human Embodiment and Psychology

Psychology has increasingly emphasized the physical, including how our physiology changes in response to the environment and what our brain does when we experience thought. A growing body of research examines our most

50. Gen. 2:7.
51. Just a few examples: Jesus touched to heal people (e.g., Matt. 8), he looked at his disciples to address them (e.g., Mark 10), and he threw over the tables of money changers in the temple (e.g., Matt. 21).
52. Jesus fell to the ground in prayer, for example, in Mark 14; he spoke thanks to God, for example, in John 6.
53. Gen. 2:7.
54. James 2:15–17 shows the interrelationship between physical behavior and faith: "Suppose a brother or sister is without clothes and daily food. If one of you says to them 'Go in peace; keep warm and well fed,' but does nothing about their physical needs, what good is it? In the same way, faith by itself, if it is not accompanied by action, is dead."
55. John 6.
56. John 6:56.
57. E.g., John 9:1.
58. E.g., Mark 1:40.

intimate thoughts within the working brain and explores how hormones and other bodily functions influence our everyday behaviors. Obviously, embodiment raises some interesting questions about how humans function.

For example, can we overcome our physical existence or mental problems by using some nonphysical part of us? Is it even possible or necessary to talk about body, mind, and soul given that research shows that our thoughts are tied to brain function? Can God actually work through physical mechanisms by altering brain activity when we relate to him?

These deep questions will be addressed in chapters 3 and 4, but what we can say at this point is that Christians need to affirm that our "earthly" and "creaturely" nature appears to be both scriptural and very consistent with contemporary understanding of human beings. Christians can also be a prophetic voice in the field of psychology by stressing that, despite our physical nature, we are more than the sum of our physical parts.

Theme 4: Humans Are Responsible Limited Agents

While theology is sometimes as conflicted as psychology on the issue of agency, people of faith generally understand that while we are limited by our physical nature, our social environment, and even God's sovereign plans, Scripture is clear that we are endowed with the ability to make choices and to act responsibly. Adam and Eve chose to rebel against God, and they were held accountable for that choice. The Bible clearly teaches that humans have choice, but our choices are far more limited than most of us like to admit. We have *agency*, meaning the ability to act as agents in the world, which involves the ability to choose, but it is *limited*.

Responsibility implies that a person has some degree of choice in their behavior, so responsibility and agency are intertwined. The ability to choose, however, does not always imply responsibility. Being *responsible* means being accountable relative to someone else. Responsibility outside of the context of a relationship makes no sense. A mother will feel more responsible for her children than for the children of a stranger. If you betray a friend's trust, you feel responsible for rectifying that situation with that person but not with someone else. In the biblical view of persons, humans are in relationship with all others as well as God and creation.[59]

59. Many passages in the Old Testament tell God's people how to care for foreigners (nonbelievers in God) who are among them (e.g., Exod. 22:21, "Do not mistreat or oppress a foreigner, for you were foreigners in Egypt"). Jesus in Matt. 25 calls people to care for people who are sick, thirsty, in prison, or without clothes.

Having agency implies not only that we make choices but also that we can change ourselves in some way. The Bible has countless stories of people changing. Change can be a gradual, lifelong process, as in the disciple Peter's life in the New Testament. Sometimes changes occur due to God's sudden and direct intervention (like the apostle Paul's experience); other times, changes happen through deliberate choices people make ("choose for yourselves this day whom you will serve. . . . As for me and my household, we will serve the LORD"[60]).

But there are also limitations on how much we are able to change since we exist in a particular time and place. For the Israelites, as much as they might have wished to be free of Roman rule at the time of Christ, there wasn't much they could do about it. When the apostle Paul and his gospel coworker Silas were in prison for preaching in Acts 16, their choices were definitely limited.

Our embodiment limits us, but our limitations are not just in terms of external forces like physical space and time. In Romans 6, Paul emphasizes that we live life as slaves—not a slavery involving physical chains but a slavery of the mind and behavior. As philosopher Robert C. Roberts[61] has noted, Paul emphasizes that we can be slaves of sin or slaves of righteousness. What did Paul mean by being a "slave"? Slavery is the polar opposite of freedom. If someone were a slave of righteousness, for example, some "choices" may not even come to mind or might be so offensive that one never pursues them. A fundamental idea of Christianity is that God is at work in people who put their faith in him, conforming them more fully to himself—becoming more and more like Christ. Conversely, slavery to sin means that righteousness is not our default behavior. One's moral character, often developed through habits, further limits thoughts and behavior. Our past choices set us in directions that dictate present and future consequences. This means not that we have no free choice but that when we make choices we are set on a path. This new path then necessarily limits other alternatives, as life is only lived once. So either righteousness or sinfulness limits our freedom because we are fundamentally limited by our earlier choices.

In addition to our embodiment and past choices, we are limited by our social groups. Of course individual accountability is still important. In criminal cases in the United States, even when multiple people are involved in a crime, defendants are judged separately to determine the amount of blame each person deserves. In the Bible, personal responsibility is also apparent; the lies of Ananias and Sapphira in Acts 5 about the money they were giving to the church resulted in each of them dying in turn after telling their lie.

60. Josh. 24:15.
61. Roberts, "Christian Psychology," 82.

But we are relational persons, and to focus on individual responsibility alone would be to miss the Bible's bigger-picture view of what it means to be human. As described earlier, groups in the Old and New Testaments were praised or condemned for their collective responsibilities. This also means that the response to sin is both personal and corporate, just like the consequences of sin. Myers puts it very clearly: "Because evil is collective as well as personal, responding to it takes a communal religious life."[62] Humans, together, have choices to make, and humans, together, are responsible for those choices. Although Western—and perhaps increasingly non-Western—culture's focus is on individual behavior and individual responsibility, the Bible has a broader scope of responsibility that extends beyond individual persons to include groups and nations.

In sum, the biblical view of responsibility is that it occurs both at the individual and at the group level. People can rise and fall on their own, but the fate of the individual is always bound up within a group because humans are interconnected. This characteristic of human nature therefore implies that how we live out our lives is shaped by being persons *and* by the groups with which we align ourselves—our families, religious groups, and countries of origin, to name a few—and for Christians, the body of Christ, which is the church. It also implies that persons have responsibility to others, whether it is just one person or a nation. God's desire is for humans to have personal and corporate relationality that is harmonious and mutually uplifting.

Human Responsible Limited Agency and Psychology

Questions of responsibility and agency come up all the time in psychology. Obviously, if a psychologist concludes that someone has no ability to choose, the notion of responsibility is irrelevant. It is impossible to be responsible without real choice. The ability to choose, however, does not necessarily result in responsibility.

Psychologists disagree about our ability to choose,[63] and thus it naturally follows that they would also disagree about the degree to which people are responsible for their behavior. Some psychologists (e.g., B. F. Skinner) assume that we have no ability to choose, which impacts the kind of research questions they ask. Rather than looking at situations in which people make choices, these psychologists study how changes in the environment change behavior. Other psychologists (e.g., Carl Rogers) assume almost unlimited agency for

---

62. Myers, "A Levels-of-Explanation View," 61.
63. Just one of a number of books that debate this question is Baer, Kaufman, and Baumeister, *Are We Free?*

humans, so these theorists might design studies that help determine what choices people make or to understand the impact of choices.

Psychological research shows that a variety of factors influence the degree to which people exercise the limited agency they have and take responsibility for their behavior. A variety of experiments, for example, indicate that some conditions and situations make it easier to follow moral codes, while other conditions and situations make that more difficult. Worthington[64] cites classic research by Stanley Milgram on obedience and Solomon Asch on conformity showing that there are particular situations under which people are much more likely to follow the ideals and desires of others rather than their own principles. In addition, differences in brain development and the consequences of brain injury imply that people differ in their ability to consider choices and to even understand the consequences of their own behavior. Research on addictions shows that how the brain responds to substances is altered by the use of those drugs, so that physical and psychological dependence results.[65] Stopping drug use is difficult because the brain has been changed. Psychological science, when it acknowledges the agency of persons and their potential for responsible behavior, gives insights into how to be responsible and how responsible we can be. We'll explore these issues more in the chapters on brain function (embodiment), social psychology, and therapy—among others. Agency and responsibility vary with a number of factors, but the Bible is clear that to the extent there is agency, persons are responsible for their behavior.

Looking ahead to later chapters of the book, we will see that debates over the extent of personal agency are pervasive in psychology. Recall Ethan from the introduction: to what degree are his behaviors the products of his choice and to what degree are they determined by factors in his environment, like his home life and school situation?

Theme 5: Humans Are Meaning Seekers

The previous four themes provide a basis for describing who and what we are, but as psychologists we also want to explore *why* we do anything. We may be relational, broken, embodied, and responsible limited agents, but if we have the capability to make choices, why do we choose certain paths over others? Are we driven forward "mindlessly" by our past and present relationships, sin, bodies, and limited minds, or can we direct our thoughts and actions with

64. Worthington, *Coming to Peace with Psychology*, 242–44.
65. Hyman and Malenka, "Addiction and the Brain," 695–703.

something more? We propose a fifth characteristic of human nature: we are *meaning seekers*, seeking to make sense of our surroundings, our experience, and our purpose.

We believe that there are at least three aspects of meaning seeking that are fundamental to human nature. First, at a most basic level, we are able to perceive patterns. We can sense and take in our world in ways that are virtually automatic but that are absolutely necessary if we are to understand what events in the environment mean and be able to respond to them. We do not merely see or hear things, however; we make sense of them. In order to care for creation, we need to be able to navigate our environment, understand how things work, and plan what to do next. Basic visual abilities like being able to perceive patterns and recognize others are also included here.

Second, we seek meaning through understanding of experiences. This aspect has a creative component because we often work at making sense of our experiences. In the Bible, people are described as understanding (and often misunderstanding) Jesus's words. For example, when miraculous events occur, the disciples discuss their meaning.[66] They, like us, want to figure things out. For the disciples, as is the case for us, fuller understanding comes through God revealing his truth to us, particularly when trying to understand God.[67] Nevertheless, as Evans[68] has stated, part of our nature is to be thinkers. This leads us to seek meaning.

Finally, there is a third dimension to meaning seeking: the human desire for a deity. Part of what makes us a unique creation is the ability to contemplate our own existence and seek its meaning. Christians believe that because we are made by God and meant to be in relationship with him, ultimate meaning comes from God who created and redeems his people. Romans 1 states that we have the ability to contemplate God.

> For since the creation of the world God's invisible qualities—his eternal power and divine nature—have been clearly seen, being understood from what has been made, so that people are without excuse. For although they knew God, they neither glorified him as God nor gave thanks to him, but their thinking became futile and their foolish hearts were darkened. Although they claimed to be wise, they became fools and exchanged the glory of the immortal God for images made to look like a mortal human being and birds and animals and reptiles.[69]

66. E.g., Mark 9:10.
67. Examples in Matt. 16:12; 17:13.
68. Evans, "Concept of the Self," 5.
69. Rom. 1:20–23.

Under Theme 2, we talked about the effects of sin separating us from God, trying to make ourselves individual gods. Attempts at individual self-fulfillment dominate people, but those individual desires can never fill the gulf that has been created between God and each person.

While people have a sense of the divine that pushes us toward worship, that sense gets misguided as we look for ultimate or even just intermediate levels of meaning in our individuality rather than in God. Note the turnabout that occurs in the last sentences of the passage from Romans 1. Rather than worshiping God, people turn to worship other things—perhaps things more easily understood, tangible, and possibly manipulated by people.

For Israel, it was worship of a homemade golden calf when Moses was away getting the Ten Commandments.[70] For us today, despite self-perceptions of being independent and autonomous, we are actually very willing to be guided, and what we serve easily becomes what we worship. To get an idea of what you serve, as Christian pastor Kyle Idleman has written, think about how you spend your time and your money.[71] What gets the most of your devotion? In what do you get your sense of identity or security? Certainly there is a distinction between spending time doing something (e.g., studying or working) and worshiping something (e.g., seeing your worth as a person rise or fall with your grade point average or financial status). The point is that for humans, it is easy to have something take the place of God.

In the end, meaning seeking is more than just how we think about things; it is what we do, and it ties directly to our propensity to worship. James K. A. Smith emphasizes that our worship takes up our reasoning and emotion, and that a Christian view of persons must emphasize our desires—our fundamental intentions that can occur in largely unconscious and strongly emotional ways.[72] As Smith has stressed, humans cannot be reduced to just our rational characteristics. People have desires, and we direct these toward what is and becomes most important to us. These desires show what we worship—what is our god.

Human Meaning Seeking and Psychology

Psychology also shows that we are meaning seekers. We do not let events go unexplained—we demand explanations for everything from the cause of car accidents (traffic investigations) to why a team won the Super Bowl (the postgame interview and analysis). People try to put the elements of a situation

70. Exod. 32.
71. Idleman's *Gods at War* takes up the notion that what Christians worship (other than God) can become an idol that becomes valued and honored.
72. Smith, *Desiring the Kingdom*, 51.

together to make a sensible story. In our desire to "make sense of our world," as Myers writes, "we are prone to perceive patterns."[73] This brings together both our simple pattern perception and our creative meaning making. As you go through this book you will see that this sort of meaning making, both accurate and inaccurate, is the basis of human sensory processes and perception, and is fundamental to what we do when thinking and to both forming and recalling memories. The idea that humans are predisposed to make meaning—to figure things out—is increasingly common within many areas of psychology. This is obvious, from cognitive and physiological psychologists studying how patterns of light captured by the back of the eye result in our instantaneously recognizing a friend's face (imposing meaning on meaningless stimuli) and from counseling psychologists exploring how people work through a strained marriage to improve it.

Looking for gods is uniquely and utterly human. Developmental research in the cognitive science of religion echoes the Bible's notion that people are born to believe. Researchers, having studied children's beliefs and citing developmental evidence that "religion is natural,"[74] have proposed that children may be "intuitive theists"[75] or "born believers."[76] In many ways, however, psychologists have neglected to consider this basic aspect of personhood. Many psychologists have maintained a mechanistic ("person as machine") view of humans. From that view, humans are driven by more simple, practical goals like survival, avoiding pain, seeking pleasure, and learning. Despite these more mechanistic views, there are also psychologists who believe humans are the only species strongly motivated to understand why we exist and to find a deeper purpose. For example, humanistic psychologists like Carl Rogers[77] and Abraham Maslow[78] proposed that people are moved to attain self-actualization, which includes meaning and purpose. Other, more recent positive psychologists like Martin Seligman[79] likewise propose that the happiest people are those who have a deep sense of meaning in their lives. There may be helpful elements in all these perspectives. We don't know about you, but we generally try to avoid pain. But we believe that Scripture points to a strong internal tendency in humans not only to seek meaning but also to act based on what we feel is meaningful.

73. Myers, *Psychology*, 20.
74. Bloom, "Religion Is Natural," 147–51.
75. Keleman, "Are Children 'Intuitive Theists'?," 295–301.
76. Barrett, "Cognitive Science of Religion: What Is It and Why Is It?," 768–86.
77. Rogers, *Way of Being*, 120.
78. Maslow, *Motivation and Personality*.
79. Seligman, *Authentic Happiness*, 14.

Psychologists have a lot to say about how we think and how we seek meaning, and some of their conclusions have implications for what we worship. Psychologists are also interested in what we desire and hold as most important in our lives and why. Some psychologists have shown that in our search for meaning, we show a self-serving bias; that is, we tend to perceive our world in a way that fits beliefs that we already have.[80] Some areas of psychology also make claims about what should be most important to us—what we desire. This is particularly the case in an area known as evolutionary psychology. How the issues of meaning and worship play out in psychology will be addressed further in several chapters.

A Look Forward

What does psychology tell us about these relationships between God, others, and creation? Psychological science is all about the exploration of our interactions with and understanding of the world—its things and inhabitants, including ourselves—and tries to characterize those scientifically. Christianity asserts that we're made not only for such physical interactions but also for a spiritual relationship with God. There are some things that psychology can tell us about our relationship with God. Psychology can empirically (e.g., using scientific observation) study our attempts to relate to God. It's possible to objectively observe activities like how often one goes to church, gather self-reports of how much one prays, or measure on a scale of 1 to 10 how important one believes God is in life, but this only gives us part of the story. We *cannot* study God's interactions with us in an empirical way. Claiming that God's actions are responsible for what someone does simply is not a scientific explanation—it does not count by science's rules, as we will discuss in the next chapter. So psychology's understanding of our relationship with God and, even more so, God's relationship with us, has a significant limitation. However, psychology's abilities to look at how we relate with humans (who are physical) and the world (also physical) are much more promising. When dealing with objectively measurable causes and consequences, science can operate. So it will be these relationships and the characteristics of humans that are pertinent to them that we will focus on as we proceed with this book.

In this chapter, we began with the significance of being made in God's image. "If humans are created in God's image, we should expect to see certain

80. Worthington, *Coming to Peace with Psychology*, 177.

characteristics appear in psychological studies of humans."[81] The biblical truths about human nature will not always allow us to accept or reject the multitude of specific theories, research, or practices in psychology, but they can direct us to accept or reject certain presuppositions or views that inform our theories and practices. Each of the major areas within psychology has a particular focus when describing humans. The remainder of this book will look at how major areas of psychology—biological, clinical, cognitive, developmental, social, and others—approach humans and how these approaches fit with the biblical depiction of humans.

DISCUSSION QUESTIONS

1. Can psychology add further insight to a biblical view of human nature? If so, how do we take up the findings of psychology yet still be true to the Bible's view of human nature?

2. Do people differ in their level of agency, depending on their psychological status? Do people with limited intellectual capacity have less agency, and if so, does one also have less responsibility?

3. Is it possible to measure God's action in this world with physical evidence?

4. How does our drive for meaning influence how we interpret actions in the world? Does our drive to make meaning influence whether we perceive physical events as supernaturally caused?

5. Did our fundamental drive for meaning lead to science?

6. What constraints are on your life? What has held you back if you ever wanted to change yourself—your study habits, your weight, your exercise patterns, perhaps something as seemingly simple as how often you say "um" in a sentence?

81. Ibid., 183.

2

Test Time!

Research Methodology

Chapter Summary: Psychological science assumes that through observation and testing, predictions can be made about human behavior. In this chapter, we discuss how these methods and assumptions relate to a Christian view of human nature. We then explore how psychology's attempts to predict human behavior correspond to responsible limited agency. In addition, we discuss how psychological science draws conclusions, particularly as related to our being meaning seekers. Finally, we look at ways that Christians might have a unique impact on psychological research through their choice of research topics.

Test them all; hold on to what is good.

1 Thessalonians 5:21

Psychologists love a good test. We're not talking about course exams, as they're not much more fun for professors to grade than they are for students to take. No, psychologists love to test a good hypothesis. Typically, this means getting data—numbers about behavioral characteristics like extroversion level (measured with a personality test), ability to learn (using response times of rats to solve a maze), or mood differences when in a red room or a green room (based on self-evaluation ratings). Psychologists love testing because they love concrete results. Results address questions psychologists investigate, such as how we are able to recognize a friend's voice in a crowd of talking people, or whether caffeine makes people more productive (or maybe just more jittery).

Psychological *Science?*

Examining the kinds of questions just mentioned might not fit the popular image of what psychologists do. In our experience as psychologists, a typical reaction when telling someone you're a psychologist is, "Well, I guess I'd better watch what I say!" People sometimes ask if we are trying to "analyze" them. Such responses are indicative of what psychologist Keith Stanovich has labeled "the Freud problem."[1] Stanovich writes that if you ask one hundred people on the street to name a psychologist, "Sigmund Freud" would be the top answer. They're partly right—although trained as a medical doctor, Freud was interested in psychology. Among the problems with this answer, however, is that modern psychology looks almost nothing like Freud's practice. Today, only a tiny minority of psychologists are concerned with Freudian psychoanalysis. Freud actually steered clear of the sort of experimental basis that is the foundation of today's psychology.

Current psychology is well characterized by the sort of definition given in today's introductory psychology textbooks, which boils down to this: *psychology is the science of behavior and mental processes.* Let's look at the components of this definition. First, *science* means that psychology uses systematic observation (also known as the empirical method) and repeatable, verifiable findings.[2] Psychology explores questions that can be tested using methods currently available to give natural (versus supernatural) explanations for those questions. In fact, this method is the common factor that holds together the diverse topics that psychologists study. How does the function of our sense of smell relate to the influence of bystanders on our likelihood to help others? It probably doesn't, yet both are studied by psychology! What puts them under the umbrella of psychology is that they are mental and behavioral phenomena that are studied using scientific methods. The word *behavior* means the externally observable actions of a person—what people do alone or with others. *Mental processes* are internal functions, particularly ones in the brain, which can be inferred from behavior, self-report, or brain-scanning techniques.

1. Stanovich, *How to Think Straight about Psychology*, 1.
2. Ibid., 8.

Science's Assumptions

Predicting Natural Phenomena

For their science to be possible, psychologists must make assumptions. First, science specifies the focus of its study: *natural phenomena*. Natural phenomena can be studied because they are assumed to be *predictable* or *regular*. For psychology to be such a science, it must be assumed that humans have a large degree of uniformity or regularity. Further, psychology must assume that nature is real (what we see, hear, etc., actually exists) and that these regularities and reality can be discovered.[3] These assumptions are the same ones chemists use when studying the molecular structure of any substance. Chemists assume that atoms function in regular, predictable ways, so that when two parts hydrogen are combined with one part oxygen, water results. If behavior was not regular in any way, as we tell students in psychology research methods courses, we may as well pull down the Psychology Department sign and go home because there would be no point in trying to figure out how humans generally act. You cannot talk about what is likely to happen if *anything* is likely.

People tend to be of two minds about this notion of the regularity of human behavior. On the one hand, we act as though we believe people will behave as expected. For example, when you drive a car, you expect that everyone else will act "normal"—they will obey traffic lights, drive on the proper side of the road, and generally not cause mayhem. When people drive in ways other than this (as we have all experienced at times), we might be surprised, frustrated, or even fearful. We anticipate consistency even of ourselves—that studying for an exam or rehearsing for a presentation will improve performance. We assume that common circumstances and behaviors will lead to usual outcomes. Causes lead to effects, even in humans.

On the other hand, the idea of regularity may seem objectionable because it implies that behavior—your behavior—is *predictable*. Psychologist John Gottman and his colleagues developed a series of tasks that, when completed by married couples, allowed Gottman and coworkers to predict with 93 percent accuracy which marriages would end in divorce over the next fourteen years.[4] He did this by determining whether a couple was behaving like couples from one of his earlier studies who had divorced.[5] That is, he determined which group a couple belonged to, and based on this, was able to predict likelihoods

3. Christensen, Johnson, and Turner, *Research Methods, Design, and Analysis*, 13.
4. Gottman and Levenson, "Timing of Divorce," 737–45.
5. Buehlman, Gottman, and Katz, "How a Couple Views Their Past Predicts Their Future," 295–318.

of divorce with amazing accuracy. We seldom like it when someone thinks they can tell us what we are going to do before we do it, but Gottman's research suggests that in the case of divorce, he and his colleagues can.

Naturalism versus Methodological Naturalism

Christians may have an additional objection to this notion of regularity in behavior, as it appears to conflict with the Bible's view of humans and God. Within the assumption of uniformity can be a further notion known as *determinism*. This is the belief that mental processes and behaviors are caused only by natural factors. Taken to its extreme, this point of view is known as naturalism. *Naturalism* is a worldview in which it is assumed that there are only natural causes to things. Strict naturalism allows for no supernatural explanations. This view says that your beliefs about God are entirely explained by your environment (e.g., what your parents did, what ideas you were exposed to) and how your brain responded to it.

Rather than embracing complete naturalism, many psychologists, and certainly most Christian psychologists, do their psychology as more limited naturalists, what can be called *methodological* naturalists. The modifier *methodological* implies that while they use the methods of science as a naturalist would, they do not necessarily assume that the causes of all events are physical in nature. This position toward science allows people from a variety of faith (or nonfaith) backgrounds, cultures, and worldviews to all conduct science in the same way, while still leaving open the possibility of realities beyond only what we see. Of course, one can be an *absolute* naturalist and reject the notion of any reality other than the physical world. That position, by definition, must reject the existence of God. This is not necessary (or really even justified) to do science, however. Science only studies natural phenomena by natural methodologies. So science, by its very method and restrictions, can neither prove nor disprove God's existence. Science simply says that the supernatural is outside of its territory.

What about Supernatural Phenomena?

If Christians want to leave room for God and supernatural phenomena, one might ask why Christians are doing any science at all. Why bother with methodological naturalism if it tends to lead us toward naturalism and determinism? Are not God and spiritual realities all that really matter? We can begin addressing this concern by first noting again that, based on its own rules, science has little to say about God. Scientific investigation can, however, produce findings that can benefit Christians in living out a life of faith. But the Bible says that along with our relationship with God, core human relationships include those with other humans and with creation.[6] Learning more about how that creation works, and how we ourselves work, should make us better caretakers of each other and creation. Doing so fits with our nature as relational persons bearing God's image (Theme 1).

Studying creation also tells us about God. This is a theological notion called *general revelation*, in which God shows something of himself in what he has created.[7] Things you have produced tell a story about you. If you look at "art" you made as a child, whether scribbles on a paper or more elaborate glue/paper/glitter self-portraits, those objects reflect who you were in terms of abilities, interests, and more. The Bible says that creation reflects who God is; he made it entirely[8] and out of nothing.[9] Likewise, the image of God carried by humans reflects who God is, again because God made us. Therefore, studying patterns in the natural world and patterns in ourselves can tell us more about God because God worked in nature: "For since the creation of the world God's invisible qualities—his eternal power and divine nature—have been clearly seen, being understood from what has been made."[10] As Malcolm Jeeves has written, creation is *theocentric*—it is meant to reveal God so that people can know God better. God is deeply interested in his creation, and humans in particular. Jeeves writes that the Bible has a theocentric emphasis that primarily deals "with humankind in relation to God their Creator, Sustainer, and Redeemer."[11]

Doing science does not conflict with Christian faith; in fact, it can reinforce faith as God's infinite abilities and care are seen in creation.[12] There is a note of caution necessary here, however. Theme 5 suggests that we have a tendency toward worship—we are meaning seekers looking for a god. Our enjoyment of creation may turn to a worship of creation or even a worship of ourselves in making discoveries (being infatuated with ourselves for ingenuity in discovery), without regard for God creating all of creation, including us. The theologian John Calvin advised: "To be so occupied in the investigation of the secrets

---

6. Jesus called his followers to pray for each other but also to take care of their physical and emotional needs (Matt. 25:43–45).

7. Worthington, *Coming to Peace with Psychology*, 76.

8. See particularly the first portion of Ps. 19.

9. Heb. 11.3. Clear statements of God's creating everything are found in several other Old Testament and New Testament verses, including Neh. 9:6; Ps. 146:6; Acts 14:17; Rev. 4:11.

10. Rom. 1:20. Yet this knowledge of God through creation does not bring salvation—Christians believe that Jesus Christ brings salvation.

11. Jeeves, *Human Nature at the Millennium*, 100.

12. See Myers, "A Levels-of-Explanation View," 50–51, for further discussion of how Christians have been leaders in science and search for truth.

of nature, as never to turn the eyes to its Author, is a most perverted study; and to enjoy everything in nature without acknowledging the Author of the benefit, is the basest ingratitude."[13]

Predictably Human?

The order and regularity seen in creation reflect the orderliness of its Creator, and these properties are sustained by God's action. This regularity and thus potential predictability have clear benefits in fields like chemistry or biology. Obviously, knowing that salt consistently dissolves in water is helpful. Cooking, for instance, would be a lot harder to pull off if you never knew what salt might do in water. Is human behavior equally predictable? Does science see humans as just mechanisms—biological robots—that respond to "laws of nature" like salt dissolving in water? Can all of psychology achieve the level of success that Gottman has had in predicting divorce?

Failures in Prediction Due to Insufficient Knowledge

We believe the short and correct answer is no. Here is the beginning of one reason why: salt does not always dissolve in water. If the temperature is below 15 degrees Fahrenheit, salt just sits on top of water (which would then be in the form of ice). Living in a snowy part of the United States, we are well aware of the fact that when it is too cold, salt does not melt ice on sidewalks, so one must tread carefully. Known chemical reactions, like salt dissolving in water, are altered depending on circumstances, although at room temperature we can be pretty sure in predicting what salt will do in water. When important dimensions of the future are not known, results are *nondeterministic*; that is, more than one possible outcome could occur. In the example of salt meeting water, our inability to predict what happens to the salt is due to our lack of knowledge about the situation in which the salt exists (in the cases outlined above, the key variable is temperature). This kind of nondeterminism is due to insufficient knowledge.[14] If all conditions were known beforehand, this kind of nondeterminism could be eliminated. Perhaps the reason that Gottman is not 100 percent correct in determining which marriages will fail and which will succeed is that he and his researchers have not identified all of the factors that influence marital success. If they did, perhaps their prediction would be perfect.

13. Calvin, *Commentaries on Genesis*, 60.
14. This is otherwise known as epistemic chance.

Failures of Prediction Due to Humans' Limited Agency

A second kind of nondeterminism may also be present when predicting the behavior of humans. The basic nature of what is being studied may include nondeterminacy because what is being studied has at least some degree of unpredictability or randomness built right into it. This is a situation of *real chance*.[15] That is, human nature may contain something about itself that can frustrate predictability because unpredictability or randomness is part of how humans work. People can do things that defy prediction, such as when a couple, following review by a Gottman-type study of their marriage quality, says, "Forget them saying that we're getting divorced; we're staying together!" and then works to do so. This is a situation of people exercising free will—as mentioned in Theme 4, humans have agency, limited though it is.

The idea of human agency is not without controversy among psychologists. Debates rage as to whether what "appears" to be choice on the part of humans is real (real chance in the sense that what someone does could not always be predicted if there was sufficient knowledge about a person) or if it just looks as though humans have free will because we don't yet know enough about people to predict behavior (insufficient knowledge about a person that will one day be complete knowledge). When it comes to telling this part of the story of human nature, psychology can sound more like the dissonance of a twenty-piece band warming up than a solo artist in the middle of a performance. Here are just a few examples from some well-known tunes in psychology. Sigmund Freud saw humans having no freedom,[16] as motivated primarily by animalistic drives (e.g., sex and hunger), but B. F. Skinner assumed that we are simply products of our environment.[17] Although having different starting points, Freud and Skinner both thought that free will was at most very limited and more likely nonexistent. An entirely different song was played by humanistic psychologist Carl Rogers,[18] who saw free will as virtually limitless. The Bible, as stated in Theme 4, depicts humans as having real choices and real responsibility. Joshua, speaking to the tribes of Israel, gives a clear example: "Choose for yourselves this day whom you will serve, whether the gods your ancestors served beyond the Euphrates, or the gods of the Amorites, in whose land you are living. But as for me and my household, we will serve the LORD."[19] In this case "choice" allows for "chance" in the sense of different possible outcomes, indicative of

---

15. What we have called "real chance" here is known among philosophers as "ontological chance." See chap. 5, "Chance," in Howell and Bradley, *Mathematics through the Eyes of Faith*.

16. Freud, *Complete Introductory Lectures on Psychoanalysis*, 49, 106.

17. Skinner, *Beyond Freedom and Dignity*, 98.

18. Rogers, *On Becoming a Person*, 203.

19. Josh. 24:15.

a nondeterminacy. Yet chance does not mean absolute randomness. Joshua knows that people will serve *something* (human nature as worshipful meaning seeking being what it is). Humans show limited agency and very regular patterns in how they behave.

Chance, in this sense of nondeterminacy, can be seen as demonstrating free will that God has given people. One way of thinking about this, argued by Howell and Bradley[20] and following the logic of Thomas Aquinas, is in terms of God as the primary cause of all things in the universe. God also created secondary agents, including people and natural processes in the universe, as well as the laws that govern these processes, to maintain his creation. Humans as image bearers are God's stewards of creation, and humans can act in creation in ways that are not fully determined. God is not micromanaging every single step we take, yet he is sovereign as he sets forth the processes and actors, and can guide the unfolding of creation while still using nondeterministic events within it.

Christians believe that God's action involves more than just setting up the rules and letting the universe run on its own from that point forward—"winding the clock," so to speak. The God of the Bible is actively involved in the world. The Bible records God speaking with people through various means,[21] directing natural phenomena,[22] and sending Jesus Christ to save believers from sin.[23] More broadly, God also shows his providence—his continued preserving and upholding of creation—through the use of natural phenomena and the circumstances provided by them.[24] Chance exists in the world, but it is not purposeless or without any direction. Chance is constrained by what is possible.

Limited Nondeterminacy

In thinking about chance, we don't want to overstate the nondeterminacy of human behavior, however. People do clearly act in systematic, regular ways, and psychology does a marvelous job of helping us understand those regularities—many of which are seen in introductory psychology textbooks. Human agency is limited, as we simply are not able to contemplate all choices at once

20. Howell and Bradley, *Mathematics through the Eyes of Faith*.

21. God spoke directly to Moses (e.g., Exod. 19:19) and Abraham (e.g., Gen. 17), for example, as well as through the prophets and Jesus (Heb. 1:1–2).

22. For example, God's assurance in Gen. 8:22: "As long as the earth endures, seedtime and harvest, cold and heat, summer and winter, day and night will never cease."

23. 1 Tim. 1:15.

24. God upholds all of creation. Acts 17:24 states that God "made the world and everything in it" and that God continues to be "Lord of heaven and earth." God maintains this world regardless of human worthiness, as shown in Matt. 5:45, which says that God "causes his sun to rise on the evil and the good, and sends rain on the righteous and the unrighteous."

(we get overloaded by choice possibilities, as we discuss in chapter 9, on think-ing), and we cannot act on more than one choice at a time (i.e., we only live each moment one time—no "redos"). Perhaps more interesting, however, is that we often fail to exercise even the limited ability we have to choose by simply doing what we usually do (without considering alternatives). A very simple example of this comes from classrooms. Neither of the authors uses assigned seating in our courses, yet by the second week of classes, most students have self-assigned themselves to a seat. People sit in the same place day after day, although there's never been a request to do so. Students in these classes have taken up a habit—the simple habit of where to sit. By going to the same seat every day, no decision needs to be made. But in doing so, each student, usually unknowingly, gives up an opportunity to exercise free will. So the *process* of learning and forming a habit may have a lawful nature to it, but the outcome does not. With most habits, people have agency to alter their behavior.

One semester, one of us brought to a class's attention that everyone sits in the same place all of the time because they are acting habitually and not exercis-ing free will. The next time the class met, many of the students switched to a different seat than usual, and two students actually sat in a new seat every day for the rest of the term! Although acts of agency appear more obvious when a person does the unexpected, exercising free will does not always mean that a person does the unexpected, however. Several of the students who stayed in their usual seats said that they could have moved but, after thinking about it, didn't want to. Going back to the example of Gottman's research on divorce, people could respond in either of these ways regarding their marriages if in-formed of what his research predicted. A person can choose to do the expected (what was predicted) simply because she wanted to pursue that option or do the unexpected because she chose to do that. That's what agency is.

Predicting an individual's actions is actually impossible. Humans can bring about consequences using their agency (this is known as agent causation). In addition, psychologists compare groups with other groups (or occasion-ally they compare a single individual with a group, in the situation of a case study). However, people within groups differ from each other—not all men are identical, and not all women are identical. Therefore, psychology is not so good at predicting how a particular man may differ from a particular woman. In the end, psychologists may be very good at predicting the behavior of a group (people who show behaviors like other individuals who divorced) but less accurate when it comes to predicting the behavior of any single individual.[25]

25. This idea of group versus individual prediction is also apparent in insurance rates. If you have car insurance, you pay a particular premium because of the group to which you belong. If

Taken together, insufficient knowledge and human limited agency help provide the basis for why predictions in psychology are *probabilistic*: prediction is in terms of what is likely, but not guaranteed, to occur. Using the knowledge that they have, psychological scientists attempt to predict what *most* people are *likely* to do in particular circumstances. That is quite different from being able to predict what *all* people will *definitely* do.

Seeking Meaning through Science

Issues of nondeterminacy aside, modern psychology's definition and method of study (even the use of methodological naturalism) imply that what is learned from systematic testing and observation should be totally straightforward and objective. Based on evidence, either a theory is objectively accurate or it is not. Designed to give the facts and nothing more, science's general stance is to be neutral regarding moral and ethical questions.[26] Therefore, psychological science, by its method and reliance on only natural explanations, is unable to answer moral questions.

Values and beliefs, rather than science, are the basis for morality. This is not to say that science (and good reasoning, for that matter) has nothing to do with morality. Science can inform a moral question—that is, it can provide useful information about what is likely to occur should one course of action be taken rather than some other possibilities. Knowing the consequences of actions could help you decide what to do, but it cannot tell you if that decision is right or wrong. For example, a parent may be trying to decide whether punishing a misbehaving child by giving a time-out (separating from the child with no interaction for a few minutes) is more cruel than yelling at a child. Psychology could shed some light on this issue by providing statistics on the outcomes of these two parenting techniques—for example, how does each affect the parent-child relationship, does the child act more responsibly following one than the other, and so on. How the parent prioritizes these outcomes, however, is ultimately a question of values. While scientific information can be used to give insights in making

---

you are currently unmarried, you pay more for car insurance than if you become married. It's not that part of the marriage ceremony includes a course in better driving; people who are married tend to have fewer accidents than those who are not married. That's why they pay less. The insurance company does not know whether you will have fewer accidents when you're married. It does know that in the past, people who are married have had fewer accidents than those not married, so such people cost less to insure.

26. See chap. 3, "Should There Be a Christian Psychology?," in Myers and Jeeves, *Psychology through the Eyes of Faith* for further explanation of this.

the judgment, it cannot actually judge what makes an outcome ultimately good or bad.

Psychology's findings regarding human behavior and moral questions are better seen as *descriptive*—telling or describing how things are—rather than *prescriptive*—telling us how things should be. As David Myers, author of a best-selling introductory psychology textbook, writes, the "ultimate" questions of life—How should I live? What is the purpose of life?—are not answered by psychology. "Instead, expect that psychology will help you understand why people think, feel, and act as they do. Then you should find the study of psychology fascinating and useful."[27] Questions regarding life's ultimate purpose are, for Christians, addressed in the Bible and in the contexts of relationships with God and God's people.

Meaning Seekers Conducting Research

Values, therefore, are critical in determining whether to use scientific information. Worldviews inform morality by shaping what will be studied, how people will interpret the findings, and even how they might implement the findings. However, as philosophers of science have noted, the beginning of the scientific process is also full of values, and even the process of doing science is not as unbiased as may be presumed.[28]

Perhaps you have wondered just how a psychologist decides what behavior is worth examining. You might think the answer is "all behavior," but the history of psychological study, like the history of any other discipline, shows that not everything is judged equally worthy of time and effort.[29] Just as any student prioritizes study time based on unique criteria (like personal interest in a class, difficulty of previous tests, and current course grade), psychologists use their own set of criteria to choose what they will research. Scientists' interests and research agendas flow from what they value, and values arise from many sources, including one's nationality, current psychological state, and religious worldview,[30] as well as very practical matters like availability of funding to do studies. The training and experience of psychologists also shape how they address a question. Here's an example of how this can play out: If you're a psychologist trying to study ADHD in people like Ethan in the introduction,

27. Myers, *Psychology* (2010), 10.

28. Kuhn, *Structure of Scientific Revolutions*, 77–79.

29. Explore the history of psychology section of any introductory psychology textbook to see these changes.

30. Wolterstorff, *Reason within the Bounds of Religion*.

your background and assumptions might direct you toward what you study and how to treat him. A developmental psychologist would probably be interested in how ADHD changes over the course of Ethan's life, while a cognitive psychologist might study how Ethan would differ from people without ADHD on other cognitive abilities like memory. A social psychologist may look at how people interact differently with people like Ethan if they think he does or does not have ADHD, while a physiological psychologist would focus on how Ethan's brain differs from someone without ADHD.

The reason for these differences in interests, we believe, goes back to Theme 5: we are meaning seekers. All of us, regardless of religious convictions, seek to make meaning. With this sort of creative meaning seeking, people are trying to understand the world, so it follows that different people will have different priorities in doing so, based on their experiences and worldviews. For Christians, acting out of their faith commitments should impact what is deemed worthy of study in psychology and what to do with those findings. A pivotal question for a Christian to ask when contemplating a potential psychological study should be, Will this honor God? That can include asking whether the core relationships humans have will be built up in God-honoring ways by the work done. Myers and Jeeves give the following example: "Just as physics can be used to trigger nuclear explosions or to relieve suffering through radiotherapy, so psychology can be used to manipulate individuals or groups or to relieve anxiety and depression."[31] We believe that Christian psychologists must continually use their faith as a beginning point for using psychological research.

An example of the influence that a Christian worldview might have on research comes from the research path of one of our colleagues, Blake Riek, who has specialized in studying interpersonal relationships. In reviewing and analyzing the research literature on forgiveness, he found that psychology's predominant emphasis has been on the effects of granting forgiveness.[32] In particular, past research had explored the benefits that come to the person who forgives—impacts on health and happiness, for example. The Christian view of forgiveness is broader and deeper than this, emphasizing the restoration of relationships. For forgiveness to occur in a relationship, along with granting forgiveness, seeking and receiving forgiveness are also needed.[33] The Bible repeatedly emphasizes seeking forgiveness from others and God to heal

31. Myers and Jeeves, *Psychology through the Eyes of Faith*, 12. Myers, "A Levels-of-Explanation View," also gives a helpful set of examples of ways that Christian faith can relate to psychological research.

32. Riek and Mania, "Interpersonal Forgiveness," 304–25.

33. "Forgive, and you will be forgiven" (Luke 6:37).

broken relationships, stressing this as the motivation for forgiveness.[34] Acting out of his Christian worldview, Riek saw inadequacies in the literature on forgiveness and has developed a research program that is beginning to explore these additional components of a deeper biblical picture of forgiveness. His faith perspective led him to see these further components of forgiveness. For a Christian, the goal of work is to glorify and serve God. Working to have a more complete understanding of how relationships can fit with God's design for our interactions can certainly be part of that.

Approaching Research with Respect and Care

Differences in priorities, extending even to how we see the world, can be labeled *biases* or simple prejudgments in favor of one alternative or another.[35] That is, we like one thing or idea more than another from the outset, and that influences the work that we do. Biases influence how people draw conclusions based on research findings.[36] Our general tendency toward seeking meaning deeply influences our interpretation of research.

What are we to do if we do not like what the research "says"? Because psychology is about you (and us), there may be ideas we personally hold that are confronted by psychological research, and the two do not line up. For example, classic research by Stanley Milgram shows that average people will obey an authority figure even to the point of acting immorally.[37] A person may look at such research and say, "People aren't like that; no one can make me do something I don't want to do," and reject it out of hand (regardless of the amount of evidence supporting it). Similarly, what is a Christian to do if a research finding goes against her Christian beliefs? For example, some research on prayer has shown it to be ineffective in helping physically heal people who were being prayed for,[38] concluding that prayer is ineffective. The Bible clearly

34. Many passages emphasize repentance—being sorrowful and contrite about past behavior. Repentance is tied to forgiveness. A great example of this is Ps. 51, where King David begs God for forgiveness following his adultery with Bathsheba.

35. We have a lot more to say in chap. 9 about how psychology has studied human biases as they influence thinking and decision making.

36. Bastardi, Uhlmann, and Ross, "Wishful Thinking," 731–32, is a good example of where people's evaluations of scientific evidence were strongly influenced by what they hoped to be true.

37. Milgram, "Behavioral Study of Obedience," 371–78.

38. No positive effect of prayer was found by Benson et al., "Study of the Therapeutic Effects," 934–42. Another study reviewed ten studies that had tested over seventy-five hundred participants, and showed that in some studies, prayer was associated with positive outcomes, although the majority did not show prayer to have effects; see Roberts et al., "Intercessory Prayer."

stresses the importance and effectiveness of prayer.[39] In the research both on obedience and on prayer, an important personal belief appears to be contradicted by research. Again, what should be the response?

Christian research psychologist Scott VanderStoep writes that the first, gut response that you might have—to simply reject it, saying "I don't believe it!"—is unacceptable if we are to take any psychological research seriously.[40] Research needs to be critiqued on its scientific merit. If it is scientifically unsound, rejection is very appropriate, but if we allow our personal preferences alone to dictate the validity of research, science has little hope of finding anything because we will use what we like and dismiss what we do not like (even if what we dismiss is actually valid). Malcolm Jeeves writes that when Christians encounter research findings that either contradict or confirm our beliefs, we must above all tell the truth about what we have found, honestly exploring what God shows in creation, even if we may not like everything we see.[41] First, this means that when Christians are evaluating research, we must do so respecting science's rules. Assessing research quality begins with examining whether the research methodology in the study allows for the conclusions that were made by the experimenters. In our psychology department, students in the major are required to take a course in research methodology (as is the case in most psychology departments) so they can learn this important skill. How to do this assessment well, however, is beyond the scope of this book.

If the research was done well and the conclusions follow from the method used, the consumer of the research can then decide whether action should follow. As we discussed earlier, research findings are descriptive, not prescriptive.[42] Therefore, even if a study shows that prayer is not effective in the context in which that study was done, such a finding does not mean that people need to stop praying. One may decide that prayer is important whether a prayer is answered in the way that one hoped it to be answered or not. In addition, prayer may be not so much about making God do something as about recognizing one's own inadequacy and drawing the person praying closer to God.[43] This also gets at another important issue: just what research question was being asked and how was it answered—that is, what research agenda was involved and what assumptions behind that agenda influenced the research? Evaluating

39. First Thess. 5:17 encourages people to "pray continually"; James 5:16 encourages believers to pray for those who are sick as "the prayer of a righteous person is powerful and effective."

40. VanderStoep, "Psychological Research Methods," 100–104.

41. Jeeves, *Human Nature at the Millennium*, 235.

42. VanderStoep, "Psychological Research Methods," 102.

43. Myers and Jeeves, *Psychology through the Eyes of Faith*, 91–102, has a very helpful discussion of the research on prayer's effectiveness.

the physical effects of prayer may not fit with a biblical understanding of prayer, particularly if trying to measure how it brings about healing.[44]

A final way that Christians should approach research that appears to conflict with one's deeply held beliefs may involve examining one's own beliefs.[45] For example, what does the Bible say regarding prayer, and does that differ from what a particular person believes about prayer? As Everett Worthington writes in his book *Coming to Peace with Psychology*, all people—scientists, Christians, and Christians who are scientists—are living in a broken world. This means that humans can make errors in doing and interpreting science, as well as in their interpretation of Scripture.[46] Human understanding of Scripture involves potential errors in how God's Word is translated into modern language and in terms of how theologians and laypeople are influenced by their context, including politics, history, society, and culture.[47]

Seeing in the Midst of Bias

If values influence how research is done and the conclusions that are drawn, is there any hope for seeing reality as it actually is, and untainted by bias? Christian philosopher Arthur Holmes wrote, "All truth is God's truth," saying that God is the author of all truth, so that any truth that is discovered is from God.[48] While Holmes's book title has a great sentiment to it, is it possible for broken, sinful people to clearly discover that truth?

Bert Hodges offers a helpful set of suggestions for a Christian approach to dealing with the many problems of bias.[49] According to Hodges, knowledge is fundamentally contextual. That is, a piece of information counts as being "knowledge" in a certain time to a certain group of people, with certain biases included. Hodges says that at the center of the story of humanity's fall into sin is a rejection of our being creatures—humans wanted to be able to know "like God."[50] As Theme 2 implies, sin resulted in broad consequences. The account of humanity's fall in Genesis resulted in humans becoming "painfully self-conscious (3:7). Then they became afraid (3:8–10). Then social cohesion and trust were ruptured (3:12). Finally, humans became alienated from their own environment (3:17–19). Ironically, their attempt to know more led to a

---

44. Ibid.
45. VanderStoep, "Psychological Research Methods," 102–3.
46. Worthington, *Coming to Peace with Psychology*, 116.
47. Ibid., 117.
48. Holmes, *All Truth Is God's Truth*.
49. Hodges, "Knowing and Doing the Truth."
50. Gen. 3:5.

lessening of their ability to know and do."[51] A profound disconnection from the central relationships, including the relationship with being a person, occurred. Hodges says that this alienation "reduces each individual to his or her own perspectives with a consequent loss of comprehensiveness."[52] We are each trying to figure out everything on our own but fail because we have some degree of separation from everything that we are studying or trying to relate to. We tend toward being individuals, rather than persons, as we discussed earlier.

To attain more lasting knowledge, to move toward the truth of reality and God, we need to embrace and live out our characteristic of being relational persons as described in Theme 1. Hodges points out that God revealed himself and the relationship between himself and creation through multiple perspectives: creation, varieties of voices in Scripture, and the life of Jesus Christ. These multiple perspectives allow humans to discover God's character and being. Hodges further suggests that this revelation of God happens over time as he works through history to bring about the redemption of sinful people and a fallen world. Finally, because there are these multiple (though intertwined) forms of God's revealing himself over time, in order to understand him and his creation, people need to come together in community to share these multiple perspectives. "Knowledge is embodied more in community than in any single perceiver."[53] Knowledge is attained through the diversity of viewpoints, says Hodges.

Thinking about the example of Ethan with ADHD, the insights of a developmental psychologist along with cognitive, social, and physiological psychologists will give a far more complete and accurate picture of his abilities and treatment than would that of any one of these specialists alone. In embracing our interrelatedness (and actual interdependency), we can come to know and better understand our reality. This does not necessarily get us all the way to true knowledge of God and his work, as God is not temporally or contextually limited. Christians do believe that there is real, objective truth in the universe and that their pursuit of truth can be guided by God's work in his people through the Holy Spirit. This happens best in the body of believers.

Implications and Applications

We have tried to make the case that psychological science does not provide a basis for faith or morality but that it can significantly enhance our understanding of ourselves and others. Research findings can even potentially help

51. Hodges, "Knowing and Doing the Truth," 69.
52. Ibid., 70.
53. Ibid., 74–75.

Christians clarify their own beliefs when findings differ from those beliefs. Does psychology offer anything in the way of showing people how best to live? Christians believe that the clearest source of knowledge for Christian living is the Bible. As 2 Timothy 3:16 says, "All Scripture is God-breathed and is useful for teaching, rebuking, correcting and training in righteousness." The Bible, Christians believe, leads people to God through Christ and informs them how to live life. As Christian philosopher Nicholas Wolterstorff has succinctly written, "To be Christian is to be fundamentally committed to be a Christ-follower," and the Scriptures are "authoritative guides for the thought and lives of those who would be Christ-followers."[54]

Is then the Bible's explanation of Christian living complete, telling Christians all that they need to do on a day-to-day basis? While the Bible is meant for all people for all times, as C. S. Lewis wrote in *Mere Christianity*, it does not set out a particular method of living that would be effective through all circumstances and all of history. Lewis writes:

> When it tells you to feed the hungry, it does not give lessons in cookery. When it tells you to read scriptures, it does not give you lessons in Hebrew and Greek, or even ordinary English grammar. It was never intended to replace or supersede the ordinary human arts and sciences: it is rather a director which will set them all to the right jobs, and a source of energy which will give them all new life, if only they would put themselves at its disposal.[55]

Scripture outlines God's will for our lives, but it is not an indexed how-to manual for all situations. How one ought to go about their Christ following varies based on who a person is and the time in which they live. "What I ought to be doing today by way of following Christ differs from what you ought to be doing, and from what I ought to have been doing when I was younger," writes Wolterstorff.[56]

God's relationship with people is both eternal and in the present. Christians are called by God to care for and be in relationship with each other and creation. In that vein, Scripture instructs parents to love their children and teach God's plan for living to them.[57] It gives some general guidance in parenting, such as exhorting fathers to "not exasperate your children; instead, bring them up in the training and instruction of the Lord."[58] However, parents are not told the

54. Wolterstorff, *Reason within the Bounds of Religion*, 71–72.
55. Lewis, *Mere Christianity*, 64.
56. Wolterstorff, *Reason within the Bounds of Religion*, 71.
57. E.g., Prov. 22:6; Deut. 6:6–7.
58. Eph. 6:4.

answers to very practical questions such as whether or not to use day care, which type of feeding schedule to use, or how to help a child having speech difficulties. Nor are there answers to broader questions such as how human memory works or what the nature of consciousness is. Psychologists, employing rigorous research methodology, can help Christians and all people answer these questions. In so doing, they can help enhance the lives of everyone. Such understanding also can help Christians to be Christ followers by increasing their understanding of people. This can improve their effectiveness in ministering in very practical areas of life, such as helping parents parent, as well as helping inform the understanding of ourselves, creatures made in the image of God.

DISCUSSION QUESTIONS

1. Why are people bothered by the idea that their behavior is predictable?

2. Why do we seldom experience the feeling of being predictable?

3. Will there be psychology (or perhaps any science at all) in heaven?

4. How is evidence for claims made in the Bible different from evidence in psychological science? How are they similar?

5. Should a Christian understanding of human behavior be different and/or require a different research methodology because Christians take spiritual realities seriously?

6. Can scientists who are Christians learn from non-Christians and vice versa? Why or why not?

3

"Bodies Revealed"

Brain and Behavior 1

Chapter Summary: If we are embodied, as we discussed earlier, what are the implications for understanding human behavior? Is this really a strong biblical perspective? Isn't the mind or soul what really counts? The answers will not only stress the biblical emphasis on embodiment but will also explore how this needs to be understood in the context of relationality, our basic condition, and our other basic human characteristics.

If the body be feeble, the mind will not be strong.

Thomas Jefferson, to Thomas Mann Randolph, 1786

After all, no one ever hated their own body, but they feed and care for their body.

Ephesians 5:29

Antonio was fascinated by the traveling museum exhibit "Bodies Revealed."[1] If you are not familiar with this exhibit, it was a somewhat surreal display of plasticized human bodies and body parts, designed to educate us about the human body. As he observed these interesting, but slightly disturbing,

1. Bodies Revealed, Premier Exhibitions, http://www.bodiesrevealed.com/.

displays, the biblical question—"What is mankind that you are mindful of them?"—came to his mind. He was taught as a child that God can see us on the inside, so as he looked at these displays he imagined God being able to see our bones, blood, muscle, and internal organs all the time—how unattractive is that! This raised other questions in his mind, such as, "Why do we have these frail and somewhat disgusting bodies at all? Why didn't God make us more like angels or perhaps to be pure spirits?"

Think about all the advantages of not being a body. We wouldn't have to worry about being hot, cold, hungry, tired, and so on. Perhaps we could fly or transport ourselves to distant places or walk through walls; the possibilities are endless! However, the Bible places a great deal of emphasis on bodies, so they must be important for something. Christ's bodily resurrection and the bodily resurrection of believers are central themes mentioned in countless passages. Many other passages stress the value and importance of the body (see 1 Cor. 15:35–54; Eph. 5:28–30; Phil. 1:20; 3:21). But there are puzzling aspects to the scriptural emphasis on bodies. We are also told that we will receive *new* bodies in the next life, and over the centuries most Christians have assumed that the restored body rejoins a "disembodied" soul in heaven, following the second coming of Christ. But if bodies are so important, why, as some suggest, can we exist as disembodied beings for a period of time? If they aren't important, why do we need to rejoin a pile of flesh and bones anyway—especially when it appears that we will be doing fine in heaven without it? (We will return to the disembodied soul question in the next chapter.)

Rejecting the Body

Despite the emphasis placed on material bodies in Scripture, many Christians have downplayed the body. In the early days of the Christian church, gnostics[2] believed that the creation was not made good, by a good God, but in fact made by an evil being and was therefore distorted from the beginning. While the early Christian church rejected this first-century heresy (which was heavily influenced by Greek philosophy),[3] some writers believe that some Christians are still influenced, in subtle ways, by this thinking.[4] Christians with these leanings often cite passages that refer to the "fleshly desires," with the implication that the body itself is evil and that the physical world is to be avoided. As we saw earlier, this view runs counter to the

2. Brakke, *Gnostics*, x.
3. Pearson, *Ancient Gnosticism*, 12–19.
4. See Bloom, *American Religion*.

strong scriptural view that God's creation—including human beings—was created good.

This "world-rejecting" emphasis of gnosticism has two very important implications for psychology. First, it suggests that many activities of this world (e.g., science, psychology, technology, and cultural development) are of little value; we should focus instead on saving individual souls. Second, this perspective suggests that bodies are of little consequence when considering human nature, and therefore we should focus on the spiritual. So while we may have difficulties as the result of our weak and sinful bodies, we can rise above or escape from these realities by *transcendence*. This fancy, but useful, term refers to a person's ability to rise above or beyond the physical existence and to experience ideas or feelings in an abstract world. This transcendent view implies that science can tell us very little about human nature because the body is simply an imperfect vessel for the "real" me—the spiritual me. Furthermore, the real "transcendent me" is where I make moral decisions, make my faith commitments, and willfully decide the course of my life. Since science cannot possibly address the nonmaterial aspects of my being, then psychological science must be an extremely limited discipline, or perhaps it has no value at all.

However, we the authors assume that God did make a good creation, which includes human beings who are made of "dust."[5] Therefore, we believe that bodies should be taken very seriously, and our "earthly composition" should have a huge impact on our understanding of human nature. But before we explore more about what Scripture teaches about the body, let's examine some fascinating things that neuroscience and psychology have revealed about bodies—that we humans think, feel, live, and act with our bodies. To quote David Myers and Malcolm Jeeves, "Without our bodies, we are nobodies," and "we do not have bodies, we *are* bodies, bodies alive with minds."[6]

Embodied Experience

Consider the unusual case of the woman known as "S" (her name is withheld to protect her identity). S was described by neurologist Antonio Damasio as a "tall, slender, and extremely pleasant young woman."[7] But two structures in her brain known as the amygdalae were completely calcified and ultimately destroyed because of a rare disease. The amygdalae are known to be involved in fear responses, along with other types of emotion and learning. Surprisingly,

---

5. See Ps. 90:3.
6. Myers and Jeeves, *Psychology through the Eyes of Faith*, 30.
7. Damasio, *Feeling of What Happens*, 62–67.

S maintained good memory, and her general intelligence (e.g., language, problem solving, and planning) remained strong. The biggest change to her personality was with her emotions and social actions. For example, she became unusually cheerful and was eager to interact with almost anyone she met. She regularly hugged and touched people whom she had just met and would almost never show anger, agitation, or fear—even when the situation called for it. Careful testing showed that she was not able to identify the expression of fear from pictures of faces, even though she could identify emotions such as surprise, happiness, and sadness. She could also not display a fearful facial expression on command—despite being able to display other emotions on command. When asked to rate the trustworthiness of a large number of faces shown to her, she rated all of them as trustworthy, even though half of the pictures had been rated as untrustworthy by other people. S was good at drawing faces, and when asked to draw faces showing different expressions she could do so easily, but she was unable to draw faces that displayed fear. Most surprising of all was that S seemed to lack any conscious understanding of the *concept* of fear. In other words, the problem went beyond the inability to express fear or to feel fear—she had no memory or awareness of fear. One real-life consequence of her disability was that she was often taken advantage of by untrustworthy people.

The case of S reveals several interesting features about our "mindful" brains. First of all, it illustrates that our conscious experience (that part of us we sometimes call the soul) is very much part of what the body does. Emotions are known to be influenced by brain areas but are also very much felt in the body (e.g., increased pulse, blood rushing to our face). So S lacks the normal brain regulation, the necessary body response, *and* the conscious experience needed to fully know fear. If conscious experience is only related to a transcendent, nonmaterial "mind/soul," S should be able to re-create the conscious experience in her mind even without the brain regulation or body response. However, S has no conscious mental experience of fear because of her *body's* inability to create this. S *was* able to intellectually describe situations that might cause a fearful response in others, but she simply couldn't create the mental experience for herself. She had lost the ability to transcend her bodily existence to create the abstract concept of fear.

The second issue illustrated by the case study is that S seems incapable of *willing* herself to experience fear despite being able to show willfulness in other areas (e.g., she could will herself not to eat candy). This loss of willfulness can occur in other situations that are less drastic. For example, a very intelligent young woman whom one of the authors met several years ago was experiencing severe depression. After receiving medication and several weeks of counseling, her symptoms of depression began to diminish. She communicated some time later that, for the first time in her life, she knew what the experience of happiness was all about. She had observed this emotion in others and could intellectually describe what conditions would normally cause happiness in others, but she could not experience this emotion at what psychologists call a "phenomenological" (i.e., experiential, personal, internal, and conscious) level. Again, this young woman could not transcend her bodily experience in order to appreciate the abstract concept of happiness, nor could she experience happiness by sheer force of will or by greater self-determination. Asking this student to will herself into happiness, or the woman S to will herself into fear, would be like asking a woman born blind to will herself into imagining a visual scene.

What *Are* Bodies For?

Elizabeth Lewis Hall, in her very thoughtful essay, "What Are Bodies For?," suggests that we cannot determine how to understand or use any object or being until we know the purpose for which it was made. Her thesis is that bodies were designed for "interacting in the world around us, including other people."[8] She believes that both psychology and Scripture confirm that we were created *as* bodies because that is what allows us to have relationships. She provides several illustrations for how and why bodies work this way. For example, she describes how we form relationships with others in our infancy by first mirroring another person's actions mentally and then using that experience to understand the intentions of others. So we do not learn about these intentions through abstract mental reasoning but through observation and action. A large amount of research shows that when other people perform an action, groups of cells in our brain called mirror neurons activate the circuits in our brain that normally produce the same movement we observe in others.[9] (If you want to observe this phenomenon yourself, demonstrate to someone how agile you are at pointing your tongue in different directions, and then watch their mouth and tongue as the observer unconsciously mimics you.) This mirroring of others is what allows us to understand what others are intending to do because our brains and bodies are re-creating their actions. Studies on child development point out how important it is that very young children mimic the emotional expression of parents in close, face to face interaction.

8. Hall, "What Are Bodies For?," 165.
9. Rizzolatti and Craighero, "Mirror-Neuron System," 169–92.

Children who are deprived of these forms of mimicking activities show poor development in brain circuits that are involved in empathy, and they show a lack of empathy in their behavior as they get older.[10] By mimicking the actions and emotions of others, we come to understand the actions and the meaning of the actions. Clearly, this embodied response to action is a big part of the way we learn to experience and control emotions, and eventually to experience relationships.

Hall provides another intriguing example from studies on the hormone oxytocin. This hormone is released in response to a variety of specific types of bodily stimulation. For example, women release this hormone during sexual intercourse, childbirth, and breast feeding. In all of these cases there are specific physiological benefits from the hormone (e.g., functions supporting labor and delivery, and the production and "release" of milk in the breast), but it also is known to activate emotion centers in the brain that promote bonding. In other words, it promotes a sense of emotional closeness and attachment to the baby or sexual partner. So we feel this emotion in our entire being (i.e., body and mind).

To further understand the purpose of our body, we can also draw from the field of evolutionary psychology. While some Christian readers may react negatively to any notion of evolution, one does not have to accept all elements of this field to find useful applications to human behavior. In addition to explaining how behavior came to be, this discipline also tries to explain the main purpose or function of a behavior. A simple example of this functional approach is to ask why we get sweaty when we give a speech. One reason is that the function of fear was originally to help us prepare for life-threatening emergencies, such as a wild animal coming at us. When we need to run from a wild animal, our bodies heat up and we need to cool them—hence the sweat. As it turns out, modern humans interpret standing in front of people as threatening, so our body kicks in and causes sweat. The sweat is unhelpful here because we don't really need to engage in any strenuous physical activity in this situation.

Another interesting functional explanation for bodies comes from studies on sexual attraction. During the course of a woman's menstrual cycle, various hormones fluctuate. The level of one hormone, estrogen, is high just before ovulation, when women are most fertile (i.e., most likely to conceive because the egg has been released from the ovary). In one study, women were shown pictures of men at times during their hormone cycle when estrogen levels were highest or lowest.[11] The faces of the men were altered by

10. Schore, "Evaluative System in the Cortex," 337–58.
11. Penton-Voak et al., "Menstrual Cycle Alters Face Preference," 741–42.

computer graphics to look more masculine (e.g., square jaw, more prominent eyebrows) or more feminine (e.g., softer jaw, less prominent eyebrows).
During high estrogen periods, women thought the more masculine-looking
males were more attractive, but during low estrogen periods they rated the
more feminine-looking male faces as more attractive. How and why would
estrogen levels make a difference? First of all, we know from brain studies
that estrogen can alter the function of neurons in areas of the brain devoted
to emotions[12] and face perception.[13] Second, the functional explanation from
evolutionary psychology is that women prefer masculine faces during high
fertility levels because this most clearly represents the opposite sex, which
represents the best possible mate. They represent the best mate because
masculine-looking males are generally the healthiest and most likely to produce a good amount of sperm. There may be additional explanations for this
pattern, but it certainly does suggest that some of our deep desires and tendencies (e.g., attraction to the opposite sex) are directed by deep-seated bodily
processes.

Does this mean that we can reduce all of our intentions, emotions, and
desires to simple physical events? Neurologist Antonio Damasio provides a
thoughtful response: "Does this mean that there is no true love, no sincere
friendship, no genuine compassion? That is definitely not the case. Love is
true, friendship is sincere, and compassion is genuine, if I do not lie about
how I feel, if I *really* feel loving, friendly, and compassionate."[14] Damasio is
suggesting that while these amazing experiences are accomplished with bodies, we cannot fully reduce these experiences to the simple "nuts and bolts" of
bodily function; in other words, they are greater than the sum of the neuro-
biological parts. This holistic approach does not mean that these experiences
are somehow outside of ourselves (i.e., in a separate mind/soul) but that the
personal, subjective nature of mental experience is real and meaningful and
that our whole being is capable of authentically choosing these feelings. As
we described earlier, we are meaning seeking creatures (Theme 5), and as
such our embodied minds are very capable of establishing the meaning and
significance of our experiences.

What these examples of bodily functions *do* imply is that we understand
our world and relate to one another with our whole being, not just with an
abstract or disconnected mind. Can you imagine a robotic being, or a ghost-
like spirit, forming deep relationships the way we do? Without the intricate

12. Osterlund, Keller, and Hurd, "Human Forebrain," 333–42.
13. Hong et al., "Aberrant Neurocognitive Processing of Fear."
14. Damasio, *Descartes' Error*, 125.

workings and interactions of brain and body in the context of personal experiences, how could they truly understand another being, relate to one another, and truly develop feelings about one another?

The Embodied Church

A fresh reading of the Bible may awaken us to the "earthy" nature of our human nature and the purpose that God has for our bodies. Again, Hall provides beautiful language to capture this purpose: "We are told throughout Scripture that creation exists for God's glory (Isa. 43:4–7, Eph. 1:11–12, Rev. 4:11). In other words creation, and humans as part of that creation, exist to show who God is in all His glory."[15] She puts some "flesh and bones" on this idea by showing that we reflect God's glory when we are in relationship with him. As 1 Corinthians 6:15 suggests, "Do you not know that your bodies are members of Christ himself?" Notice that the apostle Paul doesn't say, "Your *souls* are members of Christ," suggesting that it's not some transcendent part of you that belongs to Christ but *all* of you. Earlier in chapter 6, Paul suggests, "The body, however, is not meant for sexual immorality *but for the Lord*, and the Lord for the body" (v. 13; emphasis added). Finally Paul ends this chapter with, "Therefore, honor God with your bodies" (v. 20). This passage is not suggesting that we should "rule over our bodies" by exerting our will, as if we need to beat the body into submission. Rather, it's a positive message suggesting that our embodied selves can honor God because we are in fellowship with him, and in fact we are embodied with him.

The church is often described in Scripture as "the body of Christ" (Rom. 12:3–8; 1 Cor. 6:13; 12:27). This is not simply an interesting metaphor, as Hall points out, but a deeply meaningful connection that illustrates ancient Hebrew thinking. The Hebrews viewed a cohesive group of people as a complete unity, not just a collection of individual bodies. So to be cut off from the body of Christ would be a truly horrible thing, just as a finger cut off from the body would die. Just as we cannot imagine having a deep relationship with one another without being a physical body, how can we have any meaningful relationship with God outside of our bodily existence or outside of his collective body? As we discussed earlier, being made in the image of God is not simply an individual concept but is a collective concept. In other words, it is not really the individual body that reflects God's nature but the collective or unified body of believers in fellowship with their Maker.

15. Hall, "What Are Bodies For?," 167.

Implications

What are the practical implications for revealing the purpose of bodies and our embodied relations? To start, let's go back to the story of Ethan in the introduction—who you may recall had many difficulties (e.g., ADHD, social isolation from others, etc.). His friend Shawna suggested that Ethan should just take on adult responsibility and that the real issue lies with his heart and soul. We have some sympathy for Shawna's view because, before the face of God, we ultimately bear responsibility for our actions (see chap. 1). However, we also believe that Shawna fails to appreciate that we cannot transcend our bodily selves. Our bodies and brains sometimes don't work the way they are supposed to. Just as S cannot *will* herself to experience fear, it's entirely possible that Ethan cannot *will* himself to act in a completely different way. So, human beings are limited agents (Theme 4); we are both enabled and constrained by our bodies in very significant ways. Even when bodies function optimally and we are able to freely choose, many aspects of our bodily existence limit or shape our thinking and behavior (think about oxytocin and estrogen as two examples).

In addition, if we understand that bodies allow us to be relational creatures, we may come to appreciate that our relational experiences (e.g., the divorce of Ethan's parents) become part of us—in other words, part of our bodily function. So our thoughts, actions, memories, and learned patterns of behavior influence our hormones, bodily reactions, brain activity, and even how our brain is "wired." These physical changes and internal responses in turn impact how we think about and relate to one another. Therefore, Ethan is embodied in community, and it is the community that should bear the struggles with him. So the "cures" for Ethan's problems come from many sources; not only from a pill—which may be helpful in restoring elements of his bodily function—but also from restored and renewed relationships, and from new ways of thinking and behaving that come through these relationships.

In conclusion, the reason people—including Christians—should care about bodies is that we ultimately care about relationships; first our relationship with God, then our relationships with one another. God commands us to love him above all and our neighbors as ourselves. Applying this idea to our previous examples, the main reason we should care about S's problem is that her lack of fear results in her having difficulty being in healthy relationships with others. The young woman with depression is debilitated not only because she can't experience happiness but also because she has difficulty relating to others—including God—in her current state. While psychological science is unlikely to find ultimate answers to the deeper meaning of our existence, it can help us to better understand the function and purpose of our bodies. It can help us appreciate how and why our embodied minds function as they do. As you will learn from studying this book, as well as from studying the entire discipline of psychology, there are many predictable, even lawful, elements to our behavior that spring from being embodied individuals.

There is one more implication from being embodied. We believe that the "redemption of our bodies" does not end with the gift of eternal salvation. This is only the beginning. This salvation frees believers to be of service, to bring healing to our current existence, to restore relationships to what God intended, and to embody Christ's Spirit. Because of our embodiment, we are also very much in relationship with God's good creation—since we are very much part of it. Therefore, Christians should care about our earthly existence and the impact of hunger, poverty, disease, and injustice on bodies and relationships. People are Christ's hands and feet in this world, and he expects his followers to get moving and not waste their bodies for themselves. As Christian psychologists we are not particularly interested in *just* saving individual souls. We are interested in saving and restoring the *whole person*—body, mind, relationships—and bringing a person into the whole body of Christ. We can thank the Lord that he had the wisdom to fashion these rather unappealing bits of flesh and bone into a collection of creatures that beautifully reflect his image.

DISCUSSION QUESTIONS

1. What are some specific physical experiences (e.g., hunger, pain) or qualities (e.g., chronic anxiety) that have influenced how you have thought or felt?

2. How have relationships been influenced by your physical life, and how have relationships impacted who and what you are physically today?

3. What would you say to someone who says that "curing" almost any life problem involves becoming more spiritual and connecting more with God?

4

The Ghost in the Machine

Brain and Behavior 2

Chapter Summary: If we are embodied individuals (as we discussed in chap. 3), does this mean that we are determined by our genetic and physical existence—and therefore have no free choices, no specialness, and no meaning? This chapter addresses these deeper questions about mind, body, and soul—how scientists have recently portrayed these ideas—and various approaches to these issues by Christian psychologists and scholars.

> True religion is real living; living with all one's soul, with all one's goodness and righteousness.
>
> Albert Einstein, as cited in Maker of Universes
by H. Gordon Garbedian

> No excellent soul is exempt from a mixture of madness.
>
> Aristotle, attributed by Seneca in Moral Essays

Phillipa, a capable grade-school teacher, was described by her husband as a very practical, organized, and positive person.[1] At age thirty-five she was

---

1. Ogden, *Fractured Minds*, 148–53.

assaulted by a burglar, which caused a severe head trauma that damaged parts of her frontal lobe. Despite a quick recovery from her injuries, she was a very changed person. In the rehabilitation hospital, she would call out to visitors, and if they did not respond, she would often swear at them or make comments like, "You snaky bastard, run for your life!" She did other very inappropriate things such as undressing in the ward without regard to who was present. She continued to score fairly high on IQ tests and other measures of intellect, but her husband and two young children were very disturbed by her behavior. Despite the best efforts of doctors, she remained institutionalized for the remainder of her life because of her uncontrollable behaviors.

Questions may come to mind when you read such a tragic story. Why can't a previously self-controlled person stop behaving this way? If she were a Christian (no information is given about her religious perspective), could we say that she was living in a way that was consistent with her faith? Where is the "real" Phillipa or the old Phillipa? Is she still there but hidden to us, or is she a fundamentally different person?

If you are a student of psychology, you may have read about Phineas Gage, who survived a metal tamping rod being blown through his skull and experienced a similar dramatic change in personality. However, less drastic situations than these may prompt difficult questions about human nature and personal responsibility. What about friends or family with explosive anger, addictions, chronic depression, or just annoying personalities? What about your own behavior? You may wonder why you don't have better control over your sexual urges, your emotions, your attention—or whatever unwanted behavior plagues you. Is there some inner self, "ghost," spirit, or soul inside of us that can overcome these problems?

The previous chapter stressed the importance of the body in understanding people, and hopefully we have given you reason to think that the scriptural emphasis on body is an appropriate basis for making this emphasis in psychology. But to be perfectly honest, we danced around the issue of the mind and the soul. Since neither of the authors is a very good dancer, we decided we had best come clean and address this tough issue straight on. The plain fact is that there are many movements afoot that deny any concept of, or use for, the soul or even the mind. These movements have been strong for decades among researchers and philosophers, but they are increasingly being discussed in widely read books and popular media.

For example, Steven Pinker, the Harvard psychologist and popular writer, represents this view that the concept of soul has outlived its usefulness. In a 2004 *Newsweek* magazine opinion article he says:

> People naturally believe in the Ghost in the Machine: that we have bodies made
> of matter and spirits made of an ethereal something. Yes, people acknowledge
> that the brain is involved in mental life. But they still think of it as a pocket PC
> for the soul, managing information at the behest of a ghostly user. . . . Mod-
> ern neuroscience has shown that there is no user. "The soul" is, in fact, the
> information-processing activity of the brain.[2]

In a later *Time* magazine piece, he suggests that "scientists have exorcised
the ghost from the machine not because they are mechanistic killjoys but
because they have amassed evidence that every aspect of consciousness can
be tied to the brain."[3] He doesn't end with the implications of these ideas
for understanding human behavior; he also says that a materialist worldview
has advantages for our current actions.

> And when you think about it, the doctrine of a life-to-come is not such an uplift-
> ing idea after all because it necessarily devalues life on earth. Just remember the
> most famous people in recent memory who acted in expectation of a reward in
> the hereafter: the conspirators who hijacked the airliners on 9/11.[4]

Many psychologists and neuroscientists like Pinker look at Phillipa and
say that she is a fundamentally different person. They also assume that you
can't hold people like her accountable for their actions when the "computer
hardware" doesn't work right, so we can't judge Phillipa's behavior as bad.
They would go on to argue that *all* of our behavior, even in "normal circumstances," is ultimately determined by our genetics, our brain function, and
the environments around us. We have the illusion that we freely decide what
course of action to take, but we are in fact response-generating machines
and nothing more. Taken to the logical extreme, this view would say that no
person can be held accountable for bad behavior (or that we can even define
what *bad* means); criminal behavior is just the interaction of dysfunctional
hardware (genetics and brain function), and/or bad software (environmental
influences). Just as we would assume a malfunctioning computer is not responsible for its actions, humans also have no freedom, no responsibility, and
ultimately no dignity. This view of human nature is sometimes called *monism*
because humans are viewed as just one thing—a functioning body. The other
term for the view that Pinker holds is sometimes called *materialism* because
it suggests that we are material substance and nothing more. It's a fairly

2. Pinker, "How to Think about the Mind."
3. Pinker, "Brain."
4. Ibid.

safe assumption to say that most human beings in the world maintain some form of *dualism*—meaning that there are at least two aspects of our nature (i.e., body and mind, or body and soul; for our purposes we will assume this implies a body and a soul/mind). In fact, psychologist Paul Bloom—himself a monist—suggests that human beings are intuitively dualistic because even young children have a sense that there are real (material) objects and imagined ones—which exist as mental events and therefore can't be physical.[5] Of course there are many views on this subject that exist somewhere between the extremes of materialistic monism and what is sometimes called Cartesian (from the views of philosopher René Descartes) dualism, but we suspect that most readers are still "intuitively dualistic," as Bloom describes.

The Faith Perspective

How should Christians respond to these ideas? Most Christians assume that belief in the soul is one of the cornerstones of Christian faith. Most feel that it is essential to faith because it allows us to explain:

- the simultaneous humanity and divinity of Christ,
- our own existence immediately after death,
- the physical or "fleshly" aspect of our sinful desires,
- the specialness of humans as distinct from animals, and
- the existence of free will, individuality, moral responsibility, and the meaningfulness of human life.[6]

Besides, the word *soul* is used more than 750 times in the Old Testament (King James Version) alone—so it has to be important! As a result, the majority of Christians have simply dismissed many psychologists and neuroscientists as "nonbelievers" and not worthy of our attention. They feel that the existence of the soul can never be scientifically proven or disproven any more than the existence of God—it's simply a matter of faith. So it's not worth even having a debate with scientists because we will just talk past each other anyway.

But what about the "amassed evidence" that Pinker mentions? The simple truth is that when anyone spends a lot of time looking at this evidence, even the most committed dualist has to pause and wonder what the mind is, or how soul relates to body. Christians going on to advanced studies in neuroscience

5. Bloom, *Descartes' Baby*, 199.
6. Notice that all of these issues relate in various ways to themes of this book.

or neuropsychology may find that this evidence presents such a challenge to their basic assumptions about human nature that they may begin to question other aspects of faith as well. After all, if the existence of the soul is one cornerstone of their worldview, and they begin to question this assumption, then perhaps the rest of their beliefs may begin to unravel as well. So it is very important for any person of faith who is exploring psychology to examine some of this evidence and to begin formulating a thoughtful way to respond to this apparent challenge coming from the scientific community.

Considering the Evidence

It would take volumes of information to try to capture the evidence that Pinker is referring to, so we will address just two examples here. Think about the story of Phillipa and the implications of the story. If there is a separate soul that is in control, why can't she exercise that control? One common response from a dualist perspective is that it's possible that the "real" Phillipa is still there (and perhaps God can see it), it's just that *we* don't see it. In other words, using Pinker's words, the "pocket PC for the soul" doesn't function well. So it's a simple matter of a communication problem between the body and soul with the malfunctioning brain being the block to that communication.

But there are other cases that seem even more difficult to reconcile with traditional dualist views. As Michael Gazzaniga describes the situation, consider the visual loss someone has when that person's left optic tract is severed.[7] The optic tract carries information from one side of each eye and eventually sends that information to the back of the brain, or what we call the "visual cortex," which is associated with our conscious experience of sight. If such severing occurs, patients will immediately report that they cannot see anything in their right visual field when their eyes are focused on objects directly in front of them. In other words, they are completely blind to half of the world, even though their eyes work fine. The patients are clearly consciously aware of this loss of visual experience, and this loss is obviously the result of the disrupted physical information transfer from one part of the brain to another. But what happens when damage occurs to the part of the brain that actually receives the information from the left optic tract (i e , damage to the left visual cortex)? Instead of reporting that they can't see half of the world, they report no problems at all! We know that these patients can't see half of the world because they will bump into things on the right side and, if their

---

7. Gazzaniga, *Who's in Charge?*, 65.

eyes are looking straight ahead, cannot describe anything that is presented to their right. Despite this partial blindness, they are unaware that part of the world is no longer represented in their mind.

Let's assume for a moment that the brain is, in effect, a simple calculator and transmitter of information from our bodies to the final end user—the mind/soul. If this is true, why does the lack of information transfer to the back of the brain in the case of the severed optic tract cause the person to have a conscious awareness of visual loss, when this does not occur in the case of a damaged visual cortex? Wouldn't the "end user" (e.g., the self-conscious soul) still notice something was missing? The answer that Gazzaniga provides is that there is no additional end user that we can locate; it seems that the end user *is* the cortex at the back of the brain, the self-conscious visual cortex. As he states: "The logical conclusion to these observations is that phenomenal consciousness, that feeling you have about being conscious of some perception, is generated by local processes that are uniquely involved with a specific activity."[8]

By themselves, these examples cannot undo the dualist position, and the illustration provided by Gazzaniga may say more about our mental states than about anything called the soul. Many Christian and non-Christian dualists have found ways to explain, or attempt to explain, situations such as these in a way consistent with a dualist view. However, it is also quite clear that our long-established views about the soul and mind are getting harder to reconcile with current scientific data. Interestingly, many people may not be aware that there have been a growing number of Christian psychologists, neuroscientists, philosophers, and theologians who have begun to revise or update our concept of soul. Some of these scholars still hold to a dualist view, while other Christian scholars have promoted a Christian version of the monist view. This monist view suggests that a person is a unified, living, breathing being, with nothing else "plugged in" (e.g., soul, mind, spirit, whatever) to make the person become a person.

If you are fairly new to the discipline of psychology you may be wondering if any of this discussion or disagreement really matters for everyday living. It may seem to some that debating this issue is equivalent to philosophers arguing about the existence of reality—how could this possibly matter? While they may not impact most of your lives at present, these issues do have some very big implications for issues you may encounter at some point in your life, as well as for the discipline of psychology. For example, many psychologists have had to counsel family members trying to understand moral and ethical

8. Ibid., 66.

issues raised by situations similar to Phillipa's. Likewise, many individuals have had to deal personally with significant brain diseases, sexual dysfunction, or emotional problems that cause them to wonder why they are not able to overcome these problems. If one takes a more materialist-monistic view, there is a danger of treating a person with such problems as having no value, responsibility, or meaning. If one takes a more dualistic view, there is a danger of spiritualizing all problems and not recognizing the physical, mental, and social nature of human problems. So we feel that these are very relevant questions. However, the goal of this chapter is not to defend one particular position but to see how the biblical narrative helps us to steer between the two fairly extreme views: "physicalism" (or "materialism" or "reductionism"—as expressed by Steven Pinker) and extreme "spiritualism" (which suggests that the only important thing is the soul and that this world does not matter to God at all). We will say more on the different views among Christians, and the important implications, in a moment—but first, a brief overview of the scriptural understanding of the soul.

Biblical Descriptions of Human Nature

The updated monistic view espoused by some Christian scholars (that we referred to above) is not only a response to the current data provided by neuroscience but also a revised understanding of the words used in Scripture to describe body, soul, and spirit. Many biblical scholars have pointed out that neither the Hebrew language of the Old Testament nor the Greek language of the New Testament has a word easily translated to our English word *soul*—at least as it is understood in common usage. There are two or three Hebrew words that are often translated as "soul" in older or in modern translations. One such word, *nephesh* (English spelling of the original Hebrew), was always translated as "soul" in the King James Version of the Bible, but many contemporary translations (e.g., New International Version) often don't. The problem is that the word *nephesh* is best translated as "living being." So in Genesis 2:7, we read, "God formed a man from the dust of the ground and breathed into his nostrils the breath of life, and the man became a *nephesh* [older translation: *soul*; newer translation: *living being*]." The same word, *nephesh*, is used when describing animals (see Gen. 1:20, 21, 24, 30, for examples). All through the Old Testament, *nephesh* consistently describes a living being, not a separate entity that is traditionally called the soul.

There are other Hebrew words sometimes translated as "soul." For example, *ruach*, *nishmath*, and a few other complementary words may be translated as "soul," "spirit," or "breath." However, these words are also applied to animals and may simply suggest, quite literally, that they "have the breath of life." There are many instances where combinations of these words are applied to both animals and humans, but certain combinations are used *only* for humans (e.g., Gen. 7:22). Although interpretation of these words is always difficult, this unique combination of terms may suggest that humans are unique in some way because humans have one kind of "breath" and animals another kind (see also 1 Cor. 15:39). We will return to this issue later.

Translating the New Testament is slightly more complicated since it is written in Greek, and the Greek language—influenced as it was by the dualist philosophies of Socrates and Plato—often has a dualist way of speaking. So words such as *pneuma* (most often translated "spirit") and *psuche* (sometimes spelled *psyche*, which is the basis for our English word *psychology*) are translated as "mind," "soul," or simply "person" depending on the context. Therefore do these terms represent a separate entity that can exist apart from the body?[9] There is no single answer given by Christian scholars. But as theologian N. T. Wright suggests, we don't need to have precise definitions and an agreed-upon definition for all these terms, and we shouldn't "make absolute" ("reify") any of our human-nature ("anthropological") terms. As he states:

> My basic proposal . . . is that we need to think in terms of a *differentiated unity*. Paul and the other early Christian writers didn't reify their anthropological terms. Though Paul uses his language with remarkable consistency, he nowhere suggests that any of the key terms refers to a particular "part" of the human being to be played off against any other. Each *denotes* the entire human being, while *connoting* some angle of vision on who that human is and what he or she is called to be. Thus, for instance, *sarx*, flesh, refers to the entire human being but connotes corruptibility, failure, rebellion, and then sin and death. *Psyche* denotes the entire human being, and connotes that human as possessed [for] ordinary mortal life, with breath and blood sustained by food and drink.[10]

Despite these difficulties in translation and differences among scholars, the renewed examination of the Old and New Testaments has caused biblical scholars to reassess what the Bible means by the original words we translate as "soul." Even strong defenders of a dualist view of human nature have conceded that the ancient Hebrew view was much different from current

---

9. Wright, "Mind, Spirit, Soul and Body." Also see Wright, "Mortal Soul," 447–71.
10. Wright, "Mind, Spirit, Soul and Body."

traditional Christian views. For example, John Cooper, who holds to a form of dualism, has suggested, "Careful study of the relevant Hebrew and Greek texts of Scripture does not yield the body-soul dualism of tradition. The Bible presents a more integrated, holistic view of human nature than is found in Augustine, Aquinas, Calvin and scholastic theology."[11] In commenting about philosopher René Descartes's stronger form of dualism, he goes on to say that, "As a result, body, mind, emotions and spirit have been cut off from each other both in ordinary life and in our attempts to treat the problems of ordinary life."[12] Therefore, even biblical scholars who hold to the possibility of a separation of body and soul in the next life still concede that the traditional view has gone too far in dividing our human nature as it relates to our present life.

The diversity of ideas about what the Bible really says about soul, life after death, the resurrection, and so on is far beyond the scope of this introductory book, but we can summarize two main positions among theologians and Christian psychologists. Some contemporary Christian scholars (see Cooper,[13] Evans,[14] and Stump[15] for good examples) have suggested that in this life there can be no distinction or separation between body and soul, but that at death God can, in a word, "extract" the soul (or essence of us) from the body. Others have challenged this view by suggesting that there can never be any separation because we can only think of humans as living beings—nothing more. They contend that persons are always with a body and that without some form or substance, we simply can't talk about *nephesh* (a living being). This Christian monistic view (see MacKay,[16] and Brown, Murphy, and Malony[17] for examples) points to the strong emphasis in Scripture on the resurrection of the body and the frequent reference to our mortality (i.e., "dust to dust"). Certainly there are many difficulties in understanding several scriptural passages no matter which of these two positions you take.[18] However, despite all the differing views, there is also a good deal of agreement among many Christian scholars about key aspects of our human nature. As philosopher C. Stephen Evans suggests, "There is a lot for the dualist to learn from the non-reductive materialist [i.e., "a Christian monist"]."[19] Likewise, theologian N. T. Wright

---

11. Cooper, "Body-Soul Question," 3.
12. Ibid.
13. See Cooper, *Body, Soul, and Life Everlasting.*
14. Evans, "Separable Souls," 327–40.
15. Stump, "Non-Reductive Physicalism," 63–76.
16. See MacKay, *Behind the Eye.*
17. See Brown, Murphy, and Malony, *Whatever Happened to the Soul?*
18. Giles, *Understanding the Christian Faith*, 73.
19. Evans, "Separable Souls," 340.

suggests that trying to explain this all is not the essential issue of Scripture: "I believe therefore that a Christian anthropology must necessarily ask, not, what are human beings in themselves, but, what are human beings called to do and be as part of the creator's design?"[20]

So whatever your view on the dual or unified nature of human beings, we the authors believe that deciding between these two extremes (dualism or monism) is not the most important issue, but we do hold the following truths to be nonnegotiable in understanding the biblical view of human nature.

1. We are created in God's image. Whether this means we are two separate entities or one is not the key issue. The key issue is that we reflect God's character in many ways and are able to relate to him and to one another. This also suggests that we occupy a special place in God's creation. This specialness is not simply that we are more advanced than animals, or even (necessarily) that we have an extra thing called a soul plugged in, but that God chooses to have a relationship with us.[21]

2. The resurrection of Christ and our own bodily resurrection are essential truths regardless of the means or mechanism for these events.

3. Humans possess the ability to make choices, moral and otherwise, and bear ultimate responsibility for our actions. For Christian dualists, this responsibility and morality is part of the soul, or spiritual aspect. For Christians who take the monistic approach, these characteristics are not a property of a separate soul but exist as part of an "emergent mind." In other words, the essence of our human nature is not an "end user" that exists outside of ourselves but rather is a result of the fairly mysterious "coming together" of complex neurological elements—created by an almighty God. The whole of these elements (the mind) is greater than the sum of the parts. So we can freely choose, argue the Christian monists, even without need of or reference to a separate soul.[22] While Christian psychologists from either perspective recognize the influence of genetics, brain function, and environment, the Christian also acknowledges that we cannot consider our collective social and personal behavior to be determined by physical forces alone.

4. Our humanness is very much tied to our embodiment. Both Christian dualists and monists agree that we have for too long neglected the importance of being a living body and have only stressed the spiritual. As discussed in the previous chapter, this means that Christian psychologists

---

20. Wright, "Mind, Spirit, Soul and Body."

21. Brown, Murphy, and Malony, *Whatever Happened to the Soul?*, 99–125.

22. This view is sometimes called "non-reductive physicalism" because it stresses the physical nature of humans but argues that we cannot and should not "reduce" our worth and our choices down to these physical forces alone.

need to spend more time understanding how the body functions and how this impacts our human behavior.

5. Because we are embodied, we have a lot in common with the rest of creation—including animals. God placed us firmly within the created world; we feel the wind, experience the physical changes around us, and learn to respond to those physical changes in ways that are very similar to all of God's creatures. However, as stated above, we also conclude that we are special because of God's relationship to us, because he describes us as being made in his image, and because we appear to have distinct qualities (i.e., "breath") compared to animals. The exact meaning of these concepts is not always clear to us, but our common physical nature suggests that we can learn much about ourselves from studying animals. On the other hand, if we want to fully understand the complexity of human thinking, we also have to acknowledge our distinctiveness.

Implications for Psychology

Returning to the case study of Phillipa and the typical description of human nature provided by people like Steven Pinker, how can we use this biblical understanding to answer these challenges? Rather than simply dismissing Pinker's views, a thoughtful Christian response can actually find some points of agreement with his views. Instead of using biblical counterarguments, we might respond by saying that the key issue for Christians is not whether we possess some "end user" called the soul. Rather, the key issue is our relatedness to God, our specialness, and our responsibility. We can acknowledge that Phillipa's brain injury will change her in profound ways—given the renewed understanding of embodiment—but we can also say that she is more than the sum total of her damaged neurological parts. We may also learn a lot about damaged behavior from studying brain damage in animals, but we simply cannot understand the complete nature of human behavior unless we also examine the profoundly unique qualities of human beings.

So we hope to steer between the extremes that are often present in science, psychology, and the church. We reject the one extreme, which suggests that the only part of us that matters is the soul, and that only a "spiritual" approach to counseling or any effort to change humans will be effective. This same approach also places excessive responsibility on individual behavior, as if we are all equally capable of transcending our bodies, relationships, and social existence. We also reject the other extreme, which paints human beings as nothing but biological computers, determined entirely by the physical and environmental forces that shape us, and ultimately incapable of truly responsible "agency" (e.g., the ability to freely choose). Instead, we wish to promote a more holistic view of human beings and how we should help people change their behavior. We need to focus on the whole person—their genetics, their bodies, their relationships, and their spiritual growth. As physician James L. Wright has written when referring to the unity of the person in cases of Alzheimer's disease, "Dementia confronts us with the fact that our entire person, mind and soul are as subject to decay as our heart, joints and muscle."[23] He states earlier in his paper that "As one witnesses the slow loss of personality traits, memory, independence and identity seen in Alzheimer's Dementia, one is struck by how this clearly resonates with the Psalmist's complaint, 'My soul [nephesh] melts away . . .' (Psalm 119, v. 28, NRSV)."[24]

We would like to leave you with one last challenge. Pinker also suggested that the spiritual emphasis seen in religion has caused religious people to do harm in the present life, or at least do very little good. We actually have some sympathy for this view since we believe the overemphasis on the disembodied soul has caused religious groups to sometimes neglect the important tasks that God has given us to do in this life. God does value this world he created. Why else would he create it? He also values his followers being active in all areas of his world—bringing healing to bodies and minds. As N. T. Wright has suggested in his book *After You Believe: Why Christian Character Matters*:

> The old ideas that the goal of Christian existence is simply "going to heaven" doesn't, in fact, do very much to stimulate the fully fledged virtue we find advocated in the New Testament. . . .
>
> The aim of the Christian life in the present time—the goal you are meant to be aiming at once you have come to faith, the goal which is within reach even in the present life, anticipating the final life to come—is the life of fully formed, fully flourishing Christian character.[25]

Wright suggests that this Christian character is formed not by focusing on ourselves but by being responsive to the call of the gospel and being active agents in the world that exists here and now. Thus, we believe that we are called to be transforming agents of renewal in understanding the nature of embodied human behavior and bringing restoration to the brokenness that we experience.

23. Wright, "Mortal Soul," 451.
24. Ibid., 447.
25. Wright, *After You Believe*, 32.

DISCUSSION QUESTIONS

1. Did you have a strong opinion on this issue of body, mind, and soul, or had you seldom thought about it? Have your ideas started to change on the matter after reading these chapters (or any similar source), or do you feel that your views have remained the same?

2. Regardless of which view you agree with or even which one is ultimately true, summarize some potential dangers (i.e., potential downsides or negative implications) that can occur if you apply an exclusive materialist-monist view to psychological functioning. Summarize some potential dangers you can see happening if you apply a strong dualist view to psychological functioning.

3. If someone is pronounced legally dead because they are "brain-dead," but their heart is still beating, where is that "person"? Is their "soul" (i.e., personhood) "melting away," is that person still really here, or has something already left them?

5

Who Is in Control?

Consciousness

Chapter Summary: Consciousness is our most familiar experience, but because it is private to each of us, it is difficult to understand. What is clear, however, is that much of our behavior is not under our direct conscious control or monitoring. In this chapter, we discuss the implications of unconscious and conscious thought, the relationship of both to behavior, and what they indicate about humans as responsible limited agents. We will explore how thought and behavior, shaped by deep desires that come with seeking meaning, are influenced by conscious and unconscious thought.

> We take consciousness for granted because it is so available, so easy to use, so elegant in its daily disappearing and reappearing acts, and yet, when we think of it, scientists and nonscientists alike, we do puzzle.
>
> Antonio R. Damasio, *Self Comes to Mind*

Good morning! Your alarm goes off at 7:00 a.m. You wake with a start from a dream in which you were arguing with a monkey that has stolen your new shoes. You yawn, rub your eyes, and somehow get to the bathroom to take a shower. By the end of the shower, you finally start to feel awake.

When a morning starts that way, where's the line between your being awake and being asleep? For instance, if you are asleep, how do you "hear" the alarm? And how "awake" are you when you wake? Some days you are very aware of where you are and what day it is, but on other days you may be totally confused and disoriented, at least momentarily. If you feel less awake before your shower, what changed so that you feel more awake afterward? You may say you feel more "alert," but what does that mean? Alertness might be thought of as a readiness to respond. Yet being "ready to respond" is relative—we can be somewhat more or somewhat less mentally prepared to act.

Alertness falls under the umbrella of the larger subject of this chapter, *consciousness*, which is a person's subjective, firsthand experience of reality and one's own thoughts. Although each individual's consciousness is a personal experience, not directly known by anyone else, reports of consciousness are accompanied by observable bodily responses to events, like smiling in response to a joke. In addition, if you were to record a person's brain activity, there would be characteristic patterns of neural responses that correspond with her report of being conscious. Observable bodily movements can occur without consciousness, however, and can happen without being consciously noticed by the person. In fact, many behaviors occur without conscious awareness, such as staring too long at someone who is attractive or saying "um" when thinking of what to say next (which is probably more likely when staring at someone attractive!).

Consciousness = Wakefulness + Awareness

Private experiences of our surroundings and our own thoughts, including our thoughts about our experiences, are deeply human. Some psychologists say that this characteristic of consciousness "is essential to what it means to be human."[1] Simple wakefulness (being alert) is seen in animals that show sleep and wake cycles, and animals awaken from sleep if there is a loud noise or "alarm." What may be unique to human consciousness is the awareness of our own subjective reality—what we each feel and experience from our own point of view. This dimension of consciousness is more than just knowing that something is happening—demonstrating wakefulness by being able to respond—it's a self-awareness of our own thoughts and perceptions.

These two dimensions—wakefulness and awareness—are the basic properties of consciousness and have been shown to be completely separable from each other. Our own experiences, like differences in how we feel from one day to another when waking up in the morning, show us that wakefulness and

1. Schacter, Gilbert, and Wegner, *Psychology*, 176.

awareness fluctuate. Neuropsychological research confirms these variations.[2] If both wakefulness and awareness are very low, a person would experience a coma; if both are high, the experience is conscious wakefulness. In addition, one can be high and the other low, such that they vary independently of each other. During a vivid dream, awareness is high, but wakefulness is low. Conversely, in a vegetative state, a person can appear to be awake (with eyes open), but that person lacks awareness.

If awareness or general alertness can vary so much, how can embodied persons with limited agency responsibly enact their beliefs (Themes 3 and 4)? That is, if Christians believe that they must follow the Bible in their living, how can they do that if they are not fully alert and aware in every situation they find themselves? People sleep; both psychology and the Bible are clear on this. Are self-awareness and awareness of God necessary or sufficient for faithful living, or is more needed? In the remainder of this chapter, we will explore variations in consciousness and their implications for understanding a biblical view of humans.

Limited Consciousness, Limited Agency

From a Christian perspective, consciousness, including self-consciousness, is not enough for people to live out what they believe in all times and all places. People fail to follow through on God's commands because humans are sinful (Theme 2). People sin even when aware of their own sinfulness and desiring to avoid sin. As the apostle Paul wrote in Romans: "I do not understand what I do. For what I want to do I do not do, but what I hate I do."[3] In this passage, although Paul really wants to stop his own sinning, he still continues to sin. Trying really hard did not get the job done because humans don't just make errors; people are in a state of sin. Nevertheless, Paul certainly gives directives to the churches he writes to,[4] with the obvious expectation that people have sufficient awareness to check what they are doing against what they ought to be doing and make changes as needed.

Psychology does not set out to address humanity's state of sin. Psychology does, however, provide insight into understanding how self-awareness allows

2. Laureys, "Eyes Open, Brain Shut," 32–37, further describes the dimensions of wakefulness and awareness, showing how the relative strength of each of these contributes to various states of consciousness.

3. Rom. 7:15.

4. Among the passages where Paul gives instruction in Christian living are Eph. 4–5 and Col. 3–4.

us to check whether our behavior follows our beliefs. To use consciousness in this way, it seems that we would want to maintain high levels of awareness throughout our waking hours (and hope we don't do or think about anything when unconscious during sleep!). Unconscious behaviors had best be avoided altogether because they are not consciously supervised. Psychological science and our own personal experiences, however, show that we cannot constantly check ourselves and that much of our behavior is unconscious.

Unrelenting, full awareness simply does not happen. Wakefulness and awareness vary through the day. For some, mornings tend to be rather groggy, while for others, evenings are times of drowsiness.[5] Another way that awareness fluctuates is when our minds wander as we daydream.[6] Variations in wakefulness in a well-rested person influence thinking and responding, but the effects of sleep deprivation are much more striking. Researchers in a variety of disciplines have shown sleep deprivation's effects on processes as varied as decision making, emotionality, and driving—and that the impacts are greater than most people suspect. Sleep-deprived people "nod off" during all sorts of tasks, including driving, and do so without even knowing it. As one researcher has said, sleepiness results in "inability to focus, delayed and poor decision making, indifference, lack of motivation," and general lack of self-monitoring.[7] As sleep deprivation grows, people tend to rely more on habitual, automatic responses such as stereotypes and intuitive decision making (see chap. 9 for both good and bad consequences of such decisions). Our physical state requires that we sleep. When we are sleepy (and certainly when we are asleep), we have a more difficult time exerting our will. Our already limited human agency is even more limited.

Unconsciousness

If behavior is unconsciously managed at least part of the time, are people then unable to direct their behaviors, leaving them without responsibility during those times? In contrast to Theme 4, are people then non-responsible

5. Kerkhoff, "Inter-Individual Differences," 83–112, provides a thorough review of how people differ from each other in terms of circadian rhythms through the day, also known as "morningness" versus "eveningness."

6. Mind wandering has become an area of research interest. Mason et al., "Wandering Minds," 393–95, provide information on the neural basis of our mental excursions while awake.

7. Dement, Promise of Sleep, 233. In his book, he extensively outlines the various and rather dangerous consequences of inadequate sleep. Harrison and Horne, "Impact of Sleep Deprivation," 236–49, reviewed the research on sleep deprivation's many effects on decision making; Durmer and Dinges, "Neurocognitive Consequences of Sleep Deprivation," 117–29, indicate a wide variety of cognitive deficits related to sleep deprivation, including higher accident rates, poorer learning, and slower response times.

non-agents? It's important to note that when today's psychologists are talking about the unconscious, they typically don't mean the sort of unconscious Sigmund Freud had in mind, with its underlying desires (drives or energies) seeking to be satisfied when unconscious (i.e., dreams) or "released" during consciousness in indirect ways. Freud's particular view of the unconscious was overly complicated and has not stood up well to scientific scrutiny, but it did generate a great deal of interest in the nature of the unconscious mind.[8] More important to our discussion, Freud viewed human behavior as determined by unconscious processes, leaving people without responsibility for their actions. Freud's depiction of humans was both unscientific and contrary to a biblical view of human nature in this case (see chap. 14 for a more extensive critique).

When psychologists today discuss unconscious processes, they primarily point to aspects of mental processing that are not directly experienced yet contribute to each person's thoughts, decisions, perceptions, emotions, and behavior. These include processes that cannot be brought to consciousness, no matter how much we try, as well as processes that are currently outside of awareness but that we could bring to awareness (like paying attention to the fact that we're saying "um" in conversation). Many basic processes of perception (how we detect light or configure parts of an image to determine that it is a face) and memory (how a memory is formed through altering the activity of neurons in the brain) simply cannot be consciously accessed. This aspect of the unconscious—the *cognitive unconscious*—works in ways that are more efficient and manageable than if such processes were consciously processed. Therefore, very common, "simple" processes like dividing sounds into words or perceiving the color blue are prevented from reaching consciousness due to how the brain processes information. In this understanding of unconscious processes, decisions and feelings occur without us being aware of all of the steps and thoughts involved because doing so is more efficient, not because such thoughts are repressed, as Freud suggested. As psychologist Timothy Wilson writes, "The mind is a well-designed system that is able to accomplish a great deal in parallel, by analyzing and thinking about the world outside of awareness while consciously thinking about something else."[9] Processes that don't require conscious monitoring are processed unconsciously, while those that need more careful monitoring occur consciously.

8. The scientific failings of Freud's theorizing about the unconscious are pointed out in most introductory psychology books. Scientific theories "must have specific implications for observable events in the natural world," as Stanovich, *How to Think Straight about Psychology*, 12, writes. Freud's theory doesn't make clear predictions—it merely explains human behavior after behavior occurs. Science is interested in prediction.

9. Wilson, *Strangers to Ourselves*, 8–9.

Limitations of Consciousness

The capacity of consciousness is severely limited. At most, we can consciously think about only a few items at once, and often times only one (see chap. 6 on the limitations of attention), so much of our thinking appears to be unconscious. Consider the amount of conscious relative to unconscious thought taking place in the following situation. You're walking down a street where you live, and a person sitting on the sidewalk yells, "Help!" What should you do? You need to quickly evaluate lots of information and form answers to many questions regarding the other person (Is the person serious? Is it someone I know?), the situation (Is anyone else around? Is there danger?), and yourself (Am I equipped to help? Do I feel like helping?). Most of those dimensions are evaluated unconsciously—without awareness. People simply don't consciously ask each of these questions one at a time before deciding whether to keep on walking or to stop and try to give assistance. The conscious thought, "That person needs help, I need to stop," may occur, but such a conclusion follows from and occurs alongside a lot of unconscious processing that strongly informed it (using System 1 processes[10] as described in chap. 9, on thinking). Even your response of asking, "How can I help you?" includes unconscious processes that result in the tone of voice you use, ensuring you use both a noun and a verb, and even your choice of which particular words you use. In the case of speech, "each and every conscious process is accompanied by (or is a residual of) unconscious processing."[11]

Free Will and Unconscious Thought

What does this depiction of conscious relative to unconscious processing have to say about responsible limited agency (Theme 4)? Psychologists have a variety of answers, in part because they disagree about how conscious and unconscious processing work together. A particularly disputed issue is how one type of processing might control or influence the other.

No Freedom

Some, such as psychologist John Bargh, view conscious processing as pointless. He states that the "feeling of free will is very real, just as real for those scientists who argue against its actual existence as for everyone else, but this strong feeling is an illusion."[12] This perspective reasons that although the

10. Kahneman, *Thinking, Fast and Slow*, 20.
11. Dijksterhuis and Aarts, "Goals, Attention and (Un)Consciousness," 471.
12. Bargh, "Free Will Is Un-Natural," 148.

experience of awareness is caused by the brain, this sense of awareness impacts neither the brain nor behavior. That is, being "aware" doesn't change what people actually do, so a sense of awareness does not matter, and certainly doesn't make us more responsible.[13]

Those who take this point of view argue from research indicating that human behavior is profoundly influenced by factors outside of conscious awareness, such as making automatic evaluations of situations and others in less time than it would take to be consciously aware of them.[14] This research, showing that attitudes and actions are automatically activated (primed) by objects and actions around us, can be interpreted as showing that free will doesn't really exist—people are simply responding to their environment.[15]

Those arguing against human free will also point to research on perceptions of self-control when people make a simple, voluntary movement. In some well-known experiments by Benjamin Libet and colleagues, research participants were told to move their index finger whenever they wanted, while the timing of three events was measured: (1) when brain activity related to making a finger movement occurs, (2) when the person was aware of making a conscious decision to move, and (3) when the actual finger movement occurred.[16] Using electrical sensors placed on a participant's scalp for measurement of brain activity, such experiments found that electrical activity related to planning a move began about a half second before the finger began to move, as measured by sensors measuring muscle movement in fingers. That makes sense—the brain first made a plan, then carried it out. But what about the feeling of having decided to move? To measure this, participants watched a dot move around the face of a clock to mark the moment at which the action was consciously willed. Such studies have shown that the conscious decision to act was experienced only about one-fifth of a second before the actual movement. The

13. This is the notion that consciousness is an epiphenomenon.

14. Fazio et al., "Automatic Activation of Attitudes," 229–38, showed that attitudes can be automatically activated by simply viewing objects about which a person has a strong attitude. That attitude can then act to influence evaluation of a next object to be evaluated—that is, evaluations of objects about which one has an attitude can prime responses to other objects. If research participants saw a word they had previously judged to be negative (e.g., "crime"), then were to decide if an adjective was negative (e.g., "disgusting"), they were faster at making their decision than if they saw a word that they judged positive (e.g., "gift"). Fazio et al. state that such activation appeared in their study to be "both spontaneous and inescapable" (p. 236). Fazio, "Automatic Activation of Associated Evaluations," 115–41, further reviews this literature.

15. Freud also believed that humans have no free will, but his reasoning was different. According to Freud, humans lacked free will because they were at the mercy of unconscious desires that could not be willfully controlled.

16. Libet has conducted several experiments on this topic, including Libet et al., "Time of Conscious Intention to Act," 623–42, and Libet, "Unconscious Cerebral Initiative," 529–66.

brain's planning of the action, however, began before conscious awareness of deciding to move—so the brain was active *before* even consciously thinking of the action!

Daily experiences echo such effects. Many times, our thoughts about an action occur only *after* an action has been completed. If you greet someone and a friend asks you, "Why did you say 'hi' to her?" you are likely to give a reason such as, "Because she lives next door to me." But prior to your greeting, did you actually have the conscious thoughts, "She lives next door to me. I will say hello"? You probably just said hello. For a great proportion of our behaviors, we act *without* experiencing any conscious awareness of governing our behavior, in which cases we can't claim that a behavior was caused by conscious thought: the thought never happened! Many behaviors are not the result of carefully examined and well-reasoned thought. How people act is often not intentional in the sense of behavior following a complete conscious thought. This fact may lead us to greater humility about the wisdom of our own behavior and greater grace in responding to the behavior of others.

All of these findings and examples, taken together, lead some psychologists to conclude that even when we have the sense of consciousness being in charge of our brains and bodies, that may not be what is happening. Some take this as strong evidence that humans have no agency; free choice is an illusion.

At this point in this chapter (maybe even earlier), your conscious mind may be yelling something like, "What do these people mean I don't choose? Of course I choose what I want to do! I have free will!" If you have been talking with a friend and notice the time, you may think to yourself, "Oops, I'm supposed to be at work, I have to go." In that case, it seems very sensible to conclude that your decision-making processes, at least some of which were conscious, led to your behavior. As humans, we have a natural tendency to see cause-and-effect relationships. That's part of our basic predisposition to seek meaning (Theme 5). This, along with our very real experience of having thoughts, helps lead us to believe that our thoughts cause our own action.

The Role of Free Will

Scripture shows that people do have *real* choice, however limited that agency may be (as we outlined earlier). But is there any place in psychological science for free will? Some psychologists, including Roy Baumeister, say that those arguing free will is nonexistent based on their studies of consciousness need to reevaluate what the research shows. Critiquing the research on priming and sequencing brain and movement events, Baumeister says that this work focuses on "slicing behavior into milliseconds," but doing so may "conceal the important role of conscious choice, which is mainly seen at the macro level."[17] Baumeister argues that consciousness is limited, so it would be used sparingly, only where it's necessary. Conscious planning and oversight are needed for big picture behaviors (macro level), rather than being wasted on monitoring endless, tiny details (happening over tiny fractions of a second). Free will may have more to do with deciding to walk to a particular destination than supervising the placement and action of each footstep on the trip.[18] Although we can make ourselves aware of each footstep (or in the case of Libet's experiments, each finger movement), Baumeister argues that free will is more involved in deciding *whether* to walk somewhere (or in the case of Libet's experiments, *whether* to follow the experiment's directions) than in planning each movement. In addition, as awareness varies from less to more, a simple, highly practiced behavior like moving a finger may require little awareness to be carried out.

It is important to note that by using our limited free will and setting the course of our own behavior, we also limit future possibilities. Over our lives, these changes in course (e.g., I will play basketball rather than participating in theater) yield consequences that impact the directions of life (e.g., more of my friends are fellow basketball players than folks in theater). Those directions, though later limited and seemingly without alternatives, were the consequence of conscious choices made earlier. The patterns of our lives reflect our choices; behavior that resulted from exercising our agency has long-term consequences.

Arguing in favor of free will, Baumeister points out two advantages of human agency. First, agency allows humans to have self-control, or willpower, which allows for long-term goals to be accomplished by resisting immediate desires (e.g., remaining free by not stealing money). In addition, humans have the ability for rational choice to decide, among other things, what those long-term goals might be and how to achieve them. Baumeister goes on to assert that self-control and rational choice are evolutionarily advantageous—humans who have these forms of controlling behavior are better able to function in human situations of relationships and rules than those who do not.[19] Interestingly, Bargh, who argues against free will, also looks to evolutionary theory to support his approach, stating that "consciously expressed preferences" are based on evolutionarily based preferences (modified by culture and learning), but fundamentally based in our evolved tendencies.[20] Thus, people simply act

17. Baumeister, "Free Will in Scientific Psychology," 15.

18. Ibid. He follows the logic of Gollwitzer, "Implementation Intentions," 494, in arguing to separate deciding from initiating.

19. Baumeister, *Cultural Animal*, 45–46.

20. Bargh, "Free Will Is Un-Natural," 136.

in evolved ways to respond to the environment, and our experiences of free will are meaningless.

In both cases, evidence is evaluated through interpretive lenses, also known as worldviews, which make up a fundamental orientation regarding human nature. As we have seen, psychologists are able to study experiences of conscious will—when and if people say they feel like they are causing their own actions. Psychologists cannot conclude, however, that thought (which is internal and unseen) *causes* action. Remember that in psychological science, all causes must be physical to count as scientifically valid. As Daniel Wegner, a leading researcher on consciousness and willpower, writes, "The experience of will is based on interpreting one's thought as causing one's action."[21] The experience of having caused our own behavior varies with how we interpret our situation and is not necessarily due to thought actually causing action. Those on both sides of the free-will debate acknowledge that the existence of free will is ultimately a question for philosophy and theology more than psychology.[22] However, psychological science informs this debate by gathering data that helps us better understand conditions in which humans are more likely to feel or act in ways that correspond with showing agency, as well as situations in which people are less likely to do so.

Consciousness and Christianity

The portrait of human behavior painted by psychology is one in which behavior largely is managed unconsciously, so that if there is any free will, it's quite limited. If that's the case, is human behavior primarily ruled by unconscious impulses and automatic responses to the environment (except for occasional instances in which a person's will can be exerted)? If free will is so limited by unconscious processing, then for all practical purposes we're not independent agents. When a person is able to control very little that she does, how can she be responsible for much of what she does? Human responsibility, however, is part of the Bible's depiction of humans. Can these seemingly incongruent ideas be reconciled?

As humans with limited agency, perhaps what's most important in living out what one believes is to consciously evaluate our deepest commitments.

---

21. Wegner, "Who Is the Controller?," 32.
22. For example, Baumeister, "Free Will in Scientific Psychology," 15, and Wegner, "Who Is the Controller?," 19–23, arguing the two sides regarding free will, recognize that science cannot answer the free will question. Recent books by psychologists, such as Gazzaniga's *Who's in Charge?*, continue to weigh in on the question of whether humans have free will.

Many of these deep commitments, however, are held outside of our awareness. After all, consciousness is limited. The Bible actually discusses how to deal with such thoughts and behavior, and assumes that people are responsible to change them.

Let's explore an example of this by following the logic and behavior outlined by the apostle Paul's writing to Timothy, his coworker in Christ. Paul encourages Timothy to "continue in what you have learned and have become convinced of, because you know those from whom you learned it, and how from infancy you have known the Holy Scriptures, which are able to make you wise for salvation through faith in Christ Jesus."[23] Timothy grew up in a home in which he was taught Scripture and its meaning. This was the foundation of Timothy's life, and would have influenced Timothy's behavior and thoughts in ways he would not have even been aware of. Nevertheless, Paul implies that other influences can be at work (e.g., conflicting desires, the evil of the world, etc.) that may derail Timothy from the track of his conviction to serve God. Paul tells Timothy that humans need to bring their deepest convictions to the forefront of thought, and studying the Bible can help accomplish that. Paul writes, "All Scripture is God-breathed and is useful for teaching, rebuking, correcting and training in righteousness, so that the servant of God may be thoroughly equipped for every good work."[24] Even familiar passages—ones that Timothy would have memorized—can act to change behavior and attitude (teaching, rebuking, correcting). In addition, it can train one in "righteousness," which is living in such a way that it pleases God. As Paul writes elsewhere, through studying God's commands, "we become conscious of our sin."[25] Again, Paul is implying that people can be unaware of what they do. When Christians look at what they aspire toward (living righteously), they are confronted with those deficiencies. It is important to note that the Bible says it is the Holy Spirit who ultimately allows believers to understand and believe who God is and to desire to live for God.[26]

Controlling Desire

We are relational persons (Theme 1); wanting to be in relationship is a commitment or desire held by all people. As humans, however, relational desires to be with God, others, and creation are all distorted by sin, so we look for

23. 2 Tim. 3:14–15.
24. 2 Tim. 3:16–17.
25. Rom. 3:20b.
26. 1 Cor. 2:10–16.

other ways to fill that longing. That longing, Christians believe, is fulfilled in God. Christian philosopher James K. A. Smith, in his book *Desiring the Kingdom*, asserts that humans are fundamentally driven by what they love or desire, whether they are aware of it or not. Smith says that in addition to reasoned thoughts (relatively easily brought to conscious awareness) and a set of beliefs (of which we are likely less aware), unconscious processing is pervasive. As he writes, "We don't go around all day *thinking* about how to get to the classroom or *thinking* about how to brush our teeth or *perceiving* our friends. Most of the day, we are simply involved in the world."[27]

Smith says that we act out *all* of our loves—our desires—through our actions. Being embodied, we enact our desires and meaning making in physical ways. We're not just talking about sex here. When we go to a classroom, brush our teeth, or meet with friends—all practices or habits—we are aiming our desires toward some larger end. In these examples, the behaviors may aim toward greater social acceptance in one way or another, whether by education, hygiene, or companionship. Practiced behaviors eventually become unconscious, automatic behaviors that can then take on a life of their own.[28] These desired outcomes, or *goals*, can be consciously set or automatically activated by our surroundings. For instance, most students in a course have conscious goals such as (at minimum) earning a passing grade. Students act in ways to meet that goal, and with practice that goal can operate unconsciously.[29] People act as a student without even planning to do so.[30] Sometimes, that goal gets altered—seeing a person we are attracted to can do that, as social and relationship goals might become active. Multiple goals may be active, and the student might now be advocating the formation of a study group (student plus social goals), or the student may forget about the course altogether and go straight to asking that person out on a date. Here we see action, yet it may not include full, conscious awareness of why one is doing the action. Studying may no longer be a priority in the action, although the student may still think or say it is the basis of the action.

Does this now return us to the conclusion that humans are without free will, with behavior driven by unconscious goals rather than by will? The Bible and many in psychology again answer no. In psychology, lots of research on automatic behavior has focused on how to reign in unconscious thoughts,

27. Smith, *Desiring the Kingdom*, 50.
28. See Bargh and Chartrand, "Unbearable Automaticity of Being," 465–73, for a good accounting of how repeated behaviors can become automatic.
29. Dijksterhuis and Aarts, "Goals, Attention and (Un)Consciousness," 467–90, have a thorough discussion of the relationship between unconscious processing and goals.
30. Perhaps always sitting quietly in the same spot in a classroom.

using self-control to suppress or stop "bad" behavior.[31] Many may have the impression that this fits right with what Christianity advocates: a big list of don'ts. And the Bible certainly tells us there are things to not do: "For the grace of God has appeared that offers salvation to all people. It teaches us to say 'No' to ungodliness and worldly passions, and to live self-controlled, upright and godly lives in this present age."[32] But focus on the second part of this verse: a "do" follows the "don't." Scripture advocates that behavior can be changed by redirection of the heart—one's inner desires.

God and Desire

Notice here that the Bible is *not* saying that on believers' own power alone they can "live self-controlled, upright and godly lives." God's grace, through the Holy Spirit, enables us to desire God. Look at this call from Jesus, speaking to his closest followers, his disciples: "Whoever wants to be my disciple must deny themselves and take up their cross daily and follow me. For whoever wants to save their life will lose it, but whoever loses their life for me will save it."[33] It's easy to focus on "deny" and "lose"—giving up desires—and then sin should be gone. However, just giving up desires won't work. If, as Smith asserts, we are fundamentally lovers[34]—at our core, creatures that do things according to our desires—we can't just give up desires! Christ says to give up, but then "take up their cross daily and follow me." Desire continues to exist; the Christian life isn't one of suppression but of redirection to fulfillment in Christ. As theologian St. Augustine so eloquently described the human relationship to God, "You have made us for yourself, and our hearts are restless until they rest in you."[35] As meaning seekers, we desire a deity, and this desire for God comes from God. Yet in human sinfulness, desires are easily directed toward other things, including ourselves. Through the Holy Spirit's work, however, desires can be positively directed toward God.

Perhaps a uniquely human characteristic is our desire to be a better person. This comes about from *self-consciousness*, or the ability of a person to draw attention to one's self as a thing that can be examined. Research suggests that

31. See, for example, Muraven, Baumeister, and Tice, "Self-Regulation through Practice," 446–57.

32. Titus 2:11–12.

33. Luke 9:23–24.

34. Smith, *Desiring the Kingdom*, 51.

35. Augustine, *Confessions*, 1.1.1. Smith, *Desiring the Kingdom*, 77, uses this quotation from Augustine as well, building the case that humans have a deep restlessness whereby humans end up trying to fulfill this desire for God by chasing idols.

you were able to recognize yourself in the mirror after about eighteen months of age, but let's focus on the human "tendency to evaluate yourself and notice your shortcomings."[36] Self-consciousness allows us to think about what we are like and what we can be. This ability varies between people and with levels of alertness. In addition, substances like alcohol, tobacco, heroin, and other psychoactive drugs can alter how we respond, and can lead to long-term consequences or addictions where persons crave and use substances despite their negative consequences. Drugs can alter brain chemistry, making it difficult for users to discontinue use of the substance. One may have some self-conscious awareness that one's drug use is harmful but little ability to stop that use. In fact, alcohol actually reduces self-awareness,[37] and this is likely an effect of other drugs as well. Thinking back to the case of Ethan from the introduction, his adult alcohol use problems are likely exacerbated by alterations in brain functioning and reduced self-consciousness. These changes impact his ability to exercise responsibly his limited agency. He has reduced ability to modify his desires.

Psychological research on automatic impulses and desires has tended to focus on suppression of these tendencies. Such research has shown that using self-control to suppress desire is very taxing and often unsuccessful. Evidence does suggest that the more one practices self-control, the greater the ability to be self-controlled becomes.[38] Willpower, to some degree, begets more willpower. Yet in all cases, once willpower has been exerted, people tend to be more susceptible to self-control failures afterward (working hard, then partying hard).

Redirecting Desire

Recently, psychologists have begun exploring how behavior might be altered by influencing desires. Desires need to be replaced with new desires, and conscious decisions can aid in redirecting them (not just suppressing them).[39] Desires operate largely unconsciously, but unconscious behavior can be redirected

---

36. Schacter, Gilbert, and Wegner, *Psychology*, 183, includes a discussion of self-consciousness in humans and animals.

37. Hull, "Self-Awareness Model," 586–600.

38. For example, research by Muraven, Baumeister, and Tice, "Self-Regulation through Practice," 446–57, and by Muraven and Baumeister, "Self-Regulation," 247–59, suggests that self-control is strengthened with practice.

39. This is what recent research on desires by Hofman and Van Dillen, "Desire," 318–20, shows: desires need direction. Conscious decisions can aid in redirecting desires, and that is a way of showing self-control.

toward other goals. As psychologist Peter Gollwitzer has emphasized, it is important to direct behavior at the outset—deciding what is important to do, and then, as Baumeister has emphasized, many of the small details (the automatic behaviors) occur without intention.[40] The Bible confirms that redirected actions change desires: "Those who live according to the flesh have their minds set on what the flesh desires; but those who live in accordance with the Spirit have their minds set on what the Spirit desires."[41]

When calling his disciples, Jesus bids them to "follow me."[42] If the disciples didn't know it immediately, "follow me" meant not just a change of lifestyle but a total change in what was important in life—where their desires would be directed. Jesus told Simon Peter and Andrew, the fishermen, that they would "fish for people."[43] Life's primary fulfillments would no longer come by filling nets and selling fish but by bringing people to a saving love of Christ.

Applications: "Reporting for Duty"

Christ calls his followers to line up their will with God's will. When Christ taught his disciples to pray, in what we now call the Lord's Prayer, "your kingdom come, your will be done,"[44] he was telling his followers to set their desires on God's desires, to let their desires be taken up into God's desires. As theologian N. T. Wright has said, when Christians are praying this, "We are praying, as Jesus was praying and acting, for the redemption of the world; for the radical defeat and uprooting of evil; and for heaven and earth to be married at last, for God to be all in all. And if we pray this way, we must of course be prepared to live this way."[45]

How can conscious thought influence desires toward God? We the authors have a friend named Gord who begins each day by leaning up against a wall while stretching before exercise and prays, "Good morning, Father; it's your servant Gord again, reporting for duty." Gord tells us that "then I remind him that he will have to put up with all of my weaknesses and idiosyncrasies but that I really do want to serve him." He continues in prayer and reading Scripture during his exercise routine. Gord sets the tone for each day—reaffirming and reminding himself of the big decision to follow Christ that puts in line both

40. Gollwitzer, "Implementation Intentions," 493–503; Baumeister, "Free Will in Scientific Psychology," 14–19.

41. Rom. 8:5.

42. For example, Matt. 4:19, when calling Simon Peter and Andrew.

43. Matt. 4:19.

44. The Lord's Prayer is recorded in Matt. 6 and Luke 11.

45. Wright, *The Lord and His Prayer*, 31.

his conscious and unconscious, unmonitored decisions for the day. Gord in effect is saying, "I want to be aware of you, God—use me." It's setting a tone and practice of spiritual awareness by giving over his will to God and acting on it to the extent one can.

DISCUSSION QUESTIONS

1. In what ways do you feel burdened by your conscious awareness?

2. Think of experiences in which you explained your behavior after you had done something. Was your explanation true to what you were thinking going into the behavior? How would you know?

3. What percentage of your own behavior do you think results from unconscious processing? What evidence do you have for the remainder of your behavior being under conscious control?

4. Is sin offensive to God if a person did not make a conscious decision to commit the sin? That is, can something that is just a habit be a sin? Explain.

5. Psychologist Carl Rogers (and also Nathaniel Branden, who was instrumental in highlighting the importance of self-esteem) emphasized that humans needed to bring to consciousness all of their behavior and act out of their natural core desires. How might that be problematic, both scientifically and from a Christian perspective?

6. In the last anecdote of the chapter regarding Gord, we emphasize that his statement and stance are an initial decision that can help put into play unconscious behaviors that may follow. Think of an example of how turning on a movie or opening an internet connection (or some other behavior with a distinct beginning) also sets in motion a set of automatic behaviors and responses.

6

Making Sense of Your Surroundings

Sensation, Perception, and Attention

Chapter Summary: Our abilities to sense, perceive, and pay attention are astounding, allowing us to navigate our environment and interact with each other. These abilities are so common to us and require so little of our conscious awareness that they go largely unnoticed. Our embodied sensation limits our ability to take in everything in our environment and also partially determines what we notice and find meaningful. In fact, meaning making appears to be what perception and attention are all about. This combination of great ability and marked limitation shapes the contours of our limited agency and has significant implications for relationality. This chapter explores how the limited but meaning seeking nature of our perceptual system ultimately serves our ability to maintain relationship with God, the world, and one another.

The King said, "I haven't sent the two Messengers, either. They're both gone to the town. Just look along the road, and tell me if you can see either of them."
   "I see nobody on the road," said Alice.
   "I only wish *I* had such eyes," the King remarked in a fretful tone. "To be able to see Nobody! And at that distance, too!"

Lewis Carroll, *Through the Looking Glass*

The question is not what you look at, but what you see.

Henry David Thoreau, *Journal*, August 5, 1851

For those of us with normal sight and hearing, sensory abilities are so effortless that they are easy to ignore. After all, to see, you open your eyes and look; to hear, you just listen. What we ultimately notice and how our senses serve us are anything but simple, however. In addition, our responses to these sensations are profound. Taking in the world is not the result of an inflexible, mechanical process. We have choices in how we sense and perceive what is around us, but there are also definite limitations. We therefore have limited agency in our interaction with the environment. Nevertheless, our sensory systems are our entry point to interacting with our environment, including each other, so they are critical for relationships. That being the case, sensory processes are a part of the fundamental meaning seeking of humans, shaping not only what we perceive but also what we pay attention to.

Sensation to Perception

In order to understand how sensory processes ultimately result in the kinds of outcomes mentioned in the previous paragraph, we need to look a little more at how we take in our environment. When you experience a taste or smell, bits of the actual substance being noticed must interact with you physically so that a chemical reaction can occur in your nose or on your tongue to allow for transduction (physical information converted to neural signals). Keep that in mind the next time you smell rotting garbage! In fact, if you are to sense anything about the environment, you—your sensory systems—require a physical input, otherwise known as a *sensation*. In order to experience sound, vision, and touch, physical stimuli (sound waves, light, or pressure, respectively)[1] must be converted to a code that your nervous system can begin to interpret. Such processes eventually result in a *perception*—a mental representation that is your sense of reality. Perception, like sensation, is shaped by our physical structure, as both processes are embodied (Theme 3). Our physical structures constrain our perception so that when sensory stimuli[2] are present, our perceptions are quite predictable, even lawful.[3] If a bright flashlight is shined into the eyes of a person, she will see it; the sensory system's output is undeniable. If a sensory system has no response to the environment, perhaps because the stimulus is

1. Unlike taste and smell, vision and audition do not respond to particles of the actual object being sensed to see or hear it.
2. Stimulus is a broad term for any environmental energy that a sensory system might detect.
3. An area of psychology known as psychophysics focuses on specifying and quantifying the relationship between sensations and the stimuli that bring them about and has found relationships between the strength of a sensation and the intensity of a perception, including Weber's law and Steven's power law.

too weak (an object doesn't produce sufficient air pressure change to vibrate an eardrum) or is overwhelmed by other stimuli (e.g., a very dim light gets overwhelmed in a brightly lit room), no perception of that stimulus is possible. While some stimuli are impossible to miss, other stimuli are impossible to perceive. The constraints of our sensory systems, however, mean that we do not sense or perceive everything.

Sensation connects us to creation. In several instances, Jesus's miracles involved healing sensory processes (Matt. 9:27–30 and John 9:1–12 are two examples). Think of what this meant for those healed: not just a restoration of physical capabilities, but freedom to fully engage society. These miracles reveal Jesus's power and his compassion. People can live full and fulfilling lives with some sensory loss, but if we had no sensory interaction with the world (no taste, touch, smell, vision, or hearing), our isolation from others would be complete and unimaginable.

The Bible states that people also have the possibility for spiritual perception—realities that go beyond physical sensations. God is described as able to work directly at the core of human lives through nonphysical means, bringing about changes that then can be perceived by people. Stories of God's direct impact on humans through physical, perceptual processes certainly run through the Bible, from sending food (manna) to the Israelites wandering the desert to Jesus's physical embodiment that included him audibly speaking, physically touching, and being visibly present.[4] God also is described as having spiritual impact, for instance through the action of the Holy Spirit. In one case that the apostle Paul describes, "God's love has been poured out into our hearts through the Holy Spirit."[5] Accounts of God working through visions[6] and dreams[7] and giving general direction by the Holy Spirit[8] all show that God works in people's lives in ways outside of physical means. Nevertheless, these interactions impact humans physically, as people change their interactions with God and the rest of creation.

If our sensation and perception work in very specifiable ways, ways that even God engages, do these processes dictate how we will necessarily interact with others? Do perceptual processes force us to perceive a particular stimulus in only one way?

---

4. Jesus is recorded as calming his disciples following his resurrection from death by encouraging them to "look at my hands and my feet. It is I myself! Touch me and see; a ghost does not have flesh and bones, as you see I have," in Luke 24:39.

5. Rom. 5:5.

6. E.g., Gen. 46:2, speaking to Jacob.

7. E.g., Matt. 2:19, appearing to Joseph.

8. E.g., Rom. 8.

Perception: Making Meaning of Sensation

Perceptions result when sensation is interpreted through psychological processes that take into account other factors, including meaning, past experience, relationships, and context. So while your eardrum may vibrate in a specific way due to the characteristics of a particular sound wave (sensation), you *interpret* that as the sound of a dog barking (perception). Such interpretation of the world is what makes perception central to making meaning (Theme 5).

Our sensory systems do not just record what is around us; perceptual processes prioritize and interpret our environment. Loud sounds startle us more than quiet ones; bitter is more noticeable than bland. Perceptual processes even result in us "seeing" things that may not be completely accurate relative to reality. For example, have you ever noticed that you almost never realize when you blink? Blinking makes "the lights" go out; there is no light for our visual system to respond to. Anytime you blink, that's what you should actually perceive because the sensory input of light is interrupted. However, you usually don't "see" a blink because your visual system tells you a bit of a fib about what you're actually "seeing." Typically you have the perception of *not* blinking when you blink. Since the average person blinks ten to fifteen times a minute,[9] that's helpful. If you noticed every blink, the constant interruption of normal vision by little blips of blackness could get rather annoying. You control your blinking (albeit usually unconsciously) so "seeing" a blink wouldn't give you any information you didn't already have.[10] Perhaps more important to our discussion of whether sensory processes determine how we see the world, is the fact that you don't *need* to consciously know about your blinks because part of your brain *already* does. "Seeing" the blackness of a blink is less important than perceiving ongoing reality, so the blink is ignored.

Figuring out the importance of incoming information is absolutely vital for obvious reasons, as well as for some that may be less obvious. Therefore, perceptual processes do not just let sensations be; sensation is interpreted. Clearly, some things (e.g., delicious food or a slap to the face) are likely to impact us more than other things (e.g., a tree in the distance or a gentle breeze) and should be prioritized differently. In the case of blinking, perceptual processes don't really deceive, they prioritize. Perhaps less apparent is the fact that when we interact with the environment, we are faced with an interesting paradox: it provides us with both too little and too much information to allow

9. Burr, "Vision," 554.
10. Ibid.

us to comprehend it.[11] Consider the little squiggles you're currently looking at, that eventually result in your experience of reading. On the one hand, how are these little shapes (probably black on white) supposed to mean anything? If you couldn't read, these items would remain ambiguous. If you can read, they remain ambiguous if these shapes are in an unfamiliar font or come from a language you do not know. The stimuli themselves do not carry enough information for you to perceive letters and words unless you *already* have learned about and can now recall letters and words. The sensation alone is insufficient to yield perception of words—there simply is not enough information.

The fact that a sensation does not necessarily lead to the same perception for all (readers versus nonreaders) indicates that while our embodiment limits our sensory agency (our freedom to sense anything and everything that might exist), we show greater agency with our perception. In order to figure out what to process, meaning is imposed on sensory input. If you are a keen observer of grammar, you might have noticed the passive construction in the previous sentence. We're implying that you make meaning *regardless* of whether you consciously intend to make meaning. You can simply take in information and respond in the way you automatically respond.

Experiencing Reality

Imagine this situation: a glass full of cold milk spills on what you're reading. No doubt you would immediately notice that things look different. If the milk spilled on you, you would also feel wetness and cold. Sensation drives those perceptions. This is typically called *bottom-up* processing because the initial sensory activity determines perception without being modified by *top-down*, or higher-level, processing, like expectations. Basic elements of the environment changed so that basic properties of sensory stimuli also changed—white pools of liquid, new temperature—and you notice them automatically. Sensory systems are wired to respond most vigorously to change, sending lots of nerve impulses to the brain to automatically let us know that the environment has something new.[12] As the white milk covers black letters, you now are processing more reflected light; cold milk comes in contact with your skin and receptors that respond to temperature signal a difference. In the end, the "decision" to detect what happened in the environment occurs due to nonconscious sensory

11. Smith and Kosslyn, *Cognitive Psychology*, 50–52, include an interesting discussion of "the two problems of perception in the sensory world" as being too little information and too much information.

12. Sensory systems respond maximally (with the highest rate of neuron firing) to contrast or difference. Contrast comes about by changes in time, space, or space and time together (motion).

processes. The limited agency of humans is vividly apparent here. No conscious choice was involved to yield this perception.

It is important to note that even when bottom-up processing is the primary influence on your perceptual processing at a given moment, you will have an experience of reality. When perceiving the world, you are not a disembodied mind observing from outside of your body, able to separate yourself from your physical experiences. These processes are a part of you, significantly impacting how you relate to others and the environment. Therefore, the experience of being a relational person is profoundly physical.

Limited Agency and Perception

Yet we do have some agency in how we *interpret* sensations. We understand perceptions within a context, using prior knowledge, experience, and expectation—all top-down processes. Our goals—our intentionality—influence that interpretation. That is, we reinterpret the sensory information, perhaps modifying the perception. Meaning making results from more than just increased sensory neuron responses to the environment. We are not simple machines that react to only what's loudest and brightest. Back to the cold milk example, you quickly go from the immediate sensations of visual and temperature change to an overall picture of the situation using higher-level interpretation that may result in crying over spilled milk or perhaps laughing out loud. Did you or someone else cause the milk to spill? If someone else spilled the milk, was it someone you consider a friend or a foe? Were you expecting the spilled milk, or was it a surprise? Answers to these and other questions will affect your judgment of the significance of the change you've experienced. That will shape such things as your emotional response and the physical actions you might or might not take. In the end, your response is not determined by bottom-up processes alone, but is modified by a variety of factors, including how you *choose* to respond. You are able to interpret different meanings from the same situation.

Nevertheless, characteristics of our embodiment—how our sensory systems respond to the environment—leave us predisposed to respond to what's new more than to what's been present for some time. The initial sensations from the milk spill cannot be ignored. Our nervous system lets us know what is in the environment, but in doing so it begins with an agenda. We are biased toward change, responding to difference while having a ho-hum response to sameness. Change has priority over sameness, so change is more meaningful to us than is sameness.[13]

13. Your sensory/perceptual systems also impact determining when you no longer need to notice something. Receptor cells respond most when first exposed to a stimulus. Following

Making Meaning Comes from the Bottom and the Top

It's important to think a bit more now about what it means to make something "meaningful." It's about setting priorities for what is important and what is not. This judgment process isn't just cold and logical, however; it can also be strongly emotional. Making meaning, as we said earlier, involves what we desire, but psychologists have shown that it may also signal what to avoid. Bottom-up initial perception strongly influences our goals of whether to approach or flee. These are judgments of trust versus fear, love versus hate. Evolutionary psychologists interpret this tendency as having survival value, and indeed it does.[14] It's certainly more important to know that a lion you see in the distance is running toward you than that it remains in a cage. Change more likely requires a response than does sameness. This way of prioritizing things in the environment is fundamental to how we process sensation and is part of our basic interpretive predispositions. It sets the stage for how we will achieve goals (e.g., for shelter, food, sex), and thus is deeply part of how we interpret the meaning of situations.

While perception has this bottom-up predisposition to respond more to some things than others, our tendencies are modified by prior experience and expectations. Think again about the black squiggles you are looking at right now. How do you understand that they are letters and that, in certain combinations, they make meaningful messages? Our ability to read is the result of our imposing meaning on these squiggles. As meaning seekers, humans have devised ways of communication (writing) that depend on little marks that do not look like what they stand for (e.g., the word *dog* in no way resembles an actual dog). Through lots of practice from first learning the alphabet, then learning how letters form sounds and words, and finally being able to read whole sentences and passages of text,[15] we are able to impose meaning top-down and see these black marks as words, not just shapes.

The result is that for words that are written in your primary language, reading has been so thoroughly learned that it becomes automatic. If the letters are legible and form a familiar word, you basically cannot stop reading them as a

---

that, responding tends to decline, even if the stimulus remains the same strength, allowing us to adjust to our surroundings and monitor for what is new. For example, if you enter a kitchen with freshly baked cookies, the scent is obvious. Soon, however, the scent seems less intense (if you consciously perceive it at all).

14. Itti and Koch, "Computational Modelling of Visual Attention," 194.

15. Kuhl, "Language, Mind, and Brain," 99–115, provides a nice overview of how experience alters perception.

word,[16] a basic finding from the Stroop task.[17] In this task, participants name the color of ink in which individual words are presented. If the letters form a word that names a color other than the ink's color (e.g., the word *blue* presented in red ink), participants are slower to correctly name the ink color (red) than if the word and the ink color are the same (e.g., the word *blue* presented in blue ink). This result, commonly known as the Stroop effect, occurs because people are faster at reading the word than at identifying the ink color.[18] When the color of the ink is not the same as the word, there's a conflict in what the two characteristics are saying, and people respond more slowly. People read the word involuntarily, despite the fact that reading isn't even required for the task of naming the ink color. Participants in these experiments neither decide to read those words nor can they stop doing so. In this case, people no longer have free will in how they initially deal with letters forming a word because past experience very predictably dictates processing. Advertisers have caught on to how we respond to words, and companies pay richly just to have a brand's name appear on a scoreboard or the side of a building.

Experience with letter combinations also allows us to read words and to even form expectations about what we will later read in a passage. In fact, language researchers have described text comprehension as a "search (or effort) after meaning" that arises out of expectations.[19] A drive to understand pushes reading. Here's an example of how our knowledge of the way words work can influence comprehension for those who read English:

> It deosn't mttaer in waht oredr the ltteers in a wrod are, the olny iprmoetnt tihng is taht the frist and lsat ltteer be at the rghit pclae. The rset can be a toatl mses and you can sitll raed it wouthit porbelm.[20]

Although the inner letters were scrambled in this quote, we are so familiar with how words work that we are able to relatively easily impose an interpretation on the misspellings that allows us to understand the message.

16. If there are multiple words, we can stop ourselves from reading them because reading multiple words and putting them together into a coherent thought requires more effort.

17. Named for Stroop, "Serial Verbal Reactions," 643–62.

18. MacLeod, "Stroop Effect," 163–203, provides a comprehensive review of theories on the Stroop effect.

19. Graesser, Singer, and Trabasso, "Narrative Text Comprehension," 371.

20. Here's what these sentences say: "It doesn't matter in what order the letters in a word are, the only important thing is that the first and last letter be at the right place. The rest can be a total mess and you can still read it without problem." This website of the Cognition and Brain Sciences Unit in Cambridge, UK, explains how people can read scrambled words and the limits of our ability to comprehend them: http://www.mrc-cbu.cam.ac.uk/people/matt.davis/cmabridge/. Want to try it? This website allows you to generate your own readable, scrambled letter sentences: http://www.glassgiant.com/text_scrambler/.

Practice Makes Meaning

It is clear that experience shapes perception by altering top-down processing. Experiences can occur deliberately, as in learning to read and to do math in the classroom, which shapes reactions to letters and numbers. Once those reactions are well practiced, they can become largely automatic, as in reading. We also learn through what happens to us on a day-to-day basis, as we learn that dogs bark, ice is cold, and lightning is bright. These experiences, also known as incidental learning, change how we approach things in the world, resulting in difficult-to-alter predispositions. Predispositions easily become expectations, like expecting letters to form words, so that if a set of letters is strung together, we try to read them. These are beneficial, long-term changes.

Expectations based on experience act very broadly and shape our interactions. If you look into a room of strangers and see your best friend's face, you respond to that face very differently than all of the others, based on past experience. Perceiving that face likely even influences your mood. If you were expecting your best friend to be present, you may find that face more quickly as you have developed a readiness to perceive the world in the way you expect it to appear[21] (or to misidentify someone as being your friend if you see someone who looks similar). Previous experiences with particular faces also affect our immediate perception of those faces as being friend, foe, or something in between. Obviously this has significant consequences for how we relate with each other. Interpersonal expectations play out in stereotypes and biases, both of which profoundly affect our relationships. This is discussed more in chapter 9, on thinking.

In the end, we are able to impose meaning in a top-down way on our whole existence. Our values, cultural experiences, faith perspective, and so on influence how we see the world. One person's description of a spiritual experience may be met by groans from some people and "Amens" from others, all depending on how the event is interpreted. Expectations and beliefs shape our interpretation of events, even leaving us more open or more closed to the possibility of experiences of God.

Attention's Balancing Act

We have discussed automatic perception and interpretation of perception altered by our experiences and worldview. However, far more information

---

21. This is known as perceptual set and is influenced by many factors and across cultures, as was shown by Deregowski, "Pictorial Perception and Culture," 82–88.

than we can process (or that might even be useful to process) impacts our sensory systems. Whenever you look at anything, your retina responds to all of it. Yet much of what you see simply isn't important to you when you have limited resources for dealing with your environment. For example, when you are trying to read, and you really desire to understand what you are reading, other activities around you simply distract. Unless, of course, what surrounds you is more important than what you are reading.

Attention is the process that helps you deal with the fact that you have too much information by limiting what of that information receives detailed mental activity. It's the process by which you determine what incoming information is perceived. As attention researchers Nancy Kanwisher and Paul Downing write, "Seeing the world around you is like drinking from a firehose. The flood of information that enters the eyes could easily overwhelm the capacity of the visual system," so the attention system is necessary to allow "selective processing of the information relevant to current goals."[22] The limitations that come from being embodied require that in order to make sense of your environment, you need to make sense of only what is important in the environment, not every little detail. If you precisely tracked every single movement, every individual object in your environment, your perceptual systems would be overwhelmed—the fire hose would still be flowing full blast and you would be flooded by information. The main task fulfilled by your attention system is to strike a balance between continuing to deal with what you're currently attending to and still being able to respond to new, important events in your environment.

People have some choice in where the pivot point is set in that balance. The settings of our attention are tremendously important because they determine what we will perceive (and not perceive) in the environment. As psychologist Bert Hodges has written, the limits of our perceptual abilities bring consequences in humans: "they must be selective. And choices always mean tradeoffs."[23] Attending to something requires *not* attending to a whole bunch of other things. This trading of attention to one event at the expense of attention to another event has been very well documented. One such example, inattentional blindness, occurs when, by paying attention to some events in a scene, we fail to notice when an unexpected but completely visible object appears.[24]

22. Kanwisher and Downing, "Separating the Wheat from the Chaff," 57.
23. Hodges, "Knowing and Doing the Truth," 68.
24. In one of the more famous examples of change blindness, Simons and Chabris, "Gorillas in Our Midst," 1059–74, had participants count the number of times members of a group of people passed a basketball. Shortly after the video began, a person in a gorilla suit passed through the scene, remaining there for five seconds. A startling 46 percent of participants failed

Yet as attention researchers Daniel Simons and Daniel Levin emphasize, given how successful humans generally are in interacting with the environment, it doesn't seem we even need all of that information. They write, "A system that is too precise in tracking visual details would, in the words of William James, present a 'blooming, buzzing confusion.'"[25] The attention system, however, functions to limit our input to what is important, giving the gist or basic meaning of perceptual experience across time. The ability to get a general impression helps us make sense of the world. Deriving the basic story of what is going on in a situation through attention is similar to the way memory works (see chap. 8). Yet attention can focus and give a more detailed perceptual experience at a single moment, such as when we are searching for a particular item, like a set of keys.

Getting Attention under Control

Human agency has a role in how attention functions to limit and then define what of the environment we will further process. While attention is automatically drawn to some events in the environment (such as strong sensory experiences or changes, and important items like faces), clearly we are able to *decide* about attending to other events. We can opt to start reading something or watch a movie, for example. Further, we can choose what we will read or watch—things that are enriching or things that are demeaning. Those choices matter because they affect us. For example, research has demonstrated negative influences of viewing aggression and watching sexual content in childhood and adolescence.[26] Consequently, what we watch also affects our relationships with others, even if we may think it will not. This agency means that we have responsibility for how we use our attention, but that agency is limited (Theme 4). What we attend to is what we are likely to recall as well.

The Bible also asserts that what we see and think about have important consequences for relationships. The apostle Paul advised the followers of Christ at Philippi, "Finally, brothers and sisters, whatever is true, whatever is noble, whatever is right, whatever is pure, whatever is lovely, whatever is admirable—if

---

to notice the gorilla. More demonstrations of this research can be found on The Invisible Gorilla website, http://www.theinvisiblegorilla.com/videos.html

25. Simons and Levin, "Change Blindness," 267.

26. The famous "Bobo doll" experiments by Albert Bandura (Bandura, Ross, and Ross, "Transmission of Aggression," 575–82) have shown that watching aggressive acts increases the likelihood of acting aggressively. O'Hara et al., "Greater Exposure," 984–93, suggest that early exposure to sexual content in movies promotes sexual risk taking and earlier age for initial sexual activity.

anything is excellent or praiseworthy—think about such things. Whatever you have learned or received or heard from me, or seen in me—put it into practice. And the God of peace will be with you."[27] Paul's words are an affirmation that people can make choices regarding what they pay attention to. Nevertheless, Paul also emphasizes that our general outlook and our general nature shape what we will attend to and perceive. The human propensity toward sin (Theme 2) influences how we see the world, our meaning making, and ultimately our desires. In these verses, Paul emphasizes the notion that we (including our attention) are not fully under our control. God's Holy Spirit also acts within his followers to redirect desires: "Those who live according to the flesh have their minds set on what the flesh desires; but those who live in accordance with the Spirit have their minds set on what the Spirit desires. The mind governed by the flesh is death, but the mind controlled by the Spirit is life and peace."[28]

Implications and Applications

As we have suggested above, what we attend to can have lasting impact on living. We have also stressed that much of how we attend and what we attend to (and thus what we perceive) is governed unconsciously, fitting with our embodiment and limited agency. We take in our surroundings in largely automatic ways, therefore not requiring conscious supervision. If that's really the case—and we the authors believe the literature in psychology strongly points to that—how can we influence what we attend to?

The beginning point is to understand a basic property about how perception and attention work: they are always "on." Attention is restless—it seeks out something to do.[29] Research on mind wandering—when attention drifts from an external task to internal memories and thoughts—shows that when we're not interested in what we are doing, our attention shifts to something else, quite on its own.[30] This happens particularly when we're working on automated, repetitive tasks or ones so difficult that we can't even follow what's going on. People first search externally and automatically if the current information being processed is not fully occupying their attention.[31] We're distracted when bored; we look for more interesting things if what we're currently responding

27. Phil. 4:8–9.
28. Rom. 8:5–6.
29. If you ever ask someone what she is thinking about and she answers, "Nothing," feel free to point and shout, "LIAR!" Attention is occupied because attention is always occupied.
30. One study on mind wandering is Smallwood and Schooler, "Restless Mind," 946–58.
31. Lavie, "Distracted and Confused?," 75–82, reviews the literature on distractibility.

to is not that interesting. If nothing in our environment catches our fancy, then we easily "look" inward, as the research on mind wandering shows.

This implies that we will always pay attention to *something*. What is around us "gets in." It is therefore important to avoid being naive about what we're influenced by or how much we're influenced. Information around us can become an experience that changes us, even if we have no intention for it to do so. Some stimuli, such as those containing movement and change, are most likely to grab attention. Pornography is an example of a particularly attention-grabbing stimulus. When viewing pornography, normal sexual responses occur, reinforcing the viewing. Such responses are, from a biblical view, misdirected because they are not within the context of a committed relationship; persons are instead depicted as sexual objects. Nevertheless, pornography certainly grabs one's attention.[32] Repeatedly viewing pornography easily results in a habit that can be difficult to break, and the porn industry certainly does what it can to reinforce that habit. Avoiding opportunities to view pornography can be an important, albeit potentially difficult, way to influence attention that subsequently influences desires and behavior. As we mentioned in chapter 5, on consciousness, repeated behavior becomes automated—"habitual"—so behaviors can be set into motion simply by perceiving relevant items in the environment, regardless of what someone intended to do.[33] People can show similar habits with smoking and compulsive spending, to name just two more examples. Being embodied, our limited agency is necessarily impacted by our specific situation.

You can influence your attention in the long term in other ways as well, based on your situation. Consider the impact of factors such as where you live, organizations you join, even where you shop and go for a walk. The fact that you are not able to perceive, let alone attend to, everything has significant implications for how you relate to others, creation, and God. Your situation greatly influences what you will be able to pay attention to and perceive. You simply cannot perceive or attend to things that are not around: out of sight, out of mind. If Christians want to follow God's call to care for others tangibly— to feed the poor and care for the sick—doing so is impossible if one is never around such people. Jesus lived among those who were poor and sick—both

---

32. For a good discussion of pornography and its effects, see Struthers, *Wired for Intimacy*.

33. Bargh and Chartrand, "Unbearable Automaticity of Being," 466, have shown that a great deal of a person's everyday thinking and behavior is determined not by being consciously regulated but by mental processes that operate without conscious awareness and direction. Influences from the environment can prompt behavior simply due to the fact that in the past, the similar behavior has occurred in that same environment. That is, when you see your phone, you check it because that is what you always do with your phone. Yet you did not make a conscious choice to do this.

in physical and spiritual senses—and ministered to them. When Jewish leaders questioned why he was eating with sinners, Jesus said, "It is not the healthy who need a doctor, but the sick. I have not come to call the righteous, but sinners."[34] To actively serve in the world, Christians need to be aware of the world. Christians cannot sequester themselves from the world's needs if they are going to serve God and be Christ followers. They need to know what is happening in the news and be involved in meeting concerns of their communities.

Further, active involvement in a church where prayers for others are regularly offered and God is worshiped can make these be things to which a Christian regularly pays attention. The Christian community, in which people are in meaningful, interconnected relationships with others, can provide mutual support to make changes that alter attention. As the writer of Hebrews instructs Christians, "And let us consider how we may spur one another on toward love and good deeds, not giving up meeting together, as some are in the habit of doing, but encouraging one another."[35] Note that the writer does not say "you," the writer says "we"—New Testament books and letters were written to churches more often than individuals.

Although you physically live where you live and may have little ability to change that due to limitations such as family commitments or economic circumstances, you may have the possibility of changing what you do where you live—what you attend to or bring into your environment. We are always perceiving and always attending, so it is important to seek out situations worth attending to and avoid those that are not.

DISCUSSION QUESTIONS

1. Philippians 4:13 reads, "I can do all this through him who gives me strength." How might one's perception of living be affected by embracing the apostle Paul's claim in this passage?

2. Our sensory systems prioritize change and difference. How might this prioritization make it difficult to effectively notice areas of weakness in your life?

3. What Stroop-like effects do you experience in your life, where you wish to do one thing but are distracted by others? How do things that appeal to a sinful nature detract from Christians' living righteously?

34. Mark 2:17.
35. Heb. 10:24–25.

4. Do we have responsibility for our behavior if we're not even aware of it?

5. The Bible directs Christians toward what they should pay attention to. Philippians 4:8 reads, "Finally, brothers and sisters, whatever is true, whatever is noble, whatever is right, whatever is pure, whatever is lovely, whatever is admirable—if anything is excellent or praiseworthy—think about such things." How can that be reconciled with Christianity's call for people to work among "sinners"? Specifically, consider the implications of Theme 1, humans as relational persons.

7

Change from the Heart

Learning

Chapter Summary: Learning theories and research in the early days of psychology—namely, classical and operant conditioning studies—appeared to show that animals and humans alike learn in a mechanical and passive way. In other words, we are just like glorified robots, programmed by the environment. These ideas have presented challenges to notions of free will, responsibility, and our meaning seeking nature. This chapter focuses on ways to rethink these basic mechanisms of learning and shows that the research poses much less of a challenge to free will and responsibility than is commonly assumed. At the same time, these research findings also remind us that our free choices are limited by the conditions in our environment, that we learn as embodied creatures, and that we are not quite as unique from the rest of creation as we like to think.

Any fool can know. The point is to understand.

Attributed to Albert Einstein

[Kids] don't remember what you try to teach them. They remember what you are.

Jim Henson, *It's Not Easy Being Green: And Other Things to Consider*

Let us discern for ourselves what is right; let us *learn* together what is good.

Job 34:4 (emphasis added)

A friend once said that as a child he had to drink castor oil (a very nasty substance with nasty stomach-altering effects) over several days in preparation for some medical tests. In order to tolerate the oil, his mother mixed it with an orange-flavored soft drink. Until he was in his thirties he could not stand the taste of orange-flavored drinks of any kind. Interestingly, this hatred of orange flavoring appeared to develop outside of his conscious awareness because for some time he couldn't remember why he no longer liked orange-flavored drinks—until his mother reminded him of his childhood treatments. This story illustrates some simple but potentially disturbing things about learning. It appears that humans, like animals, learn by making simple associations between events. These associations can influence our behavior in powerful ways, and they appear to happen at an unconscious level.

No doubt most readers will be acquainted with the research and theories around the two learning situations called classical and operant conditioning. Ivan Pavlov's salivating dogs together with B. F. Skinner's key-pecking pigeons are fairly well-known stories told in every introductory psychology textbook. The story above illustrates some of the principles of classical conditioning, where the castor oil represents the Unconditioned Stimulus (UCS), the aversion (i.e., ill feeling) to the castor oil represents the Unconditioned Response (UCR), the soft drink represents the Conditioned Stimulus (CS), and the aversion (i.e., ill feeling and dislike) for the soft drink represents the Conditioned Response (CR). If you need an example of operant conditioning, the explanations by the school psychologist for Ethan's behavior described in the introduction illustrate a common application of operant conditioning, since the psychologist suggests that it is simple rewards and punishments that have "made" Ethan behave a certain way. While many people are somewhat familiar with these concepts, most people don't fully appreciate why these issues are significant.

After all, who really cares if dogs can salivate to bells or pigeons can do tricks? The answer lies not only in the important contributions of these learning discoveries to all areas of psychology but also in the deeper explanation for how these situations promote learning in the first place. Many of the early researchers in these areas of study embraced behaviorism, which promoted a set of theories about learning mechanisms. However, it also represented a worldview or philosophy about basic human nature and basic ways that behavior should be understood; this worldview had a profound effect on psychology, as well as on popular notions about why humans act the way they do.

The "Challenge" of Behaviorism

The behaviorists were very excited and optimistic about the discovery of classical and operant conditioning because they were convinced they had uncovered the basic building blocks for all learning. They also felt that psychologists could use this discovery to eventually uncover all the laws of learning that would allow us to "cure" individual problems (e.g., learning difficulties, annoying personalities) as well as social ills (e.g., crime, poverty). At the level of theory, they were convinced that learning involved simple connections between events—such as a CS and a CR, or between a stimulus and a response when followed by reward (as in operant conditioning). These connections were likened to a switch that is flipped, closing an electrical circuit in the brain when two simple events happen close in time. Behaviorists were certain that these connections occur passively; in other words, we don't analyze, contemplate, or emotionally evaluate these events—they simply occur *to us* when the environmental conditions are right. Sometimes these notions were referred to as connectionism or reflexology because it was assumed that the connections created a new reflex, just like a simple knee jerk in response to a doctor's rubber hammer on the knee. These connections then cause us to behave differently in the future, just as a newly programmed computer responds differently to new input. The more complex behaviors were produced by simply adding a longer string of connections together to produce complex sequences of behavior. So in their view all learning was passive, mechanical, and happened at an unconscious level. To paraphrase and summarize B. F. Skinner's position, "We do not think, we simply respond."[1]

In addition to these basic "connectionist" ideas, behaviorists were convinced that the learning processes for animals and humans were fundamentally the same. Humans may have greater capacity to form more and better connections, but the laws that govern the process were considered identical. Not only were animals and humans considered to be governed by the same laws of learning, we share the same basic motivational goals—to avoid pain and to seek pleasure. Behaviorists suggested that this motivation, along with the associated learning mechanisms, is designed to help us survive in an ever-changing environment; so biological evolution helps species change over a long period of time, but survival motives and learned connections allow us to adapt to rapidly changing conditions. This view also implies that learning and all behavior follow prescribed laws, just as there are laws that govern the physical universe, and

1. Skinner, "Why I Am Not a Cognitive Psychologist," 1–10.

these laws would one day be fully understood and used to change behavior in whatever way the "controller" wished.

But behaviorists went beyond studying the laws of learning; many of them also characterized aspects of human nature. To many behaviorists, humans are like "blank slates" waiting to be passively altered by experience (i.e., not meaning seeking individuals, Theme 5). This behaviorist view also implies that behavior is ultimately determined by the environment (i.e., that we have no such thing as free will, Theme 4), that we are not special or unique in relation to animals (i.e., not created in God's image, Theme 1), that human nature is neutral (i.e., we are not inherently good or inherently evil, Theme 2), and—if carried to the logical extreme—that humans have no ultimate personal responsibility (i.e., not agents, Theme 4). You can see why these relatively simple concepts of classical and operant conditioning, and the behaviorist views that followed, created such a seismic shift in basic worldviews that goes well beyond salivating dogs and clever pigeons.

It should also be apparent to the reader how much these views challenge several of the major themes of human nature we laid out earlier. What makes this challenge even more troubling is how effective classical and operant conditioning principles have been when applied in psychology and everyday life. While the optimism of the early behaviorists has been diminished in recent years because we haven't cured all individual or social ills, there have been thousands of studies showing that the behavior of animals and humans can be powerfully changed by classical and operant conditioning. You don't need to be conscious, thoughtful, or even intelligent to be conditioned—even simple creatures like sea slugs can be conditioned. Besides, there have been countless successful applications to humans, bringing improvements to child rearing, training for persons with developmental disabilities, classroom teaching, reducing symptoms of emotional disorders, and many other areas. So should we conclude that the behaviorists were correct, and perhaps we are not willful, responsible, unique, relational beings?

Responses to Behaviorism

Christian psychologists have approached this topic in a variety of ways. Some have raised the possibility that a biblical perspective is actually compatible with this deterministic view, since it's possible that God in fact decided our lifelong fate before the beginning of time and that he may accomplish this plan by way of natural events. B. F. Skinner himself once suggested that he believed his position to be very compatible with the theological views of the

Calvinist theologian Jonathan Edwards,[2] who placed a strong emphasis on our sinful nature and our complete dependence on a sovereign God (i.e., a form of divine or spiritual determinism). Some individuals have also argued that the Bible is full of examples of God punishing and rewarding people for their sinful or righteous acts, respectively, which suggests to them that using these basic survival motives to change behaviors has a scriptural basis.[3]

Another approach of Christian psychologists is to suggest that while classical and operant conditioning may actually work much as these behaviorists suggest, it is only at a "low level" of human, bodily functioning. In other words, in this view we can "transcend" or overrule the mechanistic and passive influence of conditioning that occurs in the simpler parts of our brain/mind.[4] However, one problem with this view, as discussed in chapters 3 and 4, is that the findings of modern neuroscience, psychology, and even theology have made it harder to separate mind, body, and soul. Since it is harder and harder to conceive of completely separate components from both a theological and psychological perspective, this "dual-level" view of learning or willfulness is harder to accept.

While the theological and psychological issues are complicated, we do believe that the views and responses by Christians described above are certainly worthy of consideration and discussion. However, we think there may be a simpler way to solve the dilemma. As it turns out, the solution to the dilemma may arise from psychological research itself. Research over the past fifty years has consistently demonstrated that a "connectionist" view of conditioning is grossly oversimplified or just plain wrong. So the behaviorist worldview has not unraveled by way of religious challenges but has been the victim of its own successful campaign to do careful, rigorously scientific, observational research on both animal and human learning. A complete review of this vast body of literature would be impossible, but we will give you a small sample of these research findings.

The Cognitive Reinterpretation

Consider this made-up example of a learning situation that mimics several classic studies, called blocking studies, done with animals. Imagine that Clarissa has regular migraine headaches. It turns out that she drinks coffee (CS) about ten minutes before every headache (UCS), and pretty soon—because of

2. Moxley, "Skinner," 3–28

3. See Bufford, *Human Reflex*.

4. See Cosgrove, *Essence of Human Nature*.

classical conditioning—she starts to develop an aversion to (i.e., a dislike of; CR) the coffee (CS). However, because she feels obligated to drink coffee in social situations, she keeps drinking it on occasion. As it turns out, Clarissa is also trying to lose weight, so instead of sugar in her coffee she switches to artificial sweeteners. She continues to have the headaches ten minutes after drinking the coffee, just as before. However, she doesn't develop an aversion to the sweetener, but maintains an aversion to the coffee. Pavlov was convinced that she *should* make a "connection" between the sweetener and the headache because any two events that occur close together in time will get connected automatically in our brains. So why doesn't she associate the sweetener with the headache?

It's been discovered that the reason Clarissa wouldn't associate the sweetener with the headache is that it adds no new information to the situation; she *already knows* when the headache is coming—it always comes ten minutes after the beverage! So the first signal (the beverage), *blocks out* the association of the second signal (the sweetener) to the headache because the second signal involves redundant or irrelevant information. This outcome suggests that even though the sweetener is paired close in time with the headache, we don't make the automatic "connection."

However, if the above situation were slightly different, the associations change drastically. Imagine that each time Clarissa added artificial sweetener, her headaches were slightly, but consistently, worse. *In this new situation* she would in fact form a strong aversion to the sweetener. The reason she forms an association between the sweetener and the headache is that the sweetener *now* adds new information; it signals to her that she can expect an even worse headache. Studies like this show us that we don't automatically form associations; rather, we learn *about* relationships between events based on the information they tell us about the environment. Since the original blocking studies[5] were done on animals (using things like tones, lights, and mild shocks), we can't conclude that this type of learning is always conscious or even completely willful, but it does suggest that forming associations is a lot more complicated than was assumed by many behaviorists.

Consider another study with human subjects, done some years ago, that paired various tones with a mild electric shock.[6] In experiments of this type, participants eventually show a learned or conditioned response to the tone—meaning that they show a measureable emotional response whenever the tone is given. The researcher in this experiment told half of the participants

---

5. See Hulse, Fowler, and Honig, *Cognitive Processes in Animal Behavior*.
6. Dawson and Reardon, "Facilitory and Inhibitory Sets," 462.

at the beginning of the experiment that "the intelligent thing is to become conditioned," but she told the other half that "the intelligent thing is to *not* become conditioned." We should mention that the task they had to do was very easy, so actual intelligence should have had no influence whatsoever. However, giving these instructions presumably influenced the *attitude* of the participants about conditioning. In the end, the first group (told that conditioning was the *intelligent thing* to do) showed much faster learning and much stronger responses than the second group. The conclusion of the researcher is that the instructions made the first group *want* to be conditioned and the second group to *resist* conditioning because otherwise they would look unintelligent. So it appears that people are not simply conditioned against their will by passively produced connections in their brain, and that *we* control our learning destinies.

One last example involving operant conditioning (i.e., using rewards) is a phenomenon called the overjustification effect.[7] Consider two children who both receive rewards such as money for completing their homework assignment, but one gets a much larger reward than the other. If the parents eventually quit giving the reward, which child will continue to faithfully do their homework for several weeks? A traditional behaviorist explanation would suggest that the larger the reward, the stronger the "connection" between the situation and the response. So they would predict that the child with the larger reward would continue doing homework longer than the other child. As it turns out the opposite is true; large rewards often work against continued performance. Why would this be? The common explanation is that humans often look for justification for why they do things. For example, I might ask myself when doing homework, "Why am I doing this tiring task?" If I am receiving a very small reward, I may come to the conclusion that doing homework must be something I value—why else would I do it? If I am receiving a large reward, I come to the conclusion that I am only working for the reward—in other words I have too much *external* justification and no *internal* justification for doing it. So it appears that large rewards can diminish our *intrinsic* motivation for a task. This result suggests that even though rewards and punishments do change behavior, we are much more thoughtful in analyzing our basic motives than has been suggested by the behaviorists.

The predominant perspective in psychology over the past thirty years stresses a more "cognitive" understanding of learning as opposed to the behaviorist perspective. Learning theorist Jeanne Ormrod summarizes these cognitive

7. This effect was coined in a different study by Lepper, Greene, and Nisbett, "Undermining Children's Intrinsic Interest," 129–37.

principles, which we paraphrase in the following table and have contrasted to
the older behaviorist view.

Issue	Behaviorist View	Cognitive View
Animals vs. humans	Animals and humans share the same basic learning mechanisms.	Some learning processes may be unique to humans (even though some aspects of learning are common to both).
Learning research	Only objective observation is allowed; we cannot make guesses about things we can't see.	While psychologists should use objective observation to study learning, we can make inferences about internal mental processes.
Passive vs. active	Learning is a passive process.	Individuals are actively involved in the learning process.
Learning vs. performance	Learning equals behavior (if you haven't made the right connections you don't behave correctly).	Learning involves the formation of mental associations that are not necessarily reflected in actual behavior.
Knowledge representation	We can't speak of knowledge, only sequences of connections.	Knowledge is organized. We form structures or knowledge schemas.
Complex knowledge	Learning involves making new connections; previous experience has very little influence.	Learning is a process of relating new information to previously learned information.

Learning from the cognitive perspective can involve both a top-down analysis—using existing knowledge to shape and form new experiences—but also
a bottom-up process—in which completely new experiences can be organized
according to basic learning mechanisms. The cognitive perspective also stresses
that the *process* of learning may be lawful (e.g., we tend to see two events as
being causally related if certain features about the events are present), but the
knowledge structure we ultimately form, and the way we actually behave, are
not *determined* by the immediate environment.

So hopefully you can see from this list that the newer cognitive view of
learning has much greater consistency with the themes we have outlined
for this book. As we have argued, we are embodied persons (Theme 3) with
features similar to animals—yet we are special. We stressed in chapter 2,
on research methods, that systematic observation is the best way to study
behavior, but we also argued that we routinely interpret the information and
make inferences about the results. We have argued that we are responsible
limited agents (Theme 4), which is consistent with the notions that we are
actively involved in learning and that sometimes when we learn we don't
necessarily act on that learning. So there are many elements about current

psychological thinking, and the biblical view of persons, that appear to be very compatible.

This does not mean, however, that all elements of current cognitive perspectives are completely consistent with a Christian worldview. For one thing, while cognitive theorists rarely talk about the issue of determinism, most would still argue that once we know all the things that go on "inside" our heads, we will eventually be able to see that learning is determined by a number of measureable factors. Two other major differences between current cognitive views and a biblical worldview are that very little attention is given to relationality (Theme 1) and very little consideration is given to being meaning seekers (Theme 5).

The way in which relationality influences learning will be addressed later, in the chapters related to social psychology, personality theory, and therapy, since it is in these areas of study that we most see how being relational persons influences our learning and development. But we can say at this point that we believe learning always involves some form of social and interpersonal context. The issue of meaning seeking (Theme 5) is something that is a consistent theme in Scripture. One example of this idea, as it relates to learning, is illustrated in Proverbs 24:30–34:

> I went past the field of a sluggard,
>   past the vineyard of someone who has no sense;
> thorns had come up everywhere,
>   the ground was covered with weeds,
>   and the stone wall was in ruins.
> I applied my heart to what I observed
>   and learned a lesson from what I saw:
> A little sleep, a little slumber,
>   a little folding of the hands to rest—
> and poverty will come on you like a thief
>   and scarcity like an armed man.

The phrase "I applied my heart to what I observed" is an intriguing thought. It appears that the observer (notice the "empirical" observation here) not only analyzes the situation in terms of previous "knowledge structures" (as cognitive theorists like to talk about) but also *actively* applies all that he is. Biblical writers used the term "heart" whenever they wanted to talk about our deepest motives and emotions, our core tendencies, or our deepest thoughts; in other words, all that we are. So the observer is trying not only to form a new knowledge structure from this experience but also to find the deeper meaning by drawing from his emotions, motives, tendencies, and thoughts. So whenever we come to any new learning situation—be it simple or complex and whether we are fully aware of it or not—we bring our biases, worldviews, past experiences, moral perspectives, sins, relationships, and all that we are to the situation. So learning does have systematic and even lawful properties, but our learning does more than follow simple laws; it follows our heart and can end up with wrong (i.e., sinful) conclusions about reality or with correct (i.e., consistent with God's desire) views about reality.

Learning involves using all of these elements to further form our knowledge and thought structure, but wisdom takes this one step further. Wisdom involves learning with great insight, but it also involves conforming one's mind, emotions, and behavior to God's desires. For example, many people use their tremendous knowledge structures and past experience to understand Scripture, but if they don't have the wisdom to know how this should shape their existence, they really don't get it.

Implications and Applications

What are the practical implications of these perspectives for the application of basic classical and operant conditioning procedures? First, they suggest that we should be able to scientifically study the laws that govern the learning *process*, even if we will never be able to determine the final knowledge structure that an individual will create or the way that an individual will ultimately behave. This helps to avoid the confusion that newcomers to psychology often have, wondering how psychology can be scientific without treating people as being determined by physical forces (just glorified robots).

Second, we believe that it is certainly permissible for a Christian parent, educator, or therapist to use these techniques to influence the behavior of humans, since it in no way implies that we are determining some other person's internal thought process against their will. The person will shape the experience according to what they already know, feel, and do—so even if the external behavior is manipulated, the recipient of these techniques ultimately determines the outcome of their own learning structure.

Third, we believe that people should be careful about the overuse of simple motives and associations that are part of classical and operant techniques. These techniques have worked very well on children, developmentally delayed adults, and in some other limited situations. The techniques work in these situations because they present simple relationships to the learner that require less complex knowledge structures, and they create simple ways to learn when more complex ways overwhelm us. However, we need to be careful in their use because we ultimately want to change more than an outward behavior;

we want to change the person's heart. As Psalm 32:9 suggests, "Do not be like the horse or the mule, which have no understanding but must be controlled by bit and bridle or they will not come to you." Therefore, any parent, educator, or therapist should ultimately work to change understanding. (We will contradict ourselves somewhat in chap. 13, on social psychology, when we also show that changing outward behavior can have powerful effects on our inner being [e.g., attitudes, beliefs, future tendencies.]) However, while we mostly gain *understanding* by experiencing things in the environment, we also learn by examples from others. A child who experiences nothing but punishment from a parent—even if the punishment is effective in stopping incorrect behaviors—also learns that punishment is the way to "get things done." These children may become adults who use punishment in most of their relationships with potentially devastating consequences.[8] So we need to pay attention to the whole learning process and to the whole person.

In conclusion, we have tried to show that the simple learning situations that are called classical and operant conditioning do not pose any essential threat to a biblical view of persons. We have also tried to suggest that learning ultimately involves the entire person. The beliefs we possess, how we have acted in the past, and the knowledge structures we have formed all shape our learning in the future. This has serious implications. How we form ourselves now has a huge impact on how we think, learn, and behave in the future. As the father of American psychology, William James, once said:

> The hell to be endured hereafter, of which theology tells, is no worse than the hell we make for ourselves in this world by habitually fashioning our characters in the wrong way. Could the young but realize how soon they will become mere walking bundles of habits, they would give more heed to their conduct while in the plastic state. We are spinning our own fates, good or evil, and never to be undone. Every smallest stroke of virtue or of vice leaves its never so little scar.[9]

This quote also implies that when we set our hearts in the right direction, develop positive mental structures and personal habits—especially early in life—and engage in regular character-building activities, we increasingly bend our free will toward obedient habits of the mind. This mirrors the apostle Paul's suggestion in Romans 6:18, "You have been set free from sin and have become slaves to righteousness." True wisdom is not instantaneous; it is sculpted by small acts of obedience.

8. Kaufman and Zigler, "Abused Children," 186–92.
9. James, *Psychology*, 149–50.

DISCUSSION QUESTIONS

1. Can you think of ways that you have been influenced by subtle rewards or punishments that come through everyday experiences? In those situations, did it feel to you as though you were the passive victim of influences that worked against your "will," or were you in some ways "allowing" or shaping the process?

2. How has modeling from others influenced how you behave? How might the examples of your own behavior influence how others learn or behave?

3. Can you think of situations where you came to a deeper understanding of some issue or problem through "relationality"—in other words in the context of community or social interaction?

4. Think of concrete ways in which the "direction of your heart" might have influenced what you learned or how you understood what you learned.

8

Remember Me?

Memory

Chapter Summary: Memory and remembering are mentioned many times in the Bible—not usually in terms of how to memorize or how memory works, but in the context of relationships. Being relational persons requires memory—shared experiences and shared knowledge give a common basis for interacting. While it's important to remember where you have placed your jacket on a cold day, imagine the hollowness of a life in which you are not remembered by anyone else. Psychology benefits a Christian understanding of relationality by indicating the various memory types and showing how each handles different kinds of information. In this chapter, we discuss how these forms of memory impact relationships with others and God, as well as with ourselves, as embodied meaning-seekers. In addition, we explore the notion of God's forgetting, as described in the Bible, contrasted with human forgetting.

> Remember, LORD, your great mercy and love, for they are from of old. Do not remember the sins of my youth and my rebellious ways; according to your love remember me, for you, LORD, are good.
>
> Psalm 25:6–7

Memory connects us to each other. When you reconnect with a classmate from elementary school, it's the shared memories of long ago that tie you together. You may not even talk about the past, but a common history provides the foundation necessary to treat each other in a substantially different way than you would a similar person whom you've never previously met. Such connections become really obvious when sharing a memory of a fifth-grade class clown or how the boy everyone knew as "Stinky" has now gone on to a career in modeling.

Memory also connects us to ourselves. Your sense of who you are is absolutely memory dependent. This includes knowledge as simple and well practiced as your own name, and more complicated information including your list of personal likes and dislikes. That sort of knowledge helps you increase your happiness and decrease your misery. If past experience tells you that broccoli tastes good to you, you may feel free to indulge; if you despise it, you move on to something else and don't have to suffer the disappointment of broccoli each time you taste it.

The importance of memory is obvious, and people tend to think about memory a lot like they think about money: more is good, less is bad. Booksellers like Amazon.com have hundreds of titles available on how to improve memory or to avoid memory loss.[1] In addition, there are seminars, drugs, and training programs available throughout North America aimed at boosting memory and escaping its loss. Memory loss is on the minds of adult Americans, as a recent survey showed that Alzheimer's disease is the second-most feared illness in adulthood, trailing only cancer and ahead of heart disease and stroke.[2]

People also dislike and even fear being forgotten by someone else. Sure, there are exceptions like when you've done something embarrassing in the past and people forget that *you* are the answer to this sort of question: "Who was that kid who wet his pants in first grade?"[3] Yet if someone forgets your name or important details about you, it's understandable to feel at least a little unimportant. Our significance within relationships is based on what we mean to each other. One of the most disturbing consequences of memory loss, such as occurs in Alzheimer's, is when relationships are lost in a fog of forgetting. Heartbreaking stories of when "Mom didn't know who I was" or "I needed to see Dad one more time while he can still recognize me" make painfully clear that memory is what gives each of us our sense of identity.

1. In 2013, there were over 1,700 self-help book titles under the category "memory improvement" on Amazon.com.
2. Results of this 2010 national survey of 1,007 adults by Harris Interactive can be found at https://www.metlife.com/assets/cao/foundation/alzheimers-2011.pdf.
3. Okay, that's one of the authors speaking from personal experience. We won't say which one.

Memory in Scripture and Psychology

In chapter 1, we made the case that being relational persons (Theme 1) is at
the center of a biblical view of human nature—the heart of being made in the
image of God. Relating to others requires memory because it is in knowing
and loving characteristics of others that we understand how to respond and
can potentially embrace each other's personhood.[4] Scripture emphasizes the
role and purpose of memory within the context of relationships, particularly
in relationship with God.

Scripture's Emphasis

The Bible certainly refers to memory a lot. The word *remember* appears
over two hundred times across the Old and New Testaments, and the words
forget and *forgot* each show up about fifty times.[5] Only a handful of these passages directly instruct people how to remember, including this passage from
Deuteronomy, after the Ten Commandments were given to Israel: "Fix these
words of mine in your hearts and minds; tie them as symbols on your hands
and bind them on your foreheads. Teach them to your children, talking about
them when you sit at home and when you walk along the road, when you lie
down and when you get up. Write them on the doorframes of your houses and
on your gates."[6] These recommendations involve use of repetition (teaching,
talking in all times and places) and constant physical reminders (writing on
doorframes and gates) of God's laws.

Just prior to giving these instructions of *how* to memorize, however, God
gives his people the reason *why* to memorize. God's people were entering the
new land he had promised, and he assures his people that it is a land he cares
for and that "the eyes of the LORD your God are continually on it."[7] God
is reminding his people that he is with them and is calling his people into a
relationship once again (as had been the case so many times in the Bible)—
a relationship in which God is faithful to the creatures he has created. As a
final preface to the instruction for memorizing and living by the law, God
says, "Be careful, or you will be enticed to turn away and worship other gods
and bow down to them."[8] Remembering is about maintaining a relationship
with God and not "taking up" with other gods that humans, who are prone

---

4. Yannaras, *Freedom of Morality*, 23.
5. In the NIV, the word "remember" is used 231 times.
6. Deut. 11:18–20.
7. Deut. 11:12.
8. Deut. 11:16.

toward wandering worship, easily find enticing. As we have stated in Theme 5, humans are meaning seekers who desire a deity.

The Bible consists of stories of God's interactions with humans—and how humans relate to God, creation, and each other—and it speaks of memory as to how we are creatures made in God's image, crafted to be in relationships. The Bible urges God's people to remember who God is[9] and to remember each other.[10] The human need for relationship with God is apparent in human pleas for God to remember his people (particularly in the book of Psalms).[11] In all of these cases, remembering meant nurturing a relationship.

Psychology's Emphasis

Psychological science is most interested in the how and why of memory—how it is stored, organized, and retrieved, and why it fails. Scripture, on the other hand, simply does not address questions of how memory functions. Answers to the questions posed by psychological research on memory (like that presented in introductory psychology textbooks) can aid all people in understanding how to live out our relational nature by enhancing our understanding of ourselves and others, potentially improving the ways we interrelate. The topic of memory may be one of the best examples to show that the Bible is not a psychology textbook and that psychological science provides information that helps us better understand God's creation (including ourselves) and perhaps even God, as he shows his nature in creation.[12]

Among those beneficial findings from psychology is the identification of a number of subtypes of memory. Perhaps the most familiar consists of memories that include the ability to recall the sort of shared experiences that occur in relationships. These are *episodic memories*,[13] involving memories for the "episodes" of our lives—events like weddings and first days of school, as well as typically less-momentous occasions like last evening's dinner conversation. These memories for personal events include an experience of placing ourselves

9. E.g., Deut. 7:18, as God calls Israel to recall being rescued out of Egypt. Many other similar calls are given throughout the Old Testament to recall who God is. Even the birth of Jesus is a reminder of God's relationship with humans, as "All this took place to fulfill what the Lord had said through the prophet," that a virgin will have a child who will be called Immanuel, meaning "God with us" (Matt. 1:22–23).

10. E.g., Gen. 40:14, where Joseph, in prison in Egypt, interprets a dream and asks to be remembered for this deed.

11. E.g., Ps. 106:4. Examples outside of Psalms include Moses asking God to remember that Israel is God's people (Exod. 33:13) and the thief on the cross next to Jesus at his crucifixion asking, "Jesus, remember me when you come into your kingdom" (Luke 23:42).

12. Worthington, *Coming to Peace with Psychology*, 142.

13. This term was first coined by Endel Tulving in "Episodic and Semantic Memory," 386.

backward in time, allowing us to think about and share with others those earlier episodes in life. In all episodic memories, we have a representation of ourselves in the memory[14]—"I sat by a friend at a wedding" or "I was nervous on my first day of college." When talking with others who also have a memory for the same events, it is those shared memories that bring a connection. In the Bible, most references to memory refer to episodic memories that provide the basis for relationality, including remembering God's acts in relation to humans. In fact, Christian research psychologist Warren Brown mentions episodic memory as one of the critical capacities that humans possess to be relational persons.[15] Better understanding of how episodic memory functions (and sometimes fails) can have significant implications for relationships, and such knowledge comes from psychological research.

Episodic memory is one of the most obvious forms of memory to come to mind because such memories *can* come to mind. Information that we can consciously recall and retrieve is known as declarative (also called explicit) memory. Episodic memory is one of two types of this conscious memory. The other is semantic memory, which includes facts and general knowledge that do not depend on recalling a particular time or situation (such as knowing what a book is without having to remember the last time you saw a book). Semantic memories provide a shared understanding that doesn't require shared experiences. This allows people to decipher each other's language, perceive reality accurately, and draw proper conclusions. Within relationships, there is a communal nature to memory that builds on shared ability to communicate[16] and on shared experience. This shared understanding helps relationships form and, once formed, continue to work.

Memory in Practice

Not all of our knowledge about our actions or events that occur relies on these conscious, verbal systems. Many things we learn are learned without conscious awareness or control, using *nondeclarative* (also called *implicit*) memory systems. These memory types cannot be retrieved consciously, and such memories may be established without awareness—behavior is changed without any conscious recollection of learning. The word *remember* doesn't really apply to nondeclarative memory because this system does not rely on

14. See discussion in Kihlstrom, "Consciousness and Me-ness," 451–68.
15. Brown, "Cognitive Contributions to Soul," 103.
16. If there is a language barrier between people, sometimes gesture or pantomime works to convey fairly universal messages like a need to eat or drink.

or access our conscious awareness. This means that our behavior is influenced in ways and for reasons we are not aware of. In addition, we cannot verbally describe the contents of a retrieved nondeclarative memory.[17] There are several distinct forms of nondeclarative memories, each involving a different brain area.[18] For the sake of brevity, we will highlight how just two of these systems—procedural memory and priming[19]—contribute to our being relational persons.

Before working through the implications of such a memory system, let's look at *procedural* memory, a nondeclarative memory type that includes skill learning and habits. Riding a bicycle is an example of a skill that requires procedural memory (so are typing, walking, and shooting a basketball). The key ability needed to ride a bike is to maintain balance—traveling on two skinny tires without falling over. So in teaching one of our children how to ride a bicycle, one of the authors said, "You need to balance." But how do you balance? The declarative memory around the concept of balance would include words like needing to keep the bike "steady" or "upright." Of course you need to stay "upright" on a bike! Verbal instructions were useless. The nondeclarative information of how you need to slightly lean one direction or another to maintain an upright position is *not* learned verbally—it takes experience. Sensory feedback from feeling as though you're going to fall prompts changes in body position that you can't really verbalize. The only way to learn how to ride a bike is by *trying* to ride a bike—it requires nondeclarative learning and results in a memory you can't fully verbalize. While it is possible to say that you know how to ride a bike (semantic memory) and you may be able to talk about when you last rode a bike (episodic memory), words cannot adequately describe what you needed to learn to make your body be able to ride a bike (nondeclarative/procedural memory).

In the Bible, there are calls for God's people to actively worship and serve. These activities involve physically enacted, procedural memories. A particularly informative chapter in the New Testament is Matthew 6, in which Jesus during his Sermon on the Mount gives his disciples instructions for how to go about the practices of giving to the needy, prayer, and fasting. Looking at Jesus's teaching here tells us about relational aspects of memory. First, in Jesus's

17. Smith and Kosslyn, *Cognitive Psychology*, 193–235, has a helpful discussion of these systems.

18. Kandel, Kupfermann, and Iverson, "Learning and Memory," 1227–46, break down declarative and nondeclarative memory types, and indicate how they depend on different brain regions.

19. We limit the number of examples due to space limitations, but all of the nondeclarative memory systems (conditioning, sensitization, habituation, etc.) impact how people respond to others.

instructions, he begins by saying "when" rather than "if." Jesus's expectation is that his disciples regularly gave, prayed, and fasted—the issue at hand was how to do each properly. Second, these practices all have repeatable physical components that would activate and come to rely on procedural memory.

Third, when instructing his disciples, Jesus emphasized that giving, prayer, and fasting should all be done in ways not obvious to others, and even not obvious to oneself.[20] Regarding giving to those in need, Jesus says, "Do not let your left hand know what your right hand is doing, so that your giving may be in secret."[21] As Richard Foster, author of *Celebration of Discipline*, has written, such practices help God's followers to "experience a life of relationship and intimacy with God,"[22] because they are acts between God and the individual.

We are using the words "acts" and "practices" here because they are physical behaviors, conducted by embodied creatures, which humans are. Our practices form us, as James K. A. Smith writes,[23] because these practices become habits, less accessible to conscious awareness. In the terminology from this chapter, our behavior becomes increasingly governed by procedural memory. Research shows that through practice, behaviors become natural and habitual, like putting on clothes. If you've been around young children, it is obvious that dressing is a learned behavior that improves with practice. Children "teach" their arms and legs how to move properly, yet procedural behaviors like putting on clothes are not simply "mindless" habits. We each have particular rules for where to change and not to change clothes, with many of those rules centering on privacy. While there are very habitual, ritualized components to getting dressed, clothing oneself also involves active *choices* about what to wear. Christians make choices regarding their acts of devotion and worship as well. Giving, praying, and fasting involve decisions about whom to give to, what to pray about, and when and for how long to fast.

Religious behaviors can become ingrained, such as happens for well-memorized songs of praise, memorized Scripture passages, or prayers (such at the Lord's Prayer). When episodic memories fail us (they are more fragile and open to distortion, as we discuss below), such rituals can anchor us. When facing difficulties, a prayerful stance, memorized words, or other deeply

---

20. "If you do, you will have no reward from your Father in heaven" (Matt. 6:1). Rather, do these acts, so that "your Father, who sees what is done in secret, will reward you" (Matt. 6:6). This same instruction is given regarding giving (Matt. 6:4), prayer (Matt. 6:6), and fasting (Matt. 6:18).

21. Matt. 6:3b–4a.

22. Foster, *Celebration of Discipline*, 4.

23. Smith, *Desiring the Kingdom*, 55–62.

formed religious behavior can bring comfort and re-grounding in a way that trying to develop a new, novel behavior may not. Habits are fundamental to how we respond to each other because they are the default moves we make. That being the case, they impact human relationships with God, others, and even with oneself.

Another type of nondeclarative memory is *priming*, where thoughts and behaviors come to mind more easily in the future simply because they were encountered in the past. Priming can impact interrelatedness in unexpected ways because merely being exposed to ideas, objects, or behaviors changes how quickly and how positively or negatively we respond to them later. For example, we tend to more positively evaluate things that we've seen before, including people. The *mere-exposure effect*, which is a variety of priming, shows that people prefer an item they've seen before, even if they don't remember seeing it previously. In one experiment,[24] Chinese characters were briefly presented, and later in the experiment, participants were presented with items that had been shown before, as well as other, similar items that had not. Although participants were unable to tell which items had been presented before versus which were new (no reliable conscious, episodic memory), they tended to prefer the old items more than the new ones. Simply seeing something, without necessarily even being able to consciously recall it, alters our relationship with that "something." If a participant in the experiment were asked to explain why she preferred one Chinese character more than another, the reasoning given would be a conscious attempt to explain an unconsciously influenced preference! The true answer, "Because I saw it before," wouldn't be said because the person is not aware of that previous experience. In chapter 5, on consciousness, we further discussed how such unconscious processing influences relationality, as well as implications for free will and responsibility (Theme 4).

Psychology's research on nondeclarative memory shows that what we do and what we expose ourselves to may bring about changes that influence future behavior in ways that we are not even aware of. Nondeclarative memory effects also show the limited agency of people—not all of behavior is under conscious, willful control. Nevertheless, what we are exposed to changes how we respond to that idea, thing, or person. This research has significant implications, as psychological science aids our understanding of a biblical view of human nature by showing the processes by which these effects occur. For example, Christians might well consider how exposure to God and notions of faith would impact how they and others respond to Christianity.

24. Monahan, Murphy, and Zajonc, "Subliminal Mere Exposure," 462–66.

Meaning Makers Making Memories

A fundamental part of human nature is being meaning seekers (Theme 5). This is apparent throughout our memory processing, particularly in terms of our tendency toward *creative* meaning making. With our memory abilities, we are able to think about many pieces of information at once, not just what is currently being perceived, and are thus able to form new, creative ideas as we combine that information. We can do things like drawing conclusions about why an event occurred.

Organized Memories

Information that gets represented or encoded in memory is stored in an organized way, helping us make sense of our surroundings. This organization often comes simply as a by-product of having an experience and does not require effort. For example, you've learned that it hurts to touch a hot pan just out of the oven. You don't need to think, "I'll need to remember this in the future: pans out of a hot oven burn my skin," and consciously try to rehearse that idea several times, quizzing yourself again later to make sure you know it. No, you learned this immediately. More subtle forms of nonconscious learning include the mere-exposure effect that we mentioned earlier, resulting in a nonconscious memory that influences behavior. This allows a good deal of memory to happen without using our limited cognitive resources (and without taxing our limited agency).

Several factors influence what to remember and what not to remember. Some are biological predispositions, like our drive for self-preservation; other influences depend on how well the new information fits what is already stored (things we already know). Other times, deliberate strategies can be used, like organizing information under a heading (e.g., the category "themes of human nature in the Bible").[25] Whether memory is aided by natural predispositions, memory strategies, categories provided by others, or some combination of these, the thing to notice is that memory is organized. We make meaning of our experiences, sometimes by our own choices of how to do that, but also simply as a consequence of how thinking is organized.

This organization allows thinking about one idea to activate or prime related ideas so that those ideas come to mind more quickly than other ideas.[26] This is really useful, for example, in a conversation. If a friend is talking

25. Bower et al., "Hierarchical Retrieval Schemes," 323–43, published in 1969, is one of the earliest research examples showing this effect.
26. McNamara, *Semantic Priming*, 3.

about his dog, it's good that ideas about your friend, his dog, other dogs, and other relevant (meaningfully related) ideas come to mind quickly, rather than unrelated ideas like bricks, the United Nations, and bananas. Recalling and activating related ideas makes the conversation go forward in a sensible way: responding to your friend's question, "Have I shown you how my dog can play fetch?" with "I like bananas" makes for difficult interaction. The fact that ideas automatically activate related ideas improves interactions. But note something else here: if you are able to share ideas held by other persons, this means you both have similar ways of representing ideas and meaning. This indicates great uniformity in how memory works for people. Yet there are individual differences in what we each particularly remember and what we hold as sufficiently important to recall, because each person has had her own life experiences. Nevertheless, shared memories—shared representations—make us interrelated, relational persons.

Active Meaning Seeking

Meaning is also made in more active ways. When it comes to our conscious (declarative) memories, we're far from being exact recorders of information; instead, we're more like storytellers attempting to make sense of the world around us. When dealing with the world, we do not take in all information equally. Instead, we prioritize information that is important to our situation, and we disregard the rest.[27] In addition, due to limited capacity, we do not store exact copies of events as they occur.[28] Instead, we primarily store snippets and highlights—what psychologists call the "gist" of the event. For example, when we think we've remembered a quotation, it may not be exactly correct. If you're someone who likes to quote movie dialogue, have you ever had the situation where you go back and watch the movie again, only to realize you've been saying one of your favorite lines slightly wrong? Or maybe you've noticed someone else making such an error? Obviously, the original quote was not remembered in its entirety, and during recall it is reconstructed, adding information to fill in the gaps. Similar things can happen for Christians as they hand down traditions that may follow from the gist of a Scripture passage or point of theology, but with a partial notion or inaccurate quotation that may distort the original source.

Human memory also serves in an important way to give each person a sense of self. This sort of autobiographical memory that each person has of

27. See chap. 6, on perception and attention, regarding events that are important or that fit with what we already think.

28. This long-standing notion dates back at least to 1932 with Bartlett's *Remembering*.

her own life is not particularly emphasized in the Bible, but it is certainly a significant theme in memory research.[29] These sorts of memories are also known for being less than 100 percent accurate, as they "may be altered, distorted, even fabricated, to support current aspects of the self."[30] As a person fashions the story of her own life, she strives for coherence, in that she tries to make memory consistent with her "current goals, self-images, and self-beliefs."[31] This means that we may show self-serving biases, as we discussed in chapter 1. We easily misremember events and retell history in a way that leaves us looking correct.[32] Memory is fallible. As Everett Worthington writes, we should draw lessons from this, including that "we need to remain humble about whatever we think we remember clearly," and "we are liable to make errors in directions that justify our beliefs and perceptions."[33] Even our memory systems can show our brokenness and need for redemption (Theme 2).

Human memory errors involve potential problems with taking in, storing, and reconstructing information. Further, it appears that the more often we recall information, the more likely it is that the original information is altered, because memories change with each recall. We change our story of an event to fit a new audience (likely you tell jokes differently to a grandparent than you do to your closest friend), and with each retelling, the memory of the joke can be changed as the telling of the story is integrated with the memory of the story. Our propensity to make meaning and tell meaning actually changes our memory. As one researcher has described it, "If you remember something in the context of a new environment and time, or if you are even in a different mood, your memories might integrate the new information."[34]

The way we recall memories by constructing full memories out of incomplete information does have psychological benefits, even though it opens us up to some error. Psychologists are very interested in failure to take in and failure to recall information accurately. Noted memory researcher Daniel Schacter says that the ability to recall is tied to our ability to imagine the future.[35] Constructing ideas out of incomplete memories allows us to imagine future scenarios, thinking about what might happen if we do one course of action versus another. As Schacter says, imagining the future allows us to "try out" different possibilities for how our own actions might play out. Obviously, this is a lot easier and safer

29. Conway, "Memory and the Self," 595.
30. Ibid.
31. Ibid.
32. Note the research included in most introductory psychology textbooks on false memory and memory construction, such as Loftus and Loftus, "Permanence," 409–20.
33. Worthington, *Coming to Peace with Psychology*, 178.
34. Marla Paul, "Your Memory Is Like the Telephone Game."
35. Schacter, "Future of Memory," 603–13.

than actually experimenting with every option, particularly because doing a single behavior may make all other options impossible. Think of a person you were infatuated with (perhaps you are infatuated with someone right now) and the endless scenarios you may have entertained. What would be the right words and actions to express your interest? How do you look interested but not *too* interested? How do you act cool but not cold? You worked through these possibilities internally, using *episodic* information, "extracting and recombining stored information in a simulation of a novel event."[36] That information can be used flexibly to imagine future possibilities, but in doing that (one of the great cognitive capacities of humans that allows for relationality),[37] it opens us to lots of errors. Those ideas may lead you to believe the other person is more or less interested in you than is really the case as you incorporate your future plans with your existing memories. Unfortunately, those future event simulations are inaccurate because we are not particularly good at imagining just what we will be like in the future.[38] Our meaning making is decidedly finite.

Human Forgetting

As much as memory supports relationships, we can't overlook the impact of memory failure. Memory—particularly declarative memory—lets us down.[39] While episodic memory is more prone to failure than semantic memory (we often forget what we ate last week; we only occasionally forget the specific name of a kind of food—but often recall it later), we experience some degree of failure with all types of memory.

The impact of memory failure may be most stark when memory loss is severe, as in Alzheimer's disease.[40] Because memory is our connection to ourselves and to others, the profound losses of declarative memory that an Alzheimer's patient suffers can leave that person adrift. As Christian psychologist Glenn Weaver writes, such disruptions also affect relationships to God, impairing the ability to study Scripture or attend to verbal components of worship, such as sermons.[41] However, Alzheimer's spares much of nondeclarative memory—the

36. Ibid., 606.
37. Brown, "Cognitive Contributions to Soul," 113–16.
38. Daniel Gilbert wrote an entire book on this notion: *Stumbling on Happiness*.
39. Nondeclarative memory failure also can happen—priming does not always occur and we can forget well-practiced behavior (although it does seem as though people usually do not forget how to ride a bike).
40. See Weaver, "Embodied Spirituality," for further description and personal consequences of the disease.
41. Ibid., 88.

habits and practices one has had through life. Weaver writes, "The episodes of greatest spiritual assurance for Alzheimer's patients seem to arise in regular opportunities to relive very familiar *practices* that witness to the spiritual meaning of a person's life."[42] For Christians with Alzheimer's, repeated actions and behaviors (such as liturgies and hymns), particularly receiving the Lord's Supper, become "a means of grace grounded in procedural memory which can engage dementia patients late into their disease."[43] The community surrounding those with Alzheimer's can play an important role in helping those patients to enter into shared practices of faith, both spoken and physical. In this case, as is always the case for memory, the experience of being a person relies on relationships being sustained by the memory of others and of God.

God's Forgetting, God's Forgiving

Human forgetting and future planning obviously have significant flaws. God's forgetting and future planning, as described in the Bible, are entirely different from that of humans. In several places in Scripture, God is described as "forgetting" something. But if God is omniscient (a biblically based notion that God knows everything, including the future)[44] how could God possibly *forget*? The language used here is simply anthropomorphic, like the notion of "walking with God." God's "forgetting" says something about a relationship with him. God's "memory lapses" make sense if we understand memory in the way the Bible emphasizes it, as being fundamentally about relationships. When God no longer "remembers,"[45] it's about fixing the relationship between God and his people. Christianity teaches that humans are stuck in their own sin (Theme 2), unable to get out of that situation on their own. God freely chose to bring about salvation—forgiveness of sins—through Jesus Christ. Christ's sacrificial death repaired the relationship between God and his people, which no humans could do on their own.[46] So when the prophet Isaiah quotes God as saying, "I, even I, am he who blots out your transgressions, for my own sake, and remembers your sins no more,"[47] the reference is to God's faithfulness to Israel despite Israel's persistent unfaithfulness. In the New Testament book of Hebrews,[48] that prophecy is mentioned again, and it is explained that Jesus

42. Ibid., 100; emphasis added.
43. Ibid.
44. Several verses suggest God's unending knowledge, including Matt. 10:30 and 1 John 3:20.
45. E.g., Isa. 43.
46. Rom. 3:21–26.
47. Isa. 43:25.
48. Heb. 8.

Christ's coming brings about a new relationship between God and his people, in which sins are forgiven by God's grace. Christian psychologist Harold Faw, in his book on memory in the Bible, describes this situation well: "It is through Christ's once-and-for-all sacrifice that the new covenant is established and God chooses not to remember our sins."[49]

How fundamentally different from human forgetting! According to the Bible, God *chose* to bring about salvation and *chose* what he will forget. God's forgetting here means a willful change in relationship, not some failure to take in, store, or retrieve information, as is the case for people. It is because of our forgetting—due to failures in the processes just mentioned, as well as the sinful human willingness to worship things other than God—that makes working at remembering God so critical. It appears that this is why the Bible contains so many references to remembering God and remembering that he is faithful to his people.

Implications and Applications

The multiple types of memory that we have discussed in this chapter imply multiple ways that people are affected by and have an influence on their surroundings. Research on priming implies that ideas spur more related ideas. Christian symbols and practices may spur further thought and ingrained action. In addition, they may more easily be brought to mind or acted upon in times of stress, crisis, or incapacitation. Although many people steer clear of rituals and memorized prayers, perhaps such practices merit greater use.

Research on episodic and semantic memory suggests humans need to study the Bible if they wish to be faithful followers of God. Remembering God's faithfulness is subject to human memory weaknesses. We have memorized only in part—often only the gist. Christians believe that clearer knowledge of Christ comes through Scripture: "I want you to recall the words spoken in the past by the holy prophets and the command given by our Lord and Savior through your apostles."[50] Recalling what God has done is a way for people to receive God's grace to live a godly life and resist incorrect perceptions of God that come from the world: "be on your guard so that you may not be carried away by the error of the lawless and fall from your secure position. But grow in the grace and knowledge of our Lord and Savior Jesus Christ. To him be glory both now and forever! Amen."[51] Scripture reading and knowledge of the

49. Faw, *Sharing Our Stories*, 151.
50. 2 Pet. 3:2.
51. 2 Pet. 3:17b–18.

Bible are not only a redirection of current misperceptions one may have, but they also act to form people to be Christ followers.

But how are people to understand Scripture? As Everett Worthington has stated, we need to remember that "we never deal directly with the data of Scripture, namely with the original autographs that God intended to be in Scripture."[52] When we read the Bible, even if we are able to read the original languages in which texts were written (e.g., Hebrew and Greek), we would not be reading the original copies of those documents because they are no longer known to exist. We read transcriptions and translations, with inclusions of particular sections and omissions of others decided by councils, and understand these writings through the eyes of theologians (e.g., Methodist versus Orthodox versus Roman Catholic versus Presbyterian and so on) who have different understandings and agendas. "In effect, humans, who are sinful, contaminate the most basic data," as Worthington states.[53] Scripture is understood through lenses of tradition and translation, where the gist of an interpretation is influenced by these human factors.

Christians believe that the Holy Spirit, working within the broad body of Christ (the church) can guide believers in their understanding of Scripture, which is why many church traditions include a prayer for illumination (shining God's light of understanding on a text) prior to reading Scripture.[54] Further, God has not left his people alone in recalling himself. God's Spirit is said in the Bible to guide and sustain believers: "the Spirit helps us in our weakness. We do not know what we ought to pray for, but the Spirit himself intercedes for us through wordless groans. And he who searches our hearts knows the mind of the Spirit, because the Spirit intercedes for God's people in accordance with the will of God."[55] The prophet Jeremiah, speaking about the new relationship brought about by the Messiah's coming, quotes God as saying, "I will put my law in their minds and write it on their hearts. I will be their God, and they will be my people. No longer will they teach their neighbor, or say to one another, 'Know the LORD,' because they will all know me, from the least of them to the greatest." God will do this: "For I will forgive their wickedness and will remember their sins no more."[56] God's relationship stands because God forgives sin.

---

52. Worthington, *Coming to Peace with Psychology*, 116.
53. Ibid.
54. Eph. 1:17 includes the apostle Paul's words asking God to give the Ephesians "the Spirit of wisdom and revelation, so that you may know him better."
55. Rom. 8:26b–27.
56. Jer. 31:33b–34.

DISCUSSION QUESTIONS

1. Researchers are increasingly discovering ways of altering memory through the use of drugs, both to help people to remember and to aid them in selective forgetting (i.e., in patients with post-traumatic stress disorder). What are the possible positives and negatives of this? How might chemically altering one's memory impact relationality? How might it improve it?

2. How can human forgetting be a blessing (thinking again of people suffering post-traumatic stress disorder)? Can you think of situations where remembering can be a burden?

3. How does the Lord's Supper (also known as Communion or the Eucharist) utilize declarative and nondeclarative memory? Look particularly to 1 Corinthians 11:17–34 for the apostle Paul's instructions for how to conduct this meal among believers.

4. What are some examples of worship rituals or family rituals that bind Christians or families together, giving a shared church or family memory?

5. How does God's forgiveness and forgetting differ from human forgiveness and forgetting? Must they differ, based on how humans differ from God?

6. In Isaiah 49:16, speaking to Israel, God says, "I have engraved you on the palms of my hands." What does such striking language say about God's memory and commitment to his people?

9

Think about It!

Thinking—Decision Making and Reasoning

Chapter Summary: Our thinking impacts our relationships as we make judgments about others, the world, and God. In this chapter, we explore how people show amazing reasoning ability, yet also make silly misjudgments. Researchers specializing in the study of human thinking or cognition, which includes decision making, problem solving, and intelligence, consistently point to two different types of human reasoning: one that is automatic and quick, and a second that is effortful and slow. The need for these two types and when each is used are profoundly shaped by the embodied nature of being human. These different ways of thinking affect how we go about making meaning and when we can exercise our limited agency.

What a piece of work is a man, how noble in reason, how infinite in faculties, in form and moving how express and admirable, in action how like an angel, in apprehension how like a god!

William Shakespeare, *Hamlet*, Act 2, Scene 2

Two things are infinite: the universe and human stupidity; and I'm not sure about the universe.

Attributed to (but probably not actually said by) Albert Einstein

Which of the previous quotations is more true about people? A reasonable answer might be that it depends on whom you're talking about. People definitely differ in their intellectual abilities. Yet consider this: many people who, given some time, can accurately solve a multistep multiplication problem (say 27 x 86) will, in an instant, rate an item costing $2.99 as significantly less expensive than one costing $3.00—a difference of one cent![1] Maybe the question isn't *which* quotation applies but *when* each applies. The highs and lows of human reasoning are all around us and, if we're honest, are showcased in our own lives.

Why Think?

Before delving into variations in thinking, let's think about the purpose of thinking: to interact successfully with the environment. *Cognitive psychology* is particularly focused on understanding how we perceive, think about, know, remember, and use information.[2] So cognition includes perception and attention, which was covered in chapter 6; memory, which was the focus of chapter 8; and general thinking involved in reasoning, which we will discuss in this chapter. Cognitive processes involve internal (brain) states that act as go-betweens in our interaction with the environment by carrying information. In other words, cognitive processes are necessary for our existence. They are about not so much making our muscles move, but governing responses to our surroundings by formulating and implementing plans to achieve goals. Among the mental processes involved are perception of and attention to important parts of our environment, and understanding how we can navigate that environment, all the while remembering the goal of the action. So if you want to sit down on a chair, you need to perceive where you are relative to the chair, plan out how to get to the chair (e.g., walking), and recognize and avoid obstacles (is there a lamp in your way?), all while remembering that your ultimate goal is sitting. In all of these processes, you need internal mental activity that represents the environment in a useful way. Cognitive psychologists have various ideas about how people accomplish this—how representations occur and allow us to interact with our

1. Thomas and Morwitz, "Penny Wise and Pound Foolish," 54–64, showed that when the leftmost digits of the prices differ, the prices are perceived as different; this does not usually occur for a difference such as $3.09 versus $3.10. This is a good explanation for stores using prices ending in .99 rather than rounding up to the next dollar.

2. One of the founders of cognitive psychology, Ulric Neisser, defined cognition as "all processes by which the sensory input is transformed, reduced, elaborated, stored, recovered, and used" (*Cognitive Psychology*, 4).

environment[3]—but they agree that such representations happen. Such cognitive abilities have important implications within a Christian understanding of persons. As Christian psychologist Warren Brown states, these cognitive abilities allow us to be in relationship with others, creation, and God because we can communicate, remember each other and past experiences, and decide how to act.[4]

Representations also allow us to make meaning of the world (Theme 5). We make conclusions about happenings based on evidence, prior expectations, and knowledge. We draw inferences based on what we see and what we believe, and use those to make new beliefs that extend beyond the original information. Such essential processes of putting together information and drawing conclusions are what thinking is all about. They are also central to scientific psychology, as we discussed in chapter 2, on research methods. Acting intelligently comes down to being able to create representations that allow for learning (modifying representations in useful ways that allow problem solving) and using memory to appropriately apply those representations to new situations. So intelligence depends on how well representations are formed and applied in any given situation.

Creativity

Intelligence includes *creativity*, having ideas that are both novel and valuable.[5] As leading researchers on creativity have written, "Creativity is one of the key factors that drive civilization forward,"[6] implying that human creativity has a particularly significant function. Indeed, Christians believe that acting creatively in God's world (creation) is very much in line with being bearers of God's image. Caring for each other and all of creation as relational persons was part of what God tasked humans to do[7]—to be God's workers and "co-workers for his kingdom."[8] In doing that, human persons are creative as God has been creative—not actual creators, because people did not make creation, but fulfilling their roles as God's agents working in his good creation, which is God's kingdom. Just as creativity drives civilization forward, some Christians, such as Madeline L'Engle, emphasize the importance of this creative work: "Everything that we do either draws the

---

3. Markman and Dietrich, "Extending the Classical View of Representation," 471–74, outline several different ways that cognitive psychologists think about representations.

4. Brown, "Cognitive Contributions to Soul," 101–2.

5. Hennessey and Amabile, "Creativity," 572.

6. Ibid., 570.

7. Gen. 2:15.

8. Catholic Church, *Catechism of the Catholic Church*, 81.

Kingdom of love closer, or pushes it further off."[9] This is the case even in a sin-tarnished world. Therefore, the freedom to be creative—our creative agency—carries with it significant responsibility (Theme 4) as humans can work toward God's desires or at cross-purposes to his will. And while being "smart" or creative may vary between people based on previous learning and ability, as L'Engle writes, "No one is too unimportant" to join in what she calls "co-creation" with God in being his stewards on earth.[10] Each person has gifts and knowledge. Abilities vary within people as well: a person may excel at doing advanced math but be unable to fix a leaky faucet due to her particular aptitude and/or experience.

Thinking, Right and Wrong

Turning back to notions of thinking in general, it's important to note that thoughts or representations can be incorrect (relative to reality around us). We can be mistaken—we represent the world inaccurately, we misunderstand each other, we draw invalid conclusions. Although thinking can be flawed, most of the time what we do works remarkably well. Human reasoning and problem solving tend to be incredibly efficient and accurate. If asked to get a guest a drink of water, most of us succeed. That's pretty amazing, considering how many processes are involved. You need to understand language, see and hear things accurately, and draw proper conclusions to execute that movement. In addition, for one person to fulfill another person's request, mutual understanding is required—the two need to be thinking the same thing. This shared understanding of a representation brings interrelationship between persons. When that representation isn't quite the same, miscommunication happens. For example, a son of one of the authors, warm from playing, asked for water. His father got a glassful of water and brought it to him. But his father's representation of his son's desires did not match his own. When handed the glass, the son's response was, "No, pour it on my head—I'm so hot!" Each individual has his or her own thoughts. Yet shared language and culture allow those thoughts to interrelate as well. As soon as his son said this, his father knew exactly what he meant. (And although he understood his son's desire, his father didn't pour the water on him because part of his father's desire was to keep the living room carpet dry.)

9. L'Engle, *And It Was Good*, 19.
10. Ibid. By "co-creation," L'Engle is making reference to the idea that God intends for his kingdom to be restored and that humans play a role in this consummation of creation. She also encourages believers: "If we accept that God is within each of us, then God will give us, within us, the courage to accept the responsibility of being co-creators."

Fast and Slow Thinking

Thoughts can obviously differ between people. The thinking involved in solving a problem can also differ from task to task. While a parent may be concerned with the state of the carpet, that may not be a priority for a hot five-year-old who wants to be cool. We've all experienced differences with others in how they approach and perform a task. Take writing, for example. Some people use extensive outlines, while others just start writing and see where it goes. Despite such differences, striking similarities exist in people's thinking. Among these is that humans consistently show two relatively distinct types of thinking. Those two types of thinking—what they imply regarding basic characteristics of human nature and how they might be influenced—are the focus of this section.

Nobel Prize–winning psychologist Daniel Kahneman, in his book *Thinking, Fast and Slow*, explains these two kinds of thinking System 1 versus System 2.[11] *System 1* is fast, efficient, and intuitive. It's great for making snap judgments. In terms of the themes of this book, it's a quick meaning maker but has no agency. It relies on past knowledge and experience to make instantaneous judgments. *System 2*, on the other hand, is slow, requires effort, and uses reasoning. In terms of this book's themes, this kind of thinking involves experiences of agency and choice, where an individual feels she is thinking deliberately and actively making sense or meaning of information. It's important to note that these systems are just two different kinds of processes of thought—Kahneman is not implying that System 1 and System 2 are specific areas of the brain.[12]

The differences between these systems become apparent when they are used. Dealing with the environment often doesn't require System 2's reflective thought, so System 1 processes are at work. System 1 uses a variety of sources to draw conclusions: inborn abilities (like recognizing objects and preferences or avoiding pain and loss), practiced abilities (such as reading and understanding social situations), and even culturally held knowledge (such as stereotypes about gender roles). Such thinking simply happens without an individual's conscious intention or any mental effort. For example, in the price judgment mentioned earlier ($2.99 versus $3.00), System 1's intuitive thinking keys in on the leftmost number, draws a quick conclusion by "noticing" a 2 versus

11. This general type of distinction was first outlined by Stanovich and West, "Individual Differences in Reasoning," 658; more recently, Evans and Stanovich, "Dual-Process Theories," 224, have distinguished Type 1 and Type 2 processes, which correspond to the distinction between "intuition" and "reflection."

12. This point is also emphasized by Evans and Stanovich, "Dual-Process Theories," 224.

a 3, and decrees that one price is a lot less than another.[13] Once you make a decision about what something costs (and that $2.99 is considerably less than $3.00), you are likely to follow that decision with action. System 1 judgments can provide the basis for complex, multistep behaviors that eventually require slower reasoning such as when you actually make a purchase. Kahneman concludes that "most of what you (your System 2) think and do originates in your System 1, but System 2 takes over when things get difficult, and it normally has the last word"[14] in drawing a conclusion.

In general, System 2 thinking occurs when System 1 processing fails to come up with a quick answer. When you're surprised, can't figure out what something is, or a conclusion simply doesn't come to mind right away, you engage System 2 thinking. In the multiplication problem mentioned earlier, for example, most of us don't have a ready answer that has been memorized: we know 2 x 8 without mental calculation; 27 x 86 takes System 2 effort.

Negotiating Intuition and Reflection

Kahneman states that System 1 continuously generates information and conclusions based on intuition. If those suggestions are unquestioned by more reflective, System 2 processing, "impressions and intuitions turn into beliefs, and impulses turn into voluntary actions. When all goes smoothly, which is most of the time, System 2 adopts the suggestions of System 1 with little or no modification. You generally believe your impressions and act on your desires, and that is fine—usually."[15]

In the quotation above, notice the degree to which meaningful conclusions, even "beliefs," result from thinking. System 1 does it intuitively, making simple, effortless associations; System 2 does it in a more orderly and slow way. Should further reasoning or analysis be needed, System 2 uses System 1 conclusions (meaning or beliefs produced by it). For example, if System 1 concludes that a voice sounds angry, System 2 may develop a plan to deal with that "hostile" person. Reflective thinking from System 2 never actually checked to see if the other person is hostile—the initial impression and broad conclusions developed by System 1's snap judgment were simply adopted. This is what usually happens, unless the conclusions of System 1 don't work. For example, if the angry voice is followed by laughter (it was all just a joke), you reevaluate your judgment that the other person is hostile, perhaps concluding that there's nothing to fear.

13. Thomas and Morwitz, "Penny Wise and Pound Foolish," 55.
14. Kahneman, *Thinking, Fast and Slow*, 25.
15. Ibid., 24.

Our two systems tend to work very efficiently together, with System 1 minimizing effort, saving resources for situations requiring System 2 functions. As discussed earlier, just as our resources for paying attention are limited, the effort-requiring System 2 must be used sparingly. In addition, System 2 is too slow and inefficient to use all of the time. Imagine using as much mental effort and attention to walk across the room as to solve the math problem 27 × 86. Fortunately, System 1's low-maintenance, automatic guidance results in effortless walking to allow simultaneous walking and talking. Yet when System 2 is fully involved in a task, it can interrupt System 1's control of routine tasks. Then walking and solving 27 × 86 become too much for most people: one stops walking to solve the multiplication problem.[16]

Agency Even in System 1

System 2 is a resource hog (and we have limited cognitive resources), so we use it rather sparingly. Therefore, many of the judgments and decisions we make occur without conscious monitoring or even intentionality. This would seem to profoundly limit human agency or free will. How can you exercise free will when you neither plan nor monitor your behavior? However, simply because you have instances in which you do not use free will does not mean that free will does not play a part regarding when and how you use System 1–type thinking. Your beliefs, reasoning, and behaviors come out of your embodiment and your experiences—all of which are completely yours. Who you are in terms of your social and intellectual history, as well as your individual genetic makeup, influences your System 1 responses. For example, the fact that your name is meaningful to you (and far less meaningful to others who don't share your name) is the result of your experience and reacting to the repeated use of a name. This is a System 1 response. Yet you also have the option of changing your name at some point in your life. If you did, eventually you would have System 1 responses to your new moniker. Therefore, System 1 responses can change through experience. In making that change, you caused the automatic responses (over which you have little choice) to this new name.

This means that for each of us, trajectories we choose set us in the directions we currently find ourselves, even if these directions are ones over which we now have little choice. We can be responsible for our behavior despite limited agency (Theme 4).[17]

16. Kahneman, *Thinking, Fast and Slow*, 39.
17. Thanks to Laird Edman, personal communication, for insights regarding agency and history in this paragraph.

Shortcuts, Categories, and Stereotypes

Nevertheless, by relying on System 1 thinking, we give up some agency. Shouldn't we try to use System 2 as much as possible to maximize our free will? Let's explore that question by imagining this situation: You're to be an usher at a friend's wedding. Driving to the ceremony, you check yourself in the rearview mirror and discover a mess. Your teeth are blue. You check your breath—it could gag a skunk. Perhaps eating a basket of onion rings followed by blueberry pie wasn't a good pre-wedding menu! You're already ten minutes late for the ceremony, but you have your image to consider. Needing a toothbrush and toothpaste, you stop at the first grocery store you see, a huge building you've never previously entered. Hurrying down the first aisle of the store, you see a woman wearing a shirt with the store's logo. There's also a smiling man wearing a T-shirt that reads "Ford Trucks." Without a second thought, you ask the person wearing the shirt with the store logo, "Miss, could you tell me where the toothpaste is?" She immediately points you to the dental hygiene supplies, and within minutes, you're out of the store. Although this sort of shortcut search does not guarantee success (e.g., this person may have bought the store-logo shirt at a used-clothing shop), it does save the time of a System 2 search, which would involve systematically walking up and down each aisle (assuming the aisles are not labeled) or trying to find a place where you're most likely to find a store employee, like the customer service counter. System 2 processing of this situation would make you even later for the wedding. Score one for System 1 efficiency.

System 1 efficiency, however, comes from jumping to all sorts of unexamined conclusions through instantly categorizing people in terms of gender, occupation, and perceived knowledge based on the representativeness[18] of a person's characteristics as belonging in a group. Representativeness and other shortcuts in reasoning are called heuristics. You efficiently used multiple, loosely informed biases based on a logo to draw intuitive, unconscious conclusions, thanks to System 1. Consulting someone who looks like a store employee clearly makes more sense than asking someone who, based on the same reasoning, might work for Ford. In doing so, however, it's highly unlikely that you would have had the conscious thoughts: "She's a woman, she's a store employee, and she'll know where toothpaste is." Quick, logical shortcuts in the form of heuristics allow you to get on with your life by not thinking

18. Representativeness: judging the likelihood that someone belongs to a group based on similarities to that group.

too much. In fact, for successful daily living, people *need* to avoid thinking too much. (When have you ever read a line like that in an academic book?)

Categorization and Stereotypes

Categorization can be accomplished intuitively by System 1 or more systematically with System 2, and is needed in our interactions with the environment. We fit objects into our preexisting categories all of the time (such as when we recognize a new object as a chair and use it as such by taking a seat). Similarly, we use social categorization when we think about people. In the case of people, however, when we identify someone to be a part of a category and make judgments about the potential behaviors of such a person, we are using *stereotypes*. The shopping example we used contained several stereotypes regarding occupation and interests of people. Social categorization is significant for relating to others as persons, as such categories impose meaning on interactions with others. Categorization sets the tone for beginning a conversation or avoiding one, depending on the implications of such categorization.

We agree with Daniel Kahneman's assertion that social categorization is a "neutral" activity.[19] Using it to decide whether to ask one person or another for directions in a store makes a lot of sense. Yet stereotypes have a reputation for being bad—a reputation that is deserved in many situations. At a practical level, stereotypes are a problem when they are inaccurate. Perhaps the person wearing the store's shirt in the example above was simply a fan of the store, like the "Ford Trucks" fellow may be a Ford enthusiast. That sort of mistake would be relatively harmless, even if it leads to an incorrect conclusion. Wrongly assuming that someone is a store employee with particular knowledge of store items does not debase that person, as hopefully you would be courteous to someone you believe to be a store employee.

A more problematic effect can be "causal stereotyping,"[20] in which a group stereotype is applied to an individual, rather than remembering it best applies to the group (if the stereotype is accurate). Take the idea that students at a particular school have low reading abilities. It may even be factually accurate that the reading test scores for that group are lower than average. You would be using a causal stereotype if you believe that Jason, a particular student from that school, must certainly have low reading achievement. This may lead to prejudice in how you respond to Jason and even perpetuate that stereotype by

19. Kahneman, *Thinking, Fast and Slow*, 168, says that social categories consist of norms and prototypical exemplars.
20. Ibid., 167.

actually causing Jason to perform more poorly due to your expectations (e.g., if you expect Jason to be a poor reader, you may make him anxious about his abilities, resulting in poorer performance).[21]

Using any negative stereotyping, however, can result in limiting the expression of the image of God in others by reducing the other's humanity. If you have ever experienced or witnessed racism or sexism, you can see how that sort of categorization imposed on other humans can fracture relationships in a way that categorizing inanimate objects never can. Judging another's likelihood to be intelligent or trustworthy based on a single piece of information from physical appearance undercuts the expression of God's image in that person. Such stereotyping concludes that another is less worthy of being engaged in a relationship, and this devalues that person's personhood.

Not "Us versus Them"

An overarching stereotype of humans found in Christianity is that all persons are God's creation, made in his image (Theme 1). Jesuit priest Greg Boyle,[22] who employs and works to transform the lives of former gang members and convicted felons in Los Angeles, acts out this Christian worldview of humans. The people that Boyle works with are, as he has said, the "them" that people have in mind when folks think of "us versus them." Boyle bases his interaction with others on the foundational notion that each person, regardless of criminal past, is "so much more than the worst thing that you have done." That's his System 1 setting for interaction. Rather than assessing others through the stereotype of a threatening criminal, Boyle begins with God's perspective about each person. "God is compassionate, loving kindness. All we're asked to do is to be in the world who God is. Certainly compassion was the wallpaper of Jesus' soul, the contour of his heart, it was who he was. I heard someone say once, 'Just assume the answer to every question is compassion.'"[23] Boyle writes that such compassion "isn't just about feeling the pain of others; it's about bringing them in toward yourself. If we love what God loves, then, in compassion, margins get erased. 'Be compassionate as God is compassionate,' means the dismantling of barriers that exclude."[24] Reading Boyle's book *Tattoos on the Heart*, in which he relates stories of lives transformed during his

21. This is known as stereotype threat, shown in Steele and Aronson, "Stereotype Threat," 797.
22. Greg Boyle is a Catholic priest working in Los Angeles, where he founded Homeboy Industries, which employs otherwise unemployable former gang members.
23. Boyle, *Tattoos on the Heart*, 62.
24. Ibid., 75.

more than two decades of work, shows that he does indeed notice the usual categories—differences in race and gender, whether someone looks scary, angry, or just a mess. But his overarching causal stereotype goes beyond these superficial characteristics to see that everyone needs and is worthy of God's love, and this is his beginning point for relationships.

As meaning seekers, we all have a longing for God, with our hearts being restless until resting in God.[25] If we don't fill that longing through God —as was intended from the beginning—we may try to fill it through money or academic success or romantic relationships. If Christians act out their faith to allow the category of the "us" who are loved by God to be broadened to include all of those we count as "them," the consequences can be transformational. Boyle recounts a story of Mother Teresa, who spent her life working in the desperate poverty of the slums of Calcutta, India. She told "a roomful of lepers once how loved by God they were and a 'gift to the rest of us.' Interrupting her, an old leper raises his hand, and she calls on him. 'Could you repeat that again? It did me good. So would you mind . . . just saying it again.'"[26]

System 1 Sources

How do people, including Christians, develop their categories for other people? If Christianity teaches that God loves all that he has created, why do Christians so often act as though that's not true? Beliefs and knowledge that inform our thinking can come from individual experiences but also develop in a context. That is, we learn stereotypes from firsthand experience (e.g., based on experiences with our parents, we may conclude that parents can be trusted) and through shared or cultural knowledge and beliefs. As relational persons (Theme 1), the responses of others influence us (see chap. 12, on social psychology). Racial and gender evaluations are learned from multiple sources such as parents, schools, churches, and culture in general. Christians learn about faith and God—sometimes in good ways, sometimes not—in a faith community. That being the case, the church and its members have important responsibilities in terms of what they teach and how they live. The leaders of the New Testament church emphasized the importance of coming together and learning.[27]

System 1 thinking is also based on an individual's predispositions. As mentioned in chapter 10, on development, infants prefer to look at faces, and

25. Augustine, *Confessions* 1.1.1
26. Boyle, *Tattoos on the Heart*, 46.
27. See Col. 1, for example.

being drawn to faces continues into adulthood. In addition, we respond more strongly to motion than to static objects, as we mentioned in the discussion of perception in chapter 6. As Christian research psychologist Justin Barrett writes, "We naturally process some kinds of information more readily than others (such as human faces) and process some kinds of information differently than others (such as associating snakes with fear)."[28] These predispositions shape how we categorize. Categorization can become very deeply ingrained so that it becomes automatic or unconscious. This can be very useful when recognizing things, like a face. This can be very harmful, however, when responses are stereotypes that limit others. If such a stereotype is unconscious, it may be active even when one doesn't want it to occur.

Becoming Faithfully Impulsive

What can be done when System 1 responses are incorrect or even promote sinful behavior? System 1 can tell us to exclude others or ignore situations in which care for others is needed. In effect, System 1 conclusions can foster excluding "them" from "us."

Yet quick, impulsive System 1–based behavior is largely outside of our limited agency. System 2 may be able to help. Negative stereotyping is not inevitable.[29] System 1 thinking, as we have discussed, is endlessly impulsive, but as Kahneman writes, "One of the tasks of System 2 is to overcome the impulses of System 1. In other words, System 2 is in charge of self-control."[30]

Perhaps you have some larger goals that require self-control, like doing well in a class. However, habitual behavior other than studying may get in the way of your academic goals. Would you rather watch movies than study? Which do you consistently choose to do?[31] Psychologists have shown that you can employ strategies to make lifestyle changes to redirect System 1. For example, in order to overcome some cognitive biases, simply raising a person's awareness of other possible ways of thinking or living could be helpful.[32] Simply asking, Why might I be wrong about how I am living? or How do successful students live differently than I do? will lead to better thinking and decision

---

28. Barrett, *Cognitive Science, Religion, and Theology*, 39.

29. Kawakami et al., "Just Say No (to Stereotyping)," 871–88.

30. Kahneman, *Thinking, Fast and Slow*, 26.

31. Such conflicts are very common, as shown in Hofman, Vohs, and Baumeister, "What People Desire," 582–88.

32. Roese and Vohs, "Hindsight Bias," 418, discuss the hindsight bias, in which people overestimate the degree to which they believe they "knew all along" that an outcome was likely to occur. They show that if people consider other points of view, they reduce this bias.

making. Looking for differences in this way gets around System 1's *confirmation bias*[33]—seeking out information and examples that confirm what you already believe or do, like looking for others who don't study as examples for how to succeed as a student!

Clear, frequent feedback regarding one's behavior can also help override System 1 tendencies. For Christians wishing to live more faithful lives, "feedback" can come from other Christians, as well as through the guidance of God's Holy Spirit. A healthy Christian community is one in which all believers are building each other up through encouragement as well as correction. The apostle Paul urged the church in Ephesus to "live a life worthy of the calling you have received."[34] Rather than living impulsively, "tossed back and forth by the waves, and blown here and there by every wind of teaching and by the cunning and craftiness of people,"[35] Christians should speak truth to each other in love. Similarly, asking questions like, Would an intelligent, faithful person disagree with what I'm doing? can help derail the confirmation bias.

On the other hand, impulses can be good as they are. If a first impulse is to care for the needs of others, without thought for oneself, that's an impulse to be supported and nurtured. Impulsivity, by its very nature (thoughtless and automatic) is hard to detect, however, so the community of believers and the leading of God are needed to discern good from bad impulses. Practicing habits like reading the Bible for support of faithful behavior and correction and redirection of sinful behavior can open one's eyes to critically examining impulses. This is particularly the case when done with other believers who are also seeking the Holy Spirit's guidance in understanding the Bible. One can then recognize potential problems, slow down, and live more deliberately. This fits well with Kahneman's suggestions to override errors that originate in System 1.[36]

While System 1 errors can be caught and prevented by greater monitoring and effort by System 2, Kahneman suggests that constantly second-guessing our thinking would take forever. So when should System 2 be used? "The best we can do is a compromise: learn to recognize situations in which mistakes are likely and try harder to avoid significant mistakes when the stakes are high."[37]

But what is "significant"? Psychology isn't a lot of help in answering this. In research on decision making, "good" decisions are defined in terms of the

33. Kahneman, *Thinking, Fast and Slow*, 81.
34. Eph. 4:1.
35. Eph. 4:14.
36. Kahneman, *Thinking, Fast and Slow*, 417, writes, "The way to block errors that originate in System 1 is simple in principle: recognize the signs that you are in a cognitive minefield, slow down, and ask for reinforcement from System 2."
37. Ibid., 28.

decision maker's own criteria. That is, if you set out rules for what counts as a "good" decision, the only way you could make a "bad" decision is if you do not follow your own rules. By this logic, if you decide that having the most fun possible is your goal for a Saturday evening, but you make a decision that does not follow that rule (e.g., you spend the evening talking with a depressed friend), you have made a bad decision. Being irrational—making a bad decision—is when you go against your own values or criteria. In this way, psychology's stance regarding decision making is completely relativistic, depending entirely on one's own rules.

Christians believe that God's plan for living is better than what they devise on their own, so they have a different set of priorities than just deciding to do what "I want to do." For Christians, examining how well one is following Scripture would be a priority worth System 2 effort. For Christians, Scripture is not just a book; it is the authoritative Word of God. Christians believe that despite possible problems with how people interpret Scripture or differences in translations of the Bible, "the Holy Spirit has superintended the essentials of the Christian Scriptures."[38] In figuring out how to live, and acting on that belief, the Bible says that Christians are not left to their own devices to live as Christ followers. As the apostle Paul wrote to the church at Philippi, "for it is God who works in you to will and to act in order to fulfill his good purpose."[39] God works in the fellowship of believers (the church) through God's Word and the empowerment of the Holy Spirit. In so doing, Christians are able to employ their limited agency to live increasingly Christlike lives, following God's will.[40]

DISCUSSION QUESTIONS

1. Greg Boyle writes, "How much greater is the God we have than the one we think we have."[41] In what ways do you stereotype God? What are the consequences of that?

2. How can belief bias (the tendency to accept conclusions based on how believable those conclusions are, rather than based on whether they are logically valid) be influenced by others? How

---

38. Worthington, *Coming to Peace with Psychology*, 134.
39. Phil. 2:13.
40. See Rom. 6 for the apostle Paul's explanation of how God acts through the lives of Christians.
41. Boyle, *Tattoos on the Heart*, 38.

could a Christian community establish or possibly overturn such beliefs? Is there a role for being relational persons here?

3. Is knowledge different from belief? If so, what are the differences?

4. We've emphasized that fellow Christians can be helpful guides for Christians who want to change biases and behaviors. What are some necessary conditions for this to work well? Perhaps consult an introductory psychology text regarding common biases and heuristics.

5. Are people's beliefs about God based more on System 1 or System 2 thinking?

10

Moving toward a Goal

Developmental Psychology

Chapter Summary: The pattern of human development shows certain goals and tasks that are almost universal across persons, yet each of us is differently shaped by our experiences and our genetics. In this chapter, we explore developmental psychology's questions of how much and in what ways people change, as well as the relative roles of environment and genetics in making that pattern of change different for each person. In doing so, we will address issues of embodiment and responsible limited agency. Finally, we will explore how the propensity toward meaning seeking is apparent in developmental psychology theories and compare the goals, or *telos*, of those theories with a Christian understanding of the direction of development.

> Give me a dozen healthy infants, well-formed, and my own specified world to bring them up in and I'll guarantee to take any one at random and train him to become any type of specialist I might select—doctor, lawyer, artist, merchant-chief and, yes, even beggar-man and thief, regardless of his talents, penchants, tendencies, abilities, vocations, and race of his ancestors. I am going beyond my facts and I admit it, but so have the advocates of the contrary and they have been doing it for many thousands of years.
>
> John B. Watson, *Behaviorism*

Development from infancy through childhood and adolescence and on into late adulthood shows fundamental characteristics about ourselves. It is an ideal topic for exploring the relationship between Christian faith and psychology as all of the themes of this book are relevant. Human relationality (Theme 1) is apparent throughout all of life. This links to our making sense of the world and each other that begins in infancy and childhood, as well as our lifelong desire for a deity (Theme 5). In addition, in this chapter we will see that human embodiment (Theme 3) is clear in the impact of genes and environment in development and discuss whether these influences leave room for responsible limited agency (Theme 4).

First, however, we will look at whether developmental psychology has anything to say about the basic condition of humans being broken, in need of redemption (Theme 2). At the beginning of this book, we raised the question of whether persons are inherently good or bad (using Ethan as an example). Can research on children give some insight into this question? After all, newborns have yet to experience a full dose of the good, bad, or in-between effects of parents, friends, and broader culture,[1] so their original essence of humanity—their human nature—should be most evident. Although babies cannot tell us their experience, philosophers, theologians, and psychologists have all speculated on the essential core of human nature observed in infants.

A decidedly positive view of human nature was taken by philosophers such as Jean-Jacques Rousseau[2] and humanistic psychologists such as Carl Rogers,[3] who saw each individual person as complete; they saw the core of each person as good. Some developmental psychologists have concluded, based on observations of children's unprompted helping and sharing, that "young children are naturally helpful, generous,"[4] and willing to share beneficial information with others. Because children acted this way before they could have culturally learned this behavior, one could conclude that being nice is natural.

Another position, outlined by philosopher John Locke,[5] states that the environment entirely shapes a child (and adult). In that view, also held by John Watson, children have no predisposition toward goodness or badness—their only real predisposition is that they can be influenced by what surrounds them.

Christians believe that humans are sinners, living in a broken world and in need of redemption. But is this brokenness evident in infants and children?

---

1. This is mostly true, but the fetus's environment prior to birth has been shown to be correlated with later health, such as in Whitaker and Deitz, "Prenatal Environment," as well as preferences for the language of their mother at just two days after birth, presumably due to their experience with hearing their mother's language prior to birth, as in Moon, Cooper, and Fifer, "Two-Day-Olds Prefer Their Native Language."

2. Rousseau, *Emile*, 5.

3. Rogers, "Notes on Rollo May," 8.

4. Warneken and Tomasello, "Varieties of Altruism," 400.

5. Locke, *Some Thoughts concerning Education*, 74.

Over the centuries, Christians have debated whether sinfulness is apparent in the behavior of young children or if they are morally innocent, not able to choose to sin until later in life.[6] Debates continue over whether the behavior of babies shows their selfishness or their trust and innocence. Christian theology also addresses the question of goodness at a spiritual level and concludes that humans always fall short of that goodness without the reconciling work of Christ.[7] This more eternal sense of "goodness" or "badness," and the related topic of culpability for sin, is a theological issue, however, and is not our primary focus here.

Moral Babies

Psychological science actually does not allow us to conclude whether infants are born innately good or bad because these judgments vary across culture and historical time. Psychology can, however, provide valuable insight into what conditions make a behavior more or less likely to occur. If psychologists study a behavior such as grasping, they could determine when the behavior changes from being more reflexive (involuntarily occurring when anything touches an infant's palms) to more voluntary and intentional, and identify what a baby is likely to grasp (novel objects, foods they like as opposed to foods they don't). In addition, science can tell us which conditions promote culturally agreed-upon positive outcomes, such as school success or marital satisfaction.

Psychology also has much to say about morality and development, including the propensities of babies to act in ways that are either self-serving or altruistic. Research suggests that babies show a morality, and it appears to be based on cooperation. This sort of morality includes the ability to show degrees of empathy and prosocial behaviors (e.g., sharing with others), with infants doing this as soon as they have the physical skills to give objects to others.[8] As early as just two days after birth, babies show a form of empathy through simple emotional reactions to others' suffering by crying when other infants cry.[9] In addition, young babies make judgments that indicate they have a moral sense and judge whether actions by others are good or bad, deserving reward or punishment. Infants indicate these preferences by more often reaching for toys that had "acted" in morally desirable and cooperative ways

6. Bakke, *When Children Became People*, 56–109, discusses a variety of views held by early Christians.

7. Rom. 3:23: "For all have sinned and fall short of the glory of God."

8. Hamlin, "Moral Judgment and Action," 187.

9. Sagi and Hoffman, "Empathic Distress in the Newborn," 175.

than for toys that had not.[10] Babies also prefer to look at (by three months of age) or reach for (by six months of age) animal puppets (or even an object like a square) that had earlier helped another puppet achieve a goal rather than a similar puppet that hindered another puppet from achieving a goal. Further, infants as young as five months prefer puppets that harm those that previously hindered or blocked the goals of another puppet.[11] That is, babies like "helpful" puppets, but they also like puppets that punish "bad" puppets. Infants appear to develop the capacities of a moral code or a moral sense without instruction. While the content of what they are to consider moral or immoral is certainly learned and shaped by others, it appears "people are intrinsically moral creatures."[12] Christians would assert that this is "because they bear the image of God."[13]

While direct observation of infants may not tell us about the innate goodness of a child, infant and childhood development research confirms that embodied humans are naturally relational meaning seekers (Themes 1, 3, and 5). We will explore what developmental psychology says about these themes in the following sections.

Babies Are Relational Persons

Babies are born prepared for social relationship. Inborn abilities and genetically predisposed preferences drive babies into relationships from birth. For example, newborns prefer looking at human faces more than any other tested objects.[14] This inborn preference draws other human beings into the beginning of a relationship with that infant. If you have ever observed adults interact with infants, you will notice that adults light up when a baby's gaze meets their own—parents love having their babies look at them. Babies also have reflexes like grasping, which helps them hold on to others. In addition, the burst-pause pattern of feeding, present in newborns, also provides social interaction virtually every moment while infants are feeding. Babies take a few drinks and pause, at which time the feeder usually jiggles, pats, or talks to the infant.[15] After receiving social interaction, the baby resumes feeding. Babies are born with several types of cries that most adults can successfully interpret to mean

10. Hamlin, "Moral Judgment and Action," 187–88.
11. Ibid., 187.
12. Worthington, *Coming to Peace with Psychology*, 245.
13. Ibid.
14. Valenza et al., "Face Preference at Birth," 892–903.
15. Kaye, *Mental and Social Life of Babies*, 36–40.

hunger or pain.[16] They also begin intentionally smiling at human faces when they are between one and two months old, which is their first intentional act. Taken together, these abilities get babies into close contact with other humans, who care for and comfort them. Embodied relationships meet physical needs (human infants cannot care for themselves), so these relationships are critical for survival. Growing through childhood into adulthood and late life, we desire relationships with others as those connections also feed some of our deepest emotional needs as relational persons (Theme 1).

To get a sense of how foundational relationships are, think back to your childhood. Did you ever believe there were monsters under your bed or lurking in your closet, ready to pounce when the lights went out at night? Even if your bedroom was monster-free, at some time you probably woke up in the middle of the night, scared by a sound or nightmare or sick from an illness. To whom did you go? That person (or persons, depending on how big the monster!) would be among those to whom you had formed an *attachment*. As child psychologist John Bowlby claims, infants are born with behaviors that are the building blocks of these strong emotional ties to a caregiver, and these promote the baby's survival.[17] Attachment is a lifelong process, but babies do not really start to get specific about who or what they are attached to until sometime around six months of age. Attachment appears to be an inborn tendency in infants as they show a bond with those who have met their needs, as well as primary caregivers who are less responsive.[18]

Lifelong Attachment

Attachment is clear in early childhood, and as Bowlby states, "it can be observed throughout the life cycle, especially in emergencies,"[19] as it provides psychological support and often even physical aid to people. Attachment encompasses our need for belonging and intimacy that continues through childhood and adulthood. Attachments serve as a safety zone, a "home base" from which to face the world, so that when a child is scared, she goes to a parent or caregiver. Successful attachment in infancy is related to better friendships in childhood and better emotional health and romantic relationships in young adulthood.[20] Throughout adulthood, we go to friends or family when difficulty arises. As psychologists Roy Baumeister and Mark Leary state,

16. Zeskind, Klein, and Marshall, "Infant Crying," 1153–62.
17. Bowlby, *Attachment and Loss*, 223.
18. Ibid., 203.
19. Ibid., 669.
20. Sroufe, "Attachment and Development," 358.

"Human beings are fundamentally and pervasively motivated by a need to belong, that is, by a strong desire to form and maintain enduring interpersonal attachments."[21]

Attachment to God

In addition to relationships with other people, the Bible also stresses that humans are in need of relationship with God. Psychological research confirms this biblical emphasis. A leading researcher on attachment and religion states, "Much research in the psychology of religion supports the idea that religion, and particularly a perceived relationship with God, serves both the haven of safety and the secure base functions of attachment."[22] Attachment to God has been measured by examining how self-reported levels of attachment and religious beliefs relate. Researchers have shown that people who report an attachment to God continue that attachment over long periods of time, and that likelihood to turn to God in times of need was related to a person's level of attachment.[23]

Babies Are Meaning Seekers

Along with showing predispositions toward relationships with others, infants and children also demonstrate predispositions to make meaning and, as we will discuss, even to worship. Humans adapt to and try to understand whatever situation they find themselves in. The biblical theme that humans are meaning seekers can be seen in psychological research on infant preferences and childhood beliefs.

Perceiving Patterns and Making Meaning

Children, even infants, work hard at trying to figure out their world. They take cues from their caregivers to determine how to investigate the world. Babies go beyond this, as well, as they "think, draw conclusions, make predictions, look for explanations, and even do experiments," write the developmental-psychologist authors of *The Scientist in the Crib*.[24] Babies and children do not stop there. Developmental psychologist Alison Gopnik writes, "We can learn about our environment, we can imagine different environments, and

---

21. Baumeister and Leary, "Need to Belong," 522.
22. Kirkpatrick, "God as a Substitute Attachment Figure," 962.
23. Ibid., 969–70.
24. Gopnik, Meltzoff, and Kuhl, *Scientist in the Crib*, viii.

we can turn those imagined environments into reality."[25] Children transform themselves and the world around them.

These transformations begin with humans' fundamental meaning seeking search for knowledge and understanding—the drive to figure out the situations in which we find ourselves. The beginnings of such abilities are apparent in infants. Researchers who study infant preferences and memory often measure what an infant looks at as indicative of what the baby likes, knows, and does not know.[26] Unconstrained by social rules like "it's rude to stare," babies look at what interests them, staring and looking it over until they are no longer interested. Using this and related methods, researchers have concluded that babies understand a lot. For example, babies as early as four months demonstrate that they categorize objects by looking longer at members of one category than another (e.g., cats versus horses).[27] Six-month-olds make conclusions about cause and effect in scenes they observe.[28] Such abilities provide the foundation for children (and adults) to infer deeper conclusions about why things happen as they do.[29] It also allows them to categorize causes as good versus bad for making moral decisions. Children are meaning makers, and their predispositions lay the groundwork for continued development of that capacity.

Identifying Agents

A critically important meaning making skill of infants is their ability to spot an *agent* and differentiate it from mere objects. An agent is someone or something able to get things done—a possible cause that can bring about an effect. As Justin Barrett demonstrates in his book *Born Believers*, children are able to think about agency because they know about cause and effect. "Children are born with minds ready to make sense of the world around them."[30] This drive to make sense of the world helps them (and has helped all of us who are alive) survive. Children's search for patterns and making meaning of their environment results in them drawing conclusions about the nature of things. Babies, by four to eight months of age, demonstrate their agency by

25. Gopnik, *Philosophical Baby*, 7–8.
26. Oakes, "Mental Processes in Infancy," 255–59.
27. Madole and Oakes, "Making Sense of Infant Categorization," 279.
28. Leslie and Keeble, "Do Six-Month-Old Infants Perceive Causality?," 278, showed that babies looked longer at events that included an apparently causal sequence than they did at identical events without such a sequence included.
29. Gelman, *Essential Child*, explores categorization and provides one view of how it develops in children.
30. Barrett, *Born Believers*, 41.

being able to redo things that bring enjoyable consequences—repeating some simple actions like pushing a button to make a toy cat appear.

Children also distinguish between agents and other objects fairly early in life. When one of the author's sons was three or four years old, he told his dad that a favorite toy train engine was his friend and helps him do things. That was an imaginative display of attributing agency when agency obviously was not possible for the object. Children experience a sense of comfort and security in snuggling with a favorite stuffed toy.[31] Yet when push comes to shove, the child knows what is and is not possible for an object. That son never asked his train to go and get him a sandwich. He asked his mom or his dad for food. This same child once called out from his room in the middle of the night, "I'm lonely"—this despite having his favorite stuffed turtle (he had named Swimmy) in bed with him. Half asleep and wanting to be fully asleep, his dad replied, "Just hug Swimmy." He yelled back, "But he doesn't work. I need you." While the stuffed toy may be cozy and snuggly, it does not hug back.

As we have already mentioned, attachment is important for survival, but so is understanding of agency (a form of meaning making). When it comes to identifying agents, Barrett says that agents "represent both our greatest threat and our promise for survival and fulfillment."[32] Barrett goes on: "So it is little surprising that infants show signs of knowing the difference between agents and inanimate objects and that they show a great sensitivity to the possible presence of agents around them."[33]

Desire for a Deity

In that search for agents, we include the possibility of agents that are unseen and nonhuman. Cognitive psychologist Justin Barrett[34] and evolutionary psychologists including Jesse Bering[35] and Paul Bloom[36] suggest that we are born to believe in a deity or deities. These psychologists point to developmental research which they believe shows that children may be "intuitive theists"[37] or "born believers,"[38] and that "religion is natural."[39] Barrett shows that children

31. Harlow and Zimmerman, "Affectional Responses in the Infant Monkey," 421–32, famously showed the importance of physical contact, even with an inanimate object, resulting in an emotional response in monkeys.
32. Barrett, *Born Believers*, 41.
33. Ibid.
34. Ibid.
35. Bering, *Belief Instinct*.
36. Bloom, "Is God an Accident?," 105–12.
37. Keleman, "Are Children 'Intuitive Theists'?," 295.
38. Barrett, *Born Believers*.
39. Bloom, "Religion Is Natural," 147.

have a predisposition to think about deities because they tend to see purpose and recognize that purpose and order come from beings that have minds, and this "makes children likely to see natural phenomena as intentionally created. Who is this creator? Children know people are not good candidates (e.g., humans did not create the Rocky Mountains or pumas). It must have been God."[40]

Depending on one's worldview, religious beliefs can be seen to occur for other reasons. Some psychologists point primarily to our biology or our cognitive abilities to explain why people search for purpose and for causes for events. For example, if one takes a purely evolutionary view of religion's development, as Bloom does, one may conclude that religious beliefs exist as a by-product of a more useful predisposition to be on the lookout for causes of events and to more efficiently draw helpful conclusions to understand how the environment works.[41] In that view, the mechanism that looks for causes gets, in essence, carried away, and when obvious causes cannot be found, it resorts to an unseen agent—a god.

If one takes a Christian view, as Barrett does, the desire for God can be seen to arise because God has created us such that we are born to seek him out. People search for a god because humans bear God's image and are made to be in relationship with him. The Bible teaches that humans are made by God, for God. God has made us with a deep desire for him,[42] and although that desire is easily misdirected by sin, longing for God remains. In the end, both Christian and non-Christian psychologists agree that children have a predisposition to look for a god, but the two groups differ in why that predisposition exists.

Nature and Nurture throughout Life

Studying infants has shown us a number of basic characteristics of human nature. Developmental psychology, however, focuses on more than just babies. People continue to grow and change throughout their lives, and psychologists are interested in understanding the pattern of that change and factors that impact that pattern from conception to death. In doing so, developmental psychologists have identified several basic issues or questions that cut across all the topics of their field.[43] Perhaps the most basic and also most debated is how genetic inheritance interacts with our experience as we develop (genes/

40. Barrett, *Born Believers*, 135–36.
41. Bering, *Belief Instinct*, 80; Bloom, *Descartes' Baby*, 210.
42. See further discussion in chap. 5, on consciousness.
43. Santrock, *Life-Span Development*, 20–21.

nature and environment/nurture). Exploring how development is lived out physically, shaped by both genes and environment, relates to Theme 3, being embodied. In addressing that issue, however, we must also consider the involvement of each person in the course of her own development, since humans are responsible limited agents (Theme 4).

In discussing being relational persons and meaning seekers, we have focused on inborn abilities, or at the very least, ones that develop early in life. God made humans, giving us the genetic inheritance we each have. In making us, God also designed us in his image.[44] Yet these genetically based, inborn abilities (including bearing God's image) are always expressed within a specific environment. This question of nature or nurture can be complex and may best be explored using a concrete example.

As an infant, one of the author's sons almost invariably cried if the person holding him stopped walking or sat down. So long as the holder was on the move, that was all that really mattered. His other son, however, showed no such "rules" about being held as an infant and was quite content to be still. Such preferences indicate *temperament*, which is a person's particular style of reacting to situations and managing responses to the environment.[45] Differences in the quickness and intensity of responses, such as crying, as well as the ability to reign in that sort of response, are apparent very early in infancy and are thought to be part of a child's genetic heritage. As temperament expert Mary Rothbart claims, "Temperament is present in infancy and early childhood, and forms the biologically based core from which personality develops."[46] *Personality*, a person's characteristic pattern of thinking, feeling, and acting, grows out of a person's biological beginnings.

Temperament, as well as personality development, always expresses itself within a context. Each person in a relationship has her own pattern of responding, yet with development and maturation, as well as relationships with others, that pattern is modified. Psychologists believe that caregivers need to adjust their behavior to an infant's individual temperament for attachment to occur well or even at all.[47] The infant's behavior (in part stemming from temperament) influences the caregiver if the caregiver is responsive. In addition, the caregiver's response also influences the infant. As Rothbart has written, "Although temperament and personality are influenced by the genetic code, they are also influenced by variations in the child's experience, which typically

44. Gen. 1:26–27.
45. Derryberry and Rothbart, "Arousal, Affect and Attention," 958–59; Rothbart, *Becoming Who We Are*, 10–11.
46. Rothbart, *Becoming Who We Are*, 12.
47. Ibid., 107.

occur in a social context."[48] This is a lifelong pattern of each side influencing the other's behavior, and eventually their personality.

This foundational notion from developmental psychology echoes the Bible's depiction that humans exist in and are made for relationships. Being in relationships changes the people relating to each other. Just as your childhood surroundings helped shape you, you also shaped your surroundings—and that process continues throughout life. As a child, when toys were presented to you, you had a large role in choosing which of those toys became favorites. If you were like most kids, you did a good job of making your preferences known by playing with favorite toys more than non-favorites, talking about them, or asking for additional similar toys (following up on that line from many toy ads, "Collect them all!"). These experiences likely did not change your temperament, however. If you were quick-tempered without the particular toys you desired, you were likely quick-tempered even when playing with your desired toys, as this tendency shows some stability (rather than change) from childhood to adulthood.[49]

Development nevertheless is influenced by others, including individuals; smaller groups including school, neighborhood, or church; and larger communities like regions and countries that have their own cultures. The Bible echoes that the impact of others can be negative or positive,[50] regardless of one's temperament. The structural aspects of sin also get communicated and shaped in children: racism, sexism, greed—the list goes on—are displayed and even trained into children. Positive influences of family and community are also highlighted, as in the book of Proverbs: "Start children off on the way they should go, and even when they are old they will not turn from it."[51]

The fact that societies as well as genetics play a large part in shaping children should not deter parents from following the words of Proverbs in bringing up children in "the way they should go." Every person can think of counterexamples. Good outcomes can come from difficult beginnings (e.g., a child raised in poverty and neglect who goes on to a successful career and meaningful life), but a troubled life can come out of even the best homes. As David Myers and Malcolm Jeeves write, because of all the other influences on development—genetic and environmental—parents need to "love the person

48. Ibid., 5.

49. Ibid., 192.

50. Israel is commanded to not associate with groups worshiping other gods in Josh. 23; Paul in 1 Cor. 5 instructs the Corinthians to avoid associating with anyone claiming to be a follower of Christ but commiting a variety of sins. Other passages, such as Heb. 10, indicate the importance of Christians gathering together to support and build up each other—positively influencing each other in their faith.

51. Prov. 22:6.

that results,"[52] even if how she develops is not what was expected. They stress that parents' influences are limited, and thus so should the degree to which parents are blamed when children have difficulties in life. The same also goes for parents' being the cause of success: triumph happens for many reasons, and only sometimes is one of those reasons parents. In trying to understand why anyone behaves as she does, or why Ethan from the introduction has difficulties with life and suffers from ADHD, it is important to keep in mind that there are many possible genetic and environmental causes.

Nature, Nurture, and Agency

It is important to notice that, to this point, we have mentioned nothing about each person's role in shaping his or her own development. The nature-versus-nurture debate pits two deterministic extremes—genes and environment—against each other. That is, if you say a person is entirely shaped by her genes (e.g., temperament), then biology dictates who that person becomes; if you say that environment (e.g., parenting) makes the child who she becomes as an adult, then her parents and surroundings are the determining factors. Most development chapters in introductory psychology textbooks will point out that neither of these extremes is right, saying that development is always a product of the joint influences of nature and nurture working together. As one textbook states, "All that people are and all that people become is the product of an interaction between nature and nurture."[53] This more nuanced view, however, is still deterministic. Although scientifically more accurate, this position misses the important emphasis on the responsible limited agency of a biblical perspective. Theme 4 acknowledges that humans have constraints on their choices—biology and environment do not allow for unlimited possibilities, in part because we are embodied. While we are shaped by those strengths (and weaknesses) within and around us, we are also responsible to shape ourselves, to the degree that we are each personally able. For example, each child (and later the adult) has a role in developing self-regulation, leaving her able to shape her own actions, thoughts, and even ways of living. As creatures made in God's image, we are stewards of not only the rest of creation but also ourselves. A psychology of human development, to be complete, must recognize human choice and responsibility for that choice if it is to meaningfully take up a biblical view of human nature.

52. Myers and Jeeves, *Psychology through the Eyes of Faith*, 47.
53. Ciccarelli and White, *Psychology*, 231.

Focusing solely on the physical environment and human genes also misses some of God's activity in bringing about personal spiritual change. The Bible teaches that God formed humans and continues to act in the lives of people,[54] thus working through nature and nurture. As the apostle Paul wrote to the Corinthians, those who are in Christ "are being transformed into his image with ever-increasing glory, which comes from the Lord, who is the Spirit."[55] Paul also wrote that believers are being built up spiritually, "being strengthened with all power according to his glorious might so that you may have great endurance and patience."[56] God works in creation and in the lives of people living out their faith responsibly in both physical as well as spiritual ways, and these are not mutually exclusive of each other.

Telos: Where We Are Going

Reflecting on the shaping effects of environment, genetics, and each person's choices should raise a larger question always present in development: What are we developing toward? The most obvious path of development goes from the womb and eventually ends at a tomb—hopefully with some interesting stops in between. However, individual theories have particular ideas about what would be the best path for development of a person as a whole or a particular aspect of a person, such as social development or intelligence.

Consider a research article by Sarah Hamson,[57] exploring how childhood personality traits impact adulthood. Writing about adult well-being, she says that it "consists of good physical and emotional health, satisfying interpersonal relationships, and mastery in chosen fields." The goal condition in that study is well-being, and it involves an "unfolding over the life course."[58] This particular research study claims to identify processes by which people attain it. While the components of well-being included by this researcher may not fit everyone's definition of functioning well (for example, a sense of having a meaningful existence is not directly included), outlining any set of characteristics as defining "well-being" implies that these are developmental goals and that reaching and sustaining them are in some sense better than not doing so.

As developmental psychologist James Fowler has written, developmental theorists often provide a standard or norm for the "direction of the *telos*

54. Isa. 64:8 describes God as the potter and humans as the clay.
55. 2 Cor. 3:18.
56. Col. 1:11.
57. Hamson, "Childhood Personality Traits," 264–68.
58. Ibid., 264.

or goals of human life."[59] The word *telos* comes from the Greek word for "purpose" or "end."[60] Theories of development sometimes overtly, sometimes subtly, imply what counts as "good" development, despite science's attempts to be objective.

Christian philosopher James K. A. Smith says that *telos* is not simply "being 'pushed' by ideas or conclusions; rather, it grows out of our character and is in a sense 'pulled' out of us by our attraction to a *telos*."[61] In the example above regarding the development of well-being, the researchers are not referring to ideas alone but also behaviors. Those behaviors that aim toward well-being also promote the goal of well-being. We are actively involved in the goals toward which we aim, and this involvement changes us and forms us toward that *telos*.[62]

In order to see where a developmental theory is "going," Christian psychologist Ken Bussema has suggested we "turn developmental theories upside down."[63] The final stage or end point of a theory indicates the overall goal of development from that theorist's perspective. From the goal state, a developmental theorist can "work backwards, uncovering the steps along the developmental path, noting the possible disruptions, and the necessary motivation required to reach the final developmental destination."[64]

Erikson and Stages of Human Development

To further understand this, we will "turn over" the influential developmental theory of Erik Erikson.[65] His eight-stage theory of social development attempts to encompass the entire lifespan and paints a picture of what successful development looks like. Erikson's theory, as we shall see, readily relates to the biblical themes of humans being relational persons and meaning seekers (Themes 1 and 5). The culmination of development in Erikson's theory is for a person to become an independent self with meaningful relationships. That is the *telos* of Erikson's theory, found in its final stage of late adulthood. According to this theory, throughout the lifespan people progress through a series of stages, where each stage involves resolving a

59. Fowler, *Becoming Adult, Becoming Christian*, 11.

60. An area of philosophy known as teleology is the study of the purpose of things, including life.

61. Smith, *Imagining the Kingdom*, 6.

62. Ibid., 7–8, is primarily arguing this in terms of the outcomes of education.

63. Bussema, "Perspectives on Developmental Psychology," 2.

64. Ibid.

65. Erikson, *Identity*. Several other theories attempt to explain aspects of development over the lifespan, including Kohlberg's theory of moral development; Kohlberg, "Stage and Sequence," 376–83.

critical challenge for an individual to overcome before going forward to a next stage.

Independence and relationality, goals in Erikson's final stage, are also seen throughout earlier stages of the theory, so we will spend a little time here highlighting those themes in some of the stages. Erikson emphasizes the importance of experiences throughout the lifespan and how individuals deal with turning points throughout life. The more successfully a person resolves challenges of these turning points, the better that person will be able to reach a psychologically healthy state in later life. Erikson states that the first developmental challenge children face as infants is a basic question of whether the world and the people in it are to be trusted. He described this stage as a time during which a child develops a "sense of basic trust" or a "basic mistrust."[66] This issue is directly related to processes of attachment and gaining trust in a caregiver. As we discussed earlier in this chapter, attachment has been shown to have significant implications for relationality.

Erikson states that the development of trust also significantly shapes other behaviors and beliefs that will continue to develop later in life. In the child's encounter with her caregiver, the infant develops not only a sense of trust but also a sense of identity, as the relationship between the caregiver and child is "one of mutual trustworthiness and mutual recognition."[67] Then in adolescence she needs to trust adulthood, and abandon childhood, in order to develop her full personal identity (whom she wants to be and where she wants her life to go).[68] Another significant implication Erickson sees in this question of trust versus mistrust is that trust "becomes the capacity for *faith*—a vital need for which man must find some institutional confirmation."[69] This relates well with this book's Theme 5, that humans are meaning seekers, as Erikson suggests people will have faith in something. Even in this first stage of development, meaningful relationality and independence are beginning to form.

As people develop through childhood and adolescence, more tasks are encountered, as opportunities for relationships and independence grow with broadening social circles and greater knowledge and competence. Erikson made important contributions to the notion that people work to develop a meaningful life. Research on identity development has shown that this form of meaning seeking is typical in high school or college (depending on the environment) as people actively explore identity.[70] Identity formation continues, as it

66. Erikson, *Identity*, 96–97.
67. Ibid., 105.
68. Ibid.
69. Ibid., 106.
70. McLean, "Late Adolescent Identity Development," 683–91.

is a lifelong process. In midlife, people begin to take up the issue of generativity—helping subsequent generations lead useful lives—and by late adulthood, Erikson states, people must deal with the reality that "I am what survives me."[71]

According to Erikson, "In the aging person who has taken care of things and people and has adapted himself to the triumph and disappointments of being,"[72] the positive outcomes of the previous seven stages of development can grow into what he called integrity. This is achieved when a person reflects on her life and comes to "acceptance of one's one and only life cycle and of the people who have become significant to it,"[73] basically without regret or desire to have lived a different life (doubt or gloom that Erikson characterized as despair). An older person with integrity would be at peace with his life, while a person with despair would look back at the past with regret, somehow hoping it would have been profoundly different. Erikson says that those who experience integrity can accept their lives and even their impending deaths as important and satisfying. In this integrity, there can be a drive to connect with things beyond oneself through rituals that come not only from religion but also from the arts or mythology.[74]

While there is much to be seen in Erikson's theory that fits with a Christian view of human nature, in significant ways they do not fully align. First, as we have stated, the theory focuses on the importance of being relational persons. Erikson, however, views human relationality not in light of being God's image bearers who steward creation, but instead in terms of the relationship between the individual and others. Each person is on his or her own (although interacting with others) to develop a full sense of self and integrity. The Bible, on the other hand, emphasizes humans' need for relationality with God as well as with others. Second, there is a strong emphasis on meaning seeking in Erikson's theory, as he emphasized the need for humans to make sense of their environment and themselves. This is particularly seen in his eighth stage, as each person struggles between integrity and despair. Such meaning seeking "evokes 'ultimate concerns'"[75] for the purpose of one's life and potentially even an interest in God. Here again, however, a significant difference can be seen between Erikson and a biblical view of human nature in that for Erikson the struggle for integrity is each individual's alone. Christian faith emphasizes relationality here again, in that persons are meant to be upheld by others, within a creation actively upheld by God.

71. Erikson, *Identity*, 141. Pages 91–141 outline his theory of identity development.
72. Ibid., 139.
73. Ibid., 140.
74. Erikson, "Reflections," 161.
75. Erikson, *Identity*, 140.

Christian Telos

For clearer comparison between psychological theories and a biblical view of life's goals, let's turn Christianity "upside down." If we look to the goal state for Christians, it is ultimately to live forever with God. Psychology, however, necessarily focuses on this life alone, so we are overshooting its time frame of development by looking beyond the present life. It is a mistake to think that psychology could adequately address something that it never intended to address (eternity), as we would be making improper theological demands of a science. If we focus on this life's goal, in Christianity it would be to love and serve God and others. This might best be summed up in the theological term *sanctification*, which means to become holy and set apart for a special purpose, "being conformed in disposition and behavior to the image of Christ."[76] Humans started out at creation as sanctified—in full relationship with God, living out the image of God—so sanctification "refers to *living as God's people*, both ethically and spiritually."[77] Richard J. Plantinga and colleagues add, "While one important component of that work of reclamation is the forgiveness and sanctification of individual persons, these personal dimensions of salvation fit in the context of God's larger work of renovating all of created reality."[78] God's reclaiming and sanctifying all of creation go beyond a developmental theory involving individual persons, but they do point to the fundamental relationality of all persons. Human sin and its consequences have reverberated throughout creation so that humans became disconnected from God and their calling. The *telos* of humans on earth—the developmental goal—is a reconnection with God, to once again be set apart for God's perfect use as God's image bearers.

Sanctification happens in a person's life through the activity of God's Holy Spirit. If we look at the developmental path of sanctification, God is involved throughout.[79] People are unable to attain reconnection and holiness without God, so sanctification comes about through the work of the Holy Spirit in the lives of believers.[80] Theologian Abraham Kuyper wrote, "God's highest

76. Plantinga, Thompson, and Lundberg, *Introduction to Christian Theology*, 329.
77. Ibid., 330.
78. Ibid., 332.
79. This is the process of sanctification as described by Jenny, "Sanctification," 1166: "The sanctification of the world takes place at a personal and individual level. Those who choose to be sanctified by the Spirit must cooperate in the process (1 John 3:3; Rev. 22:11) just as in the water purification rites of the [Old Testament]. This process removes the sin but 'saves' the individual. The Spirit's role in sanctification begins before conversion with conviction (John 16:8–11), includes cleansing the believer at conversion (1 Cor. 6:11; 2 Thess. 2:13; 1 Pet. 1:1–2), continually washing him or her from sin after conversion (John 4:10–14; 7:38–39; cf. 1 John 1:7–9), through guiding him or her in righteous living (John 14:26; Rom. 8:5–13; 1 Cor. 2:9–16)."
80. 2 Thess. 2:13; 1 Pet. 1:2.

purposes are realized when the Holy Spirit makes man's heart His dwelling-place. Who or whatever we are by education or position, we cannot attain our highest destiny unless the Holy Spirit dwells in us and operates upon the inward organism of our being."[81] Each person is involved in her sanctification—working out faith[82]—but without God's involvement, it does not happen. Aiming desire toward the Christian *telos*, as James K. A. Smith says, "pulls" out "action that is directed toward the kingdom of God."[83]

A particularly important aspect of this development is that God is willing to act in the lives of people regardless of their age or their "significance" in the eyes of others, as we are all bearers of God's image. Christ himself was clear in emphasizing the significance of children: when people brought children to be touched by him, Jesus said, "Let the little children come to me, and do not hinder them, for the kingdom of heaven belongs to such as these."[84] Jesus showed the value of children, a notion that was very counter to the notion of children as little more than slaves or animals that was prevalent when he was on earth.[85] The Bible emphasizes the worthiness of all persons, stressing the importance of humans as relational persons, regardless of their status. In particular, care for the most vulnerable in society, including the poor, widows, and orphans, is emphasized.[86] Even in the Old Testament, Israel is called to care for the stranger and foreigners, remembering that Israel had been a foreigner at times in its history and knew the difficulty of being an outsider.[87] These acts of caregiving were not just to take care of physical needs but also to show love.[88] Each person's significance comes in light of relationality with God. The ultimate goal in the Christian life is redemption from sin and reconciliation with God. Self-fulfillment, coming to peace with one's life, and living by one's own rules do not fit the emphasis of a Christian *telos*.

Although we have explored *telos* in the work of only one theorist, Erikson, the existence of a goal state or set of characteristics is what makes such theories developmental. That theories developed by humans function in this way reflects the meaning seeking nature of people. We search for purpose in

81. Kuyper, *Work of the Holy Spirit*, 24.
82. Phil. 2:12–13.
83. Smith, *Imagining the Kingdom*, 6.
84. Matt. 19:14.
85. Bakke, *When Children Became People*, 16. At that time, women also had incredibly low social standing and, like children, were lumped together with slaves and animals as having no ability to reason. Jesus acted counterculturally toward women by speaking with and teaching women (e.g., Luke 10:38–42; John 4).
86. James 1:27: care for widows and orphans.
87. Exod. 23:9.
88. Lev. 19:33–34.

our lives. Erikson also emphasized this basic meaning seeking in people of all faiths in this life, and this is particularly apparent in his final stage in which people address integrity versus despair. The fundamental quest for integrity can be reached through a variety of paths (family, work, civic involvement, etc.). Similarly, sanctification can look different for each Christian, as people obedient to Christ are called to particular lives to use their particular gifts. Erikson's theory was an attempt to delineate an account of human development on this earth, as universally experienced. Christians include a more fundamental, theologically defined *telos* in understanding human personhood. Although Erikson's psychological model does not include theological concepts, it is not necessarily incompatible with the theological *telos* emphasized by Christians.

Born to Develop

God certainly could have made us fully developed from the moment we appeared on earth, but human persons are not born fully mature. Yet God does not leave us as infants—we have an inborn drive to develop to maturity. We see this in universal examples of mental and physical abilities (attachment and speech are just a couple of examples), as well as in Christians' development of mature faith as God pulls humans to develop. The human experience of development is universal, as we literally or figuratively go from crawling to walking in our movement and our emotional and cognitive responses. Understanding the pattern of these changes is developmental psychology's contribution to our understanding of ourselves and is the value of developmental theories such as Erikson's.

=== DISCUSSION QUESTIONS ===

1. Explaining behavior in terms of only nature or nurture (or some combination of the two) leaves us with explanations that are deterministic. How might understanding an aspect of one's personality be informed by taking seriously the role of responsible limited agency in a person's life? What about other characteristics like gender or sexuality?

2. If babies are "born believers," what becomes of that natural belief through childhood and into adulthood? Regarding your own life, how have parents and/or communities in which you

have lived influenced your notions about who or what God is or is not, including whether there is a God at all?

3. Think about the *telos* of your development to this point. Do you agree or disagree that all humans have a need for a forward-moving development into something better? What future goal(s) are you striving toward? What has been your role in your *telos*?

4. Identify the *telos* of developmental theories described in developmental psychology or introductory psychology textbooks, such as Piaget's theory of cognitive development or Kohlberg's theory of moral development. Compare these theories with the *telos* of Christianity.

5. What are some ways that meaning seeking has changed over the course of your life? What are the "big questions" you face now, and how do they differ from the ones you faced earlier in life? How do you go about making sense of the world and your existence now versus five or ten years ago?

11

Trust Your Feelings!

Emotion

Chapter Summary: Emotions have had a bad reputation for the past two thousand years—thanks in large part to the influence of Greek and medieval philosophers, who valued reason above emotions. Christians have also downplayed emotions, and many psychologists seemed uninterested in studying emotions, since they were viewed as too "messy" to measure and too much a sign of human weakness. However, in recent years, psychologists have rediscovered how essential emotions are to our basic nature. This chapter examines the embodied nature of emotions and how they are integrated into our whole being. We also explore how emotions illustrate our image-bearing quality and how they allow us to relate to God and others in ways that go to the core of our being. Finally, we also stress that we are responsible limited agents who can engage in emotional self-regulation, despite the limitations of our situations or physical existence.

Indulging in unrestrained and immoderate laughter is a sign of intemperance, of a want of control over one's emotions, and of failure to repress the soul's frivolity by a stern use of reason.

Saint Basil, *On the Vice of Laughter*

I have a Bible study that my friends and I go to here in L.A. I go to church every Sunday. I've always been a believer. I love singing. I don't have the best voice—I just love getting my emotions out.

Tweeted by actor Kellan Lutz

Grieve, mourn and wail. Change your laughter to mourning and your joy to gloom. Humble yourselves before the Lord, and he will lift you up.

James 4:9–10

Perhaps you sang this little "ditty" when you were young:

> If you're happy and you know it, clap your hands.
> If you're happy and you know it, clap your hands.
> If you're happy and you know it, then your face will surely show it.
> If you're happy and you know it, clap your hands.

These "complex and deeply moving" lyrics go on to describe additional happy actions (e.g., "stomp your feet"). Despite its painfully simple message and annoyingly catchy tune, the song captures two profound ideas. The first idea is that one can experience emotions either consciously or unconsciously ("if you're happy *and* you know it"); the second idea is that when you experience emotion it is expressed in automatic body responses ("your face will show it") and overt actions ("clap your hands"). One other interesting element about the song is that it is always sung in a group setting. The song is sung with others because, as we believe, emotions are meant to be shared and are very much a part of our relational nature.

These ideas provide a partial answer to a question that may have never occurred to you: Why should we have emotions at all? We asked a similar question earlier when we asked why we need bodies. When we ask students in our classes what they think of emotions, we get a large variety of answers. Students will say emotions have negative connotations. They say that emotions are untrustworthy, cloud judgment, hinder problem solving, make us think and act irrationally, disrupt relationships, pull us down (e.g., depression), turn us into unthinking Christians (e.g., in worship), lead us into bad or even sinful behavior (e.g., anger, jealousy, anxiety), and are a general sign of personal weakness. Other students say emotions have positive associations. They claim that emotions are more trustworthy than rational or scientific thinking, help build relationships, motivate us, help us be more authentic people—and more authentic Christians—and are a sign of personal depth.

The quotes from Saint Basil and Kellan Lutz at the beginning of the chapter also reflect these competing views that we hold about emotional experience. Even for students who value emotions, they still sometimes wonder what life would be like without emotions. Of course such a person has never existed, except in the old science fiction television series *Star Trek*. The original version of the series had a character on the show named Mr. Spock,[1] who in fact had few, if any, human emotions. While Mr. Spock was portrayed as lacking the kind of passion and courage that the spaceship's captain had, he was always portrayed as the cool, rational individual who often made better decisions because of his dispassionate nature. Although the conflicting views of our students are in many ways true (i.e., that emotions have both good and bad implications), current psychological research has shown that if a person like Mr. Spock ever existed, he couldn't live long in this world—emotions are essential to our very survival, as we describe below.

A Brief History of Emotions

Before getting to the value of emotions, it would be helpful to understand why there are so many conflicting views of emotions. Emotions were viewed quite negatively for many centuries after Greek philosophers such as Socrates and Plato suggested that the mind was part of a nonmaterial soul—and was equated with pure reason—while emotions were assigned to the body and considered less noble and worthwhile. These ideas about emotions were strengthened by seventeenth-century philosopher Rene Descartes, who taught that the body was a mechanical entity (like a clock) but that the mind was a "nonmaterial substance" that could rule over the body. However, body and mind could also interact, in that the mind has awareness of the body and the mind can influence the body. Communication and control between the two entities happened, according to Descartes, through the pineal gland, a small structure toward the center of the brain.[2] For example, "passions" could originate in the body—and might remain "in" the body and never be experienced by the nonmaterial mind—or they might create such a strong response in the body that the mind becomes aware of it. Desires of the nonmaterial mind might also translate into bodily actions and passions that influence our behavior. Descartes thought animals have passions (i.e., bodily reactions) but not emotions because these require a conscious experience of the mind (soul). Like the Greeks, Descartes's view places a high value on reason and gives emotions a much lower place of importance in human functioning. It also suggests that we can not only "transcend" our bodies, as discussed in chapter 3, but that with relatively minimal effort—a bit of reason and self-discipline—we can rule over our emotions.

1. In later, movie versions of the series, a character named Data replaced Mr. Spock as the emotionless individual.
2. Smith, *Current Systems in Psychology*, 36.

Christians have also downplayed emotions during much of church history. Being influenced by Greek philosophy, many early Christian leaders felt that emotions were associated with our "fleshly" nature. Since the "desires of the flesh"[3] were equated with sinful tendencies, it was presumed that emotions had a great potential to lead us into sin. Early Christians pointed to Bible passages that appear, at first reading, to make a direct statement about temptations that arise by way of emotions (see Eph. 2:3[4] and 4:26[5] for examples); more about this issue later.

Even many early psychological theories saw emotions as troublesome or as having little benefit. Freud and later psychoanalysts stressed the power of emotions, but also stressed how destructive they might be. They felt that "bottled up" emotions—especially anger—were damaging and should be "released" on a limited basis. However, they also believed that rational thinking should prevail in most situations. The behaviorists, such as John Watson and B. F. Skinner, stressed that emotions were simply the result of improper associations and could be corrected by simple learned mechanisms. But they still saw emotions as something to be diminished, so that more "correct behavior" could prevail. While there are many historical influences that have created more positive views about emotions within psychology, perhaps the strongest was the humanistic psychology perspective. This movement stressed that emotions were equal to, or perhaps more important than, rational thinking. "Getting in touch with your emotions" was a common refrain, and it was assumed that authentic relationships could only happen when we were aware of our emotions, expressed our emotions freely, and trusted emotions more than reason.[6]

Some movements within the church have also brought emotions into greater popularity among many groups of Christians. Movements that stress the power of the Holy Spirit have stressed the expression of emotions in order to become more Spirit filled and more authentic as Christians.

The combined influences of these historical ideas have resulted in many conflicting views and perspectives about emotions—and sometimes these conflicting views are held by the same person at the same time! Thankfully, recent research and contemporary psychology—especially neuropsychology—have done a lot to give a clearer picture of the value of emotions. We also believe

---

3. This phrase is often translated into English as "sinful nature" in more contemporary translations such as the Today's New International Version rather than "desires of the flesh" as in the King James Version.

4. Eph. 2:3: "All of us also lived among them at one time, gratifying the cravings of our sinful nature and following its desires and thoughts. Like the rest, we were by nature deserving of wrath" (TNIV).

5. Eph. 4:26: "'In your anger do not sin': Do not let the sun go down while you are still angry."

6. Shotter, "Getting in Touch," 7–22.

that contemporary research has finally rediscovered the essential nature of emotions and can help us to recapture a more complete and scriptural understanding of human nature.

Contemporary Views of Emotions

Let's first examine what cognitive neuroscience research has discovered about normal emotional functioning to help us understand what emotions do for us. Neurologist Antonio Damasio, who receives a lot of credit for the renewed interest in emotions, suggests that, "Feelings, along with the emotions they come from, are not a luxury. They serve as internal guides, and they help us communicate to others signals that can also guide them."[7] Of course, communicating to others also suggests that emotions serve a very important role in relationships.

Consider the little-known emotion mirth. Mirth is the distinctive emotion that is elicited by the perception of humor.[8] It is a subcategory of happiness, and occurs in response to unexpected but pleasant outcomes, as well as during times of "playfulness." But the more important question is, why would human beings have such an emotion? Is this something that human beings manufactured through culture, or was it given to us at the beginning of time? If it was given to us, what possible purpose does it have? To say the purpose of mirth is "to make us happy" is circular reasoning since mirth is a type of happiness. As it turns out, mirth does much for us that helps us survive. We have learned a lot about the value of mirth by studying chimpanzees. (One advantage of studying animals is that researchers don't have to worry about the influence of culture or other social issues.) Psychologist Rod Martin[9] describes how young chimps engage in lots of interactive play and even tickling. This play mimics adult chimp life in that it involves some aggressive actions (e.g., biting, pushing, etc.)—just as human children's play sometimes does. One benefit of mirth is that it is an internal signal to the young chimp that this activity is valuable (i.e., it provides an internal reward signal) because it teaches young chimps how to behave as an adult. It also communicates a signal to the other chimp that this activity is playtime and not an actual act of aggression. Finally, once the second chimp sees the first one laughing (yes, chimps do actually have a distinctive laugh), the second chimp responds with its own internal signal telling it that the first chimp means no harm. There is

7. Damasio, *Descartes' Error*, xv.
8. Martin, *Psychology of Humor*, 8.
9. Ibid., 165–67.

another value to the entire process, driven by emotional-motivational triggers: it fosters relationship. These signals not only provide information, they draw the two chimps closer together. The intimate emotional and physical exchange allows the chimps to "read" the other, to become more emotionally attached and to feel more comfortable with the other. When complex organisms form strong attachments like this, they also survive better.

Humor and mirth provide many of the same functions for humans. While emotions such as mirth provide us with important internal signals and provide important communications to others, perhaps their most important element is to create and maintain relationships. There are many other examples of normal emotional function and the purpose of emotions, but perhaps the most compelling illustration of our need for emotions comes from cases where emotions are disrupted because of disordered or damaged brains.

Emotions and Brain Damage

Individual case studies of emotional damage have made it abundantly clear that we simply don't function well without emotions. Antonio Damasio describes one such case in his highly acclaimed book, *Descartes' Error: Emotion, Reason, and the Human Brain.* He tells the compelling story of Elliot, who experienced a radical change in personality because of a brain tumor. Elliot, a very healthy man in his thirties, had been a "good husband and father, had a job with a business firm, and been a role model for younger siblings and colleagues."[10] He had attained a good deal of success in his business and in his personal life; he was considered to be very intelligent, was able to remember and keep track of important details, and made good personal and business decisions. However, after surgery to remove a tumor in the middle of the frontal lobes (i.e., right behind his forehead and above his eyes), he became a very different person. He retained his good memory, ability to talk and move effortlessly, good problem-solving ability, and overall high IQ. He also remained calm and, in casual conversation, seemed to have good social skills. However, his personal life quickly unraveled; he now made risky and ultimately disastrous business decisions, he went through two divorces, and he seemed unable to stop himself from bad decisions, even when everyone in his life advised him to do otherwise (e.g., the second marriage was to someone whom his entire family warned against).

After extensive testing, it appeared that Elliot's primary problem was that he could no longer access or appreciate his internal emotional state. He continued

10. Damasio, *Descartes' Error*, 35.

to experience some emotions (although they were diminished), but he could not seem to read or evaluate his own emotional response. So despite superior intellect, when making any significant decision—be it business, social, personal, or moral—he lacked the most important thing of all: a gut feeling. When most of us make bad decisions, we get feedback from others by way of facial expressions (e.g., frowns or angry looks) and from our own bodies (e.g., arousal or anxiety) that remind us that the decision was bad. This information, along with cognitive analysis of the situation, comes together in the middle frontal lobe area of the brain, the area affected by Elliot's tumor and surgery. We learn from these experiences that we should not repeat such actions because we not only see the consequence intellectually, we also "feel" them. Damasio knows that Elliot cannot experience these because his bodily response, as measured by a GSR (galvanic skin response) machine (which gauges the activity of the skin in response to emotions), showed a nearly flat response when confronted with events that normally create emotional reactions. Elliot simply could no longer access this feeling response, and it had devastating consequences for his life.

Emotions and Autism

Brain damage from a tumor is not the only condition that can blunt emotions. Individuals with some forms of autism spectrum disorder also have moderate to severe difficulty with emotional and social issues. These individuals range considerably in their intellectual and language abilities, but what they share in common are difficulties in reading facial expressions and understanding the social-emotional conventions of everyday interactions. Temple Grandin[11] is one such individual. She also has exceptional cognitive abilities and is well known in the worlds of engineering and animal sciences for her work in the design of humane cattle-handling systems. She possesses a remarkable intellect and amazing memory skills. However, she also has tremendous difficulty understanding the simplest of emotional cues and social rules. As told to neurologist and author Oliver Sacks, she said that while she could understand the feelings of animals, "It's different with people, . . . studying the people there, trying to figure out the natives." She also suggested to Sacks that trying to understand people was like being an "anthropologist from Mars" because they seemed like a foreign species to her; "I can tell if a human being is angry . . . or if he's smiling" she stated, but she could not really understand or relate to the emotions that she observed. Sacks recounts how Grandin compared her lack of ability to that of children: "Children, she

11. See Grandin and Scariano, *Emergence*.

feels, are already far advanced, by the age of three or four, along the path that she, as an autistic person, has never advanced far on. Little children, she feels, already 'understand' other human beings in a way she can never hope to."[12]

Grandin's difficulty is not that she lacks any internal emotional experience but that she does not have the same internal experience of emotions that others have when someone shows an emotion to her. Most individuals have an implicit (i.e., unconscious or inborn) sense about emotions, but Grandin has to "compute," as she states it, the intentions of others in order to determine their "state of mind." While she has a fulfilling career and has achieved a great deal of professional and personal success, she relayed to Sacks that it was somewhat painful to her that she had never had a close, loving relationship with another person. She does have friends that she relates to intellectually and professionally, and feels as though they are on the same "wavelength" at times, but she does not experience close, loving relationships. She suggested that she had never dated because "she found such interactions completely baffling and too complex to deal with."[13] In fact, she had a hard time even articulating what love is or what loving someone might feel like. "Maybe it's like swooning," she suggested at one point. She could also describe how others act when they say they are in love, but as with reading facial expression, it was more like a scientific analysis of events than something deeply "felt."

Individuals like Elliot and Temple Grandin illustrate to us how central emotional experience and understanding are to everyday life. There are some additional examples that we have already described in chapter 3. In that chapter we told the story about the woman known as "S," who lost the ability to be angry, and we described how people form emotional attachments because of the hormone oxytocin. Emotions assist us in virtually all of our decisions. Emotions help us to negotiate the social and interpersonal world around us, and what appears to be abundantly clear is that they make meaningful, reciprocal relationships with other people possible. Therefore, perhaps the saddest aspect of these stories of brain and emotional dysfunction is the disruption of meaningful relationships.

Biblical Pictures of Emotion

As we have suggested throughout the book, God designed us for relationships (Theme 1). So the embodied emotions (Theme 3) that we possess are part of

12. Sacks, *An Anthropologist on Mars*, 270.
13. Ibid., 285.

that grand design. These qualities also mirror God's character in so many ways. An electronic Bible search reveals countless passages about God's emotions. God is described as angry in over two hundred passages, and that doesn't count the times he is described as "slow to anger." God, as Father or as Son, shows a wide range of emotions that humans also experience including concern (Exod. 2:25), happiness (1 Chron. 29:17), sorrow (Matt. 26:37), and envy (Deut. 4:24). There is also a wealth of emotional language throughout Scripture. If you want to see how emotional Scripture can be, examine 2 Corinthians 7 and count the emotion-related words (we count thirty-two). What this suggests to us is that when God created us in his image and with characteristics that allow us to have relationships, emotions were a very significant part of that creation. In order to have a deep and meaningful relationship with any other person (including God), we need to be able to communicate (using language), represent ideas in our mind (cognitively), and understand the intentions and ideas of the other (sometimes called theory of mind),[14] but we also need to communicate our emotions and to form emotional bonds. So we believe that emotions are an essential part of our created image and our relational nature. While this idea makes the case studies of disordered emotions all that much more painful—since relationships with God and fellow humans are distrupted—Warren Brown has suggested that even when some individuals struggle in relating to God, God can still maintain that relationship with them.[15] God continues to provide us with his love and care and maintain his promises to us, even when we can't feel it.

"Problem" Emotions?

So it appears that both psychological science and Scripture emphasize the essential nature of our emotional life. However, our experience tells us that emotions may sometimes create problems for us or even lead us to sin. Isn't it still the case that emotions can cloud judgment and make us do irrational things at times—or even cause us to become superficial (i.e., nonthinking) people or Christians? Isn't it still the case that some people express too much emotion, or not enough, or don't control their emotions? Psychology and Scripture are on the same page in addressing these concerns about emotions. Both Scripture and psychological science point to the harmful impact that very extreme negative emotions can have, and the need to "rein in" our more powerful emotions.

14. Brown, "Cognitive Contributions to Soul," 108.
15. Ibid., 123–24.

Certainly some biblical passages suggest that emotions can be a vehicle for sinning. Emotions such as anger, envy, anxiety, and others appear to be condemned in some parts of Scripture. But a closer examination of many scriptural passages suggests that the problem comes from the way we use these emotions, not with the emotion itself. After all, God shows every one of those same emotions at times, so it doesn't appear that the emotion is the main problem. It appears that the reason or causes for experiencing a particular emotion, and how we act when we become emotional, are the key concerns of many passages. Take worry or anxiety, for example. There are several passages that seem to command us not to worry or have anxiety (see Matt. 6:25–34; Phil. 4:6). But if you examine the context of most of the passages, the focus is on what people were anxious about—money, clothing, and other aspects of material daily existence—rather than condemning all anxiety. The point of such passages is to show that the main attention of Christians should be focused on God's kingdom, not on all these things of lesser importance. We can also contrast these ideas to passages in which there is a clear indication not only that some legitimate concern or worry is appropriate (such as 1 Sam. 9:5–6, where Saul is worried that his father would be concerned about his whereabouts) but also that the lack of concern seems to be the greater sin (such as Prov. 6:9–11, where the lack of concern over property maintenance brings on poverty).

Much the same could be said about anger, where the problem isn't the anger itself but what the anger is directed toward and how people react when angry (1 Cor. 13:4–6; James 1:19–20). There are also clear admonitions about how long people stay angry and what they do when angry (Eph. 4:25–27). So none of the emotions we experience appear to be sinful experiences by themselves, but our own sinful tendencies can distort why we experience certain emotions and how we react when we have the emotions. There is also clear indication that how we act when we have powerful emotions can damage relationships. Therefore, Scripture clearly teaches that people also need to be in control of their emotional response and consider the impact of emotions on relationships.

From the psychological community, it is intriguing that therapists also increasingly understand that we need to exercise control over our emotions. This is a significant change from the days of Freud, who felt that unbridled "release" of problem emotions was almost always a good thing (called catharsis by psychoanalytic therapists), and from the humanistic psychologists, who felt that most emotions should be accepted for what they are and rarely considered as good or bad. Much of current therapy practice recognizes that unregulated emotions can be destructive and that we need to, and that we are able to, learn how to manage them. For example, a study by Kevin Ochsner and colleagues showed that participants were able to cognitively "retrain" or self-regulate their emotional responses. More importantly, this retraining had profound effects on their brain activity in response to an emotional event.[16] Therefore, with an emotion like anger, the current view in psychology is that neither releasing it, repressing it, nor expressing it whenever we want are particularly helpful. Rather, when we experience strong emotions like anger, we need to identify the real source or situation to which we are reacting, learn to constructively deal with that issue, and learn to regulate the intensity and direction of the emotions we experience.[17]

So we believe that the variety of God-given emotions that help us form meaningful relationships can be distorted by our own sinful tendencies, but they can also be distorted simply because we live in a broken world (think of Elliot and other case studies presented). But whatever the cause of our emotional turmoil, God's desire is that we learn to understand the source of our emotions, balance our emotional responses, and learn to restore relationships damaged by emotions.

The Pursuit of Happiness?

When we control our emotions and when we seek to shape our own emotional experience, should the goal always be to achieve happiness and avoid the more negative emotions? Most people in Western societies value happiness, and even the Constitution of the United States speaks of each person's right to pursue his or her happiness. Many therapists also strive to bring about greater happiness in their clients (see chap. 16, on therapy), but are negative emotions always something to be avoided? Psychologist Joseph Forgas reviews a series of studies showing that negative mood states (mostly sadness) have many positive effects on people.[18] Sadness was associated with more accurate memories of events, more polite behavior, increased sensitivity to social cues, and greater fairness in social situations. Forgas is not arguing that we should remain in these states, since there are different positive benefits for positive moods as well, but he suggests that we should not attempt to eliminate all of our up and down emotional experiences, since these moods may be a response to a life situation and be just what we need at that time.

In a very different way, author Kathryn Greene-McCreight, who writes about her own struggle with clinical depression, suggests that her lengthy bout

16. Ochsner et al., "Rethinking Feelings," 1215–29.
17. See Travis, *Anger, the Misunderstood Emotion.*
18. Forgas, "Don't Worry, Be Sad!," 225–32.

of depression and sadness had some surprising benefits in the end. While she would never wish such struggles on anyone, she suggests that having gone through this struggle made her have "deeper compassion for the sick, bedridden, and homeless."[19] She had always thought that she had been a compassionate person, but after she experienced these negative moods that caused her great pain, she realized that this was not true. As she says, "How, after all, can one put oneself into the shoes of another who is suffering without having suffered personally?"[20] Deeply negative and even painful emotions can be part of a growing experience. But in her case, and in the case of many with mental illness, such negative mood states seemed ever present, robbing her of the benefits and important consequences of positive states that we also need.

Scripture also points out the value of experiencing guilt,[21] remorse,[22] and other negative moods[23] from time to time. While God may not desire for us to remain in painful emotional states, we often learn from the variety of emotional states that God has created for us to experience. Just as a bad taste in our mouth from spoiled food helps us to learn that we should avoid such foods in the future, so a negative mood state may help us learn about our current situation and about ourselves. So we can be thankful that, by God's grace, psychological science has also pointed to ways that we can learn from our emotional experiences and also learn to manage or restore some emotional balance and self-regulation to our lives.

Implications and Applications

These scriptural and psychological insights into the value and purpose of emotions don't necessarily help in dealing with all of the practical issues related to emotions, but here are a few practical applications that we believe grow out of these larger ideas.

1. Develop your God-given emotional life by nurturing relationships with God and with others—which requires you to "practice" understanding emotional cues from others, using appropriate emotional expression, and engaging in appropriate self-regulation. (It's also worth noting that

19. Greene-McCreight, *Darkness Is My Only Companion*, 156.
20. Ibid.
21. See Ps. 32:5: "Then I acknowledged my sin to you and did not cover up my iniquity. I said, 'I will confess my transgressions to the Lord.' And you forgave the guilt of my sin."
22. See 2 Cor. 7:8: "Even if I caused you sorrow by my letter, I do not regret it. Though I did regret it—I see that my letter hurt you, but only for a little while."
23. See James 4:9–10, quoted at the beginning of this chapter.

Temple Grandin nurtured these abilities through careful observation and constant practice—even though she struggled with using emotions "naturally.")

2. Be mindful and aware of your own emotional responses. Some emotions are very automatic and can occur outside of our immediate conscious awareness (being embodied as they are). Becoming aware of when and why you have strong emotional reactions is the first step in regulating your own experience and expression of emotions.

3. Evaluate the reasons for your emotions. Is the issue you are emotional about (be it a positive or negative emotion) really as important as you think? Scripture and psychological practice agree that it's very important to rethink—or as some psychologists suggest, reframe—your priorities. This reframing may cause you to realize that your emotions are really inappropriate or totally out of proportion to the situation. For example, are you angry about a true injustice or a true sinful action (which is what God gets angry about), or are you angry about some rather minor issue that affects only you? Scripture would admonish us to set others first and to reduce how emotional we get about our own personal issues.

4. Determine (perhaps with insights from wise friends or professional therapists) if your emotional experience or expression is beyond your current ability to regulate by yourself. The embodied nature of our emotions, along with our learned tendencies that may make some emotions strong habits of the mind, may limit our ability to manage our emotions on our own. Perhaps your difficulties with emotions are due to intense or long-term experiences that have had a strong impact on your ability to self-regulate (e.g., post-traumatic stress disorder, long-term depression). These more extreme examples of emotional difficulty may require the support and assistance of others—and perhaps medication—to help regulate your emotional experience.

5. Finally, learn to observe the impact that your emotional experience has on your relationships. If emotions were given to us to foster our relationships, make sure that your emotional life is being used to enhance, not destroy, those very relationships that are so valuable to God.

Discussion Questions

1. Think about how emotions influence small and large decisions you make (i.e., choosing an outfit to wear, which person to talk to, which career to select, etc.). Identify times when these emotions influenced you in positive ways and in negative ways.

2. How have emotions been beneficial to you in your interpersonal relationships, spiritual life, or worship experiences? Would you have been diminished in each of these areas if you had not been able to feel emotion?

3. Have there been times in your life where you really "lost it" emotionally (i.e., strong anger, extreme anxiety, or intense sadness)? Were you surprised at your own response? Did you feel "out of control," and did you regret or feel embarrassed by your intense emotion?

4. How could you have "reframed" your experience in question number 3? How could you have responded more constructively?

12

We're in This Together!

Social Psychology 1

Chapter Summary: An overarching theme for this book is that we are, at our core, relational persons. No area of psychology exemplifies this more consistently than social psychology. This chapter focuses on the powerful influence that groups can have on individuals, as well as evidence that humans are strongly motivated to seek relationships with others. Social psychology research mirrors the strong scriptural emphasis on the power of the group for good or evil. However, these influences raise significant concerns about what it means to be responsible limited agents (Theme 4) when we can be so easily influenced by groups.

We are half ruined by conformity, but we should be wholly ruined without it.

Charles Dudley Warner, *Obstacles to Living Life Fully*

As you navigate through the rest of your life, be open to collaboration. Other people and other people's ideas are often better than your own. Find a group of people who challenge and inspire you, spend a lot of time with them, and it will change your life.

Actress and comedian Amy Poehler,
Harvard University Commencement Address

A male college student we know once said that his dad was convinced that the "collective IQ of a group of adolescent boys dropped steadily as the group got larger." (He was quite sure the effect applied to adolescent girls as well.) No doubt this statement was based on his experience of mostly well-behaved adolescent boys doing "dumb" or bad things when they got together. Many parents have also heard their adolescent son or daughter complain that "everyone does it," with the assumption that right or wrong is determined by percentages. The standard response that one of the authors heard from his parents was, "and if everyone jumped off a cliff, would you follow?"

Most people feel the effects of peer pressure most strongly during their adolescence, but people may experience conformity pressure at any age. The point is, if we reflect on our own actions and thoughts, we realize that we often think and act differently when we are around other people. Social psychologists have carefully documented the powerful ways that we are influenced by other people.

The Power of the Situation

The powerful influence of groups and social situations is well established in social psychology. A long list of studies have documented how frightfully easy it is to alter the behavior of everyday, run-of-the-mill people (regardless of age, education, experience, etc.) simply by changing the situation. Solomon Asch demonstrated that most people will conform and give obviously wrong answers to easy questions when influenced by a group of strangers; Stanley Milgram documented that a large majority of people would give very painful electric shocks to other human beings just because they were told by an "authority figure" to do so; Phillip Zimbardo and colleagues were able to turn average college students into brutal guards or passive prisoners by simply manipulating the roles that people played. Interestingly, participants in these types of studies are rarely aware that they are being influenced by the situation, and in fact vehemently deny that other people or the circumstances altered their natural behavior. For example, in a follow-up study to Milgram's shock experiment, he had participants first watch other people (who were in fact confederates or paid actors) *refuse* to give electric shocks to a person in another room. The rate of "shock giving" in this version of the experiment, compared to his earlier experiments, went down tremendously.[1] When he asked the participants if the action of the other people had influenced their own behavior, they were

1. Bolt and Myers, *Human Connection*, 91.

certain that there was no influence; they were convinced that they had acted of their own "free will." However, the evidence showed otherwise—they had been powerfully influenced by the situation. Apparently, we can be so caught up in a situation or with the group that we often lose ourselves.

Of course, peer pressure can also have many positive effects on people. When all your teammates keep training, you are more likely to follow suit—even when you are tired. Certainly society would be in trouble if there were no conformity pressure. In fact, some cultures value conformity far more than Americans or Europeans because they see how important it is in encouraging correct behavior. The difficulty lies in recognizing the influences—given how easy it is to miss them—and resisting the influences when they are negative.

If you have ever visited a culture very different from your own, you can also see the powerful influence of other people or circumstances. When you see how differently people in another culture live, you begin to realize that your own behavior, attitudes, and thinking patterns have been profoundly shaped by your family, your friends, and the wider culture. Our personal identity is strongly tied to our group identity. We often assume that our behavior and the behavior of those around us is "normal" (and everyone else is "strange"), but we rarely stop to think that we might have become very different people if we had been born to a different family or lived in a different culture.

These influences are directly relevant to two of the biblical themes of human nature we identified earlier—that we are relational persons (Theme 1) and responsible limited agents (Theme 4). As individuals we want to believe that we are the masters of our own fate and that we consciously and purposefully direct our actions. Previous chapters have shown that our choices are more limited than we like to think because of the constraints of our genetic inheritance, bodily existence, and learned patterns. But social psychology also illustrates very vividly that our choices and actions are very much a part of our social circumstances, *and* that we are typically unaware of these powerful influences. This thought can be especially disturbing to people of faith because Christianity stresses that people are personally responsible and accountable for their behavior and choices, especially moral choices. As we described earlier, Scripture is clear that all humans are accountable before God and that no one can simply blame their circumstances for bad or sinful behavior. We will also discuss in chapter 14, on personality, that we are individually defined and that we each have our own unique identities. However, we collectively bear God's image. God relates to us as persons, but as we described, personhood inherently involves interrelationship as God deals with us communally in groups like families, tribes, and nations.

Yet how can we be individually accountable if we are so influenced by groups? In order to resist the negative effects of conformity pressure or social influence, some people of faith may suggest that we should simply exercise more willpower or perhaps rely more on the Spirit of God. The reasoning goes that through *individual* efforts we can reduce the influence of the group and overcome our circumstances—thereby reestablishing our personal control. There are some valuable truths within this line of reasoning, as we will discuss later, but we believe that Scripture provides a more complex picture of human nature that does not easily eliminate either of these seemingly contradictory truths.

Our Relational Nature

Before exploring a scriptural understanding of this dilemma, let's examine more thoroughly what psychologists have learned about why relationships and groups are so powerful and so important to our existence. Animal-behavior psychologists have shown how important social bonds are for animal survival. Mothers form bonds with infants, which helps infants survive. Many mammalian species—including lions, chimps, apes, and others—form close bonds among groups for hunting, foraging, and protection from predators. Because of this bonding instinct, many animal species seek strong emotional attachments to others and maintain close relationships. As we described in chapter 11, on emotions, chimps even laugh in order to signal playful social interactions.

Humans have many of these same built-in tendencies, but we are equipped with many more qualities than animals to develop strong personal relationships. Psychologist Warren Brown has described how human capacities such as our cognitive ability, our ability to understand others' perspectives (i.e., theory of mind), our language capabilities, and our emotional qualities allow us to have deep interpersonal relationships with God and others.[2] But he also suggests that these qualities make having relationships an "imperative" or deep need. So we form strong emotional bonds with parents as infants, and we appear to be "programmed" to seek relationships with others (see chap. 10 for a full discussion).

Studies show that children have a powerful "need to belong," and when children have no close personal friends, they experience significant emotional turmoil.[3] Studies on adults show that the presence of other people—even

2. Brown, "Cognitive Contributions to Soul," 99–125.
3. La Greca and Lopez, "Social Anxiety among Adolescents," 83–94.

strangers—can greatly reduce stress in a fearful situation. Even recent research on brain activity and social relationships shows how powerful social interaction can be. In these studies, participants watch and participate in an animated game of catch between themselves and two other "cartoon figures." Whenever the participants were excluded from the game, by rarely getting the ball, areas of their brain devoted to emotional distress became very active.[4] Apparently human beings have a deep-seated desire for inclusion.

Humans also seem to thrive best when they have a social network or close support group—even experiencing less heart disease in these circumstances.[5] There is also evidence that people often create better solutions to complex problems and take fewer unnecessary health risks when they are part of a positive support group.

While it appears that we are programmed for relationships, and we find them deeply fulfilling, they can also be our greatest curse. When we think about broken friendships, family fights, or social rejection, we are reminded of how painful relationships can be. As described at the beginning of the chapter, other people can also influence us to act in ways that are stupid, cruel, or even sinful. So psychology verifies that relationships are important—even essential—but relationships can be painful or damaging because they are so much a part of what defines us. We simply can't think about anything in the world without thinking relationally.

The "Collective Mind"

The North American and European cultural emphasis on individual effort and individual responsibility may make it difficult for those of us from that background to appreciate how essential and somewhat "mysterious" our relational nature really is. We tend to think of groups as a collection of individuals who may (or may not) influence one another—depending on the strength of the individual personalities involved. But many different contemporary thinkers (coming from diverse disciplines such as theology, philosophy, and neuropsychology) suggest that the idea of an individual mind acting "alone" is an illusion. In this new way of thinking, a cohesive group can be thought of as a single, "indivisible unit." Theologian Alan Torrance, in his essay "What Is a Person?," describes a change in thinking about persons that has happened in recent years: "No longer defined as thinking subjects whose primary

---

4. Crowley et al., "Exclusion and Micro-rejection," 1518–22.
5. Lett et al., "Social Support and Coronary Heart Disease," 869–78.

relationship was to the world of ideas, or as mere agents defined by their relations to impersonal objects, human beings came to be defined as essentially *persons* constituted by their relations to other persons."[6]

From a very different source, neuropsychologist Alan Schore describes the extremely valuable face-to-face gaze and emotional interaction that occurs between a mother and her newborn infant. He suggests that this carefully choreographed exchange of emotional expression in the first few months of life is what helps develop the brain circuits necessary for emotional self-regulation later in life. He concludes that "for humans, as for all other species, the most salient aspects of the environment are located in not so much the physical as in the social context, the realm of interactions between one individual and another."[7] In Schore's view, our brains are designed not so much for interaction with the physical world but more for the sharing and "joining" of minds.

Likewise, researcher Raymond Trevor Bradley concludes that our personal "agency"—our ability to choose or decide—cannot be considered apart from cooperative interaction with others: "Agency requires an active brain: a self-conscious brain that can assess the significance of and assign meaning to sensory input; . . . a brain that can establish priorities and plans; and a brain that can implement, and coordinate with others, purposeful programs of social action."[8]

Therefore, psychological research confirms that being responsible limited agents (Theme 4) is not only an individual issue—it's also a collective issue. The minds of individuals can be "joined," as it were, into collective thought and action. Just as hydrogen and oxygen combine to form a substance completely unlike either part, thoughts can join to form a holistic and unique experience between individuals, with the whole being greater than the sum of the parts.

You may have experienced this "joining of minds" when working on a math problem with someone and you both suddenly realize the answer, or when several people—all at once—"get" the punch line of a joke, or when you have shared emotional experiences of sorrow or joy—and the shared glances in the room are understood by all. Perhaps the best example of this joining is married couples who, after years of marriage, complete each other's sentences or anticipate each other's thoughts. This joining of the minds can continue over time with groups of people developing a "personality." Chairpersons of committees sometimes refer to the ongoing dynamic in the group, teachers often

6. Torrance, "What Is a Person?," 202.
7. Schore, "Evaluative System in the Cortex," 337.
8. Bradley, "Theory of Quantum Vacuum Interaction," 472.

talk about the personality of their class, and pastors talk about the character of a congregation.

So a group of people can be thought of as acting as a single entity with its own developmental history (i.e., like infants growing into adults) and personality. When this "personality" does something good or bad, is some individual component responsible, or is it the whole entity? This seems like a somewhat silly question since each individual certainly has the ability to make an individual choice. Yet we can also see that when we are part of a whole, we are caught up within it; in other words we are influenced by the whole as much as we contribute to it. This truth has the potential for both positive and negative outcomes since we can sin or act obediently as individuals and as groups. We can develop "mind-sets" from the group that are obedient (e.g., service projects for the poor) or sinful (e.g., racial prejudice).

Social Identity

In addition to influencing our behavior and thinking, groups influence how we think about ourselves. We often define ourselves according to unique qualities (e.g., "I am short"), but also according to the group or organization to which we belong (e.g., "I'm from California," "I go to church X," "My family is . . ."). Thus, social identity helps answer the question, Who am I? But these self-descriptions can begin to change who we are. One study did extensive interviews of physiology graduate students at the beginning and end of their graduate program. Most, if not all, of the students started in the program as a stepping-stone to medical school. But over time they began to identify less and less as premed students and more and more as physiology students. They also developed value systems that were similar to their professors and fellow students and less like those of medical students.[9]

Perhaps you have experienced this form of transformation where, having settled on a particular academic major, you began to act and think more like people in that major. Maybe you selected one college over a rival college. Initially, the choice may have been a close call, with both schools being attractive, but after being at your selected college, you begin to disparage the other. If you ever changed churches or joined new groups of friends, not only does your self-identity change, you quickly adopt the thinking patterns of those around you, and you often contrast yourself to others not in your circles. Again, this implies that this social identity can have positive influences on your

9. Ashforth and Mael, "Social Identity Theory," 20–39.

thinking (e.g., "My church is very involved in outreach and social justice") or be potentially damaging (e.g., "My friends are really into buying lots of material goods"). If a person belongs to a group that develops very destructive thoughts (e.g., hatred toward certain groups, excessive materialism, aggressive or violent ideas), to what extent does that person bear responsibility for their own tendencies?

Covenantal Relationships in Scripture

It's fascinating that Scripture also captures many of these contradictions about groups and individuals that psychologists have studied—the good and bad influence of groups, as well as the amazing, almost mystical, joining of minds that can happen within a group. Scripture describes the mutual accountability in relationships and how responsibility is both individual and collective. Countless Scripture passages stress the responsibility of the individual (e.g., "Choose for yourselves this day whom you will serve"[10]), but just as many show the power of the group for promoting good or evil. Families, tribes, churches, and nations are often treated as a single entity and singled out for praise or blame. Certainly not all individuals within these families, churches, or nations were equally responsible for all of the actions of the whole, yet all are held accountable for the actions of the whole. Many biblical scholars have pointed out the extent to which God "covenants" (i.e., forms a reciprocal promise) with both individuals and groups, and that God works through groups in very profound ways.

The New Testament is also full of references to the fact that Christians are part of the "body of Christ." Some believe that this phrase speaks to a kind of unity of spirit, similar to the camaraderie that you might find being part of a sports team. But careful reading of the passages reveals that this unity of the body of Christ is much richer and deeper than the fellowship a person might feel with a group of friends. For example, 1 Corinthians 12:18–20 says: "But in fact God has placed the parts in the body, every one of them, just as he wanted them to be. If they were all one part, where would the body be? As it is, there are many parts, but one body." This passage captures the uniqueness of each person but also the unity of the whole. Even though one human body is a collection of "entities," we still talk about the whole person acting; likewise, a body of believers has parts, but can also be considered as one whole "person." The notion of having a "collective mind" is captured in Philippians

10. Josh. 24:15.

2:2, which says: "Then make my joy complete by being like-minded, having the same love, being one in spirit and of one mind."

Practical Implications for the Church

There are many practical implications of social psychological findings and scriptural revelation about group membership. For one thing, North American Christians tend to focus a lot of attention on their individual sins and personal failures, but they rarely look at how they were led to sin within a family, group, or culture. Sinful tendencies of individuals can be developed and incorporated into groups to which the individual belongs, and groups in turn shape and modify these tendencies. For example, individuals who love to buy things tend to find each other and become friends. Before long the influence of the group accentuates this desire in each member of the group to the point that they may all develop excessive materialism.[11]

So can we escape the impact of the group when and if the group is leading us astray? The bottom line is that we are "embedded" creatures. We cannot fully escape the reality of our family, group, church, tribe, or nation. So asking how to escape from group influence is similar to asking how we can escape our own bodies—it simply can't be done. This is one part of the "limited" aspect of being responsible limited agents. We can't transcend our circumstances, but what we can do is to change our group membership. As Christian psychologist Martin Bolt noted, "We think the solution is found in developing greater independence; we teach our children, 'Dare to be a Daniel; dare to stand alone.'"[12] But he suggests that living as Christians is actually a community task and it can't really be done alone:

> It requires social support. Without a sustaining environment it is hard to develop and even more difficult to maintain a Christian lifestyle. Being created social means that we need to be nourished; we must be encouraged by each other to live our commitments. It's tough to maintain one's Amish identity while living in San Francisco.[13]

He goes on to suggest that churches often fail at this community building because "it is certainly a lot easier to 'attend church' than to 'be church.'"[14]

---

11. This tendency is sometimes called group polarization and has been demonstrated in many studies. See Myers and Lamm, "Group Polarization Phenomenon," 602.

12. Bolt and Myers, *Human Connection*, 91.

13. Ibid.

14. Ibid., 93.

So social psychology and Scripture are telling us a very similar message: we humans are so relational that we cannot think of ourselves outside of our situation. In fact, it makes little sense to even talk about the individual outside of her experience. Of course there are key differences in the way Scripture refers to the body that is the church and the way social psychology describes group dynamics. As the well-known theologian Dietrich Bonhoeffer suggested, "Because Christian community is founded solely on Jesus Christ, it is a spiritual and not a psychic reality."[15] But he also goes on to suggest that the church needs to develop a greater psychic unity (i.e., become of "one mind"), so there are many ways in which Christian communities do function very much like other communities.

Problems with Christian Communities?

There is a serious and legitimate concern that may arise from being in a Christian community. Does this unity of the body mean that Christians should separate themselves from the rest of the world and live in a monastery, an Amish community (as Bolt alludes to above), or a Christian commune? While many find this a tempting scenario, we do not believe that Scripture is necessarily telling us to engage in extreme separatism (although there may be great value in doing this for a time). In fact, there are some significant dangers in becoming an isolated community. Social psychology research on social identity (discussed earlier) and "in-group" and "out-group" bias suggests that we have a strong tendency to quickly view our group as superior and all other groups as less valuable.[16] For example, in one study, fans watched a video recording of their favorite football team playing a rival team.[17] Fans of the rival team watched the same recording. Fans for *both* teams thought the referees were more biased against players from their own team than from the other team. This tendency can extend to families, schools, cultures, and races. Christians run the risk of developing an in-group bias and a sense of superiority over other communities if they separate themselves from others too much.

The cure for this dilemma is to be grounded in community, but not completely separate from other communities. Scripture paints a picture of Christians being involved in the Christian community and then using that foundation to be a "blessing" to others. The apostle Paul seems to suggest in 2 Corinthians 1:12 that Christians need to be active in the world while they maintain

15. Bonhoeffer, *Life Together*, 21.
16. Otten and Moskowitz, "In-Group Bias," 77–89.
17. Hastorf and Cantril, "They Saw a Game," 129.

strong relationships within the church: "Now this is our boast: Our conscience testifies that we have conducted ourselves *in the world*, and especially in our relations with you, with integrity and godly sincerity. We have done so, relying not on worldly wisdom but on God's grace" (emphasis added). In Romans 12:2 Paul also suggests: "Do not conform to the pattern of this world, but be transformed by the renewing of your mind. Then you will be able to test and approve what God's will is—his good, pleasing and perfect will." Christians can be transformed in community with other Christians, but this transformation needs to be put into practice beyond that community. Therefore, we can combat the potential in-group bias that can arise even in positive communities when we remember to also be active in the world.

A second serious concern about being in community is that even mostly positive communities can still influence us in harmful ways. Humans easily become blind to negative influences that can become woven into a community, including the church. Remember that participants in many social-psychology experiments were not aware of how much the group influenced them, so most of us often miss the fact that negative group tendencies exist and that they influence us (e.g., "I'm not influenced by movies I watch"). Christians sometimes come to believe that the practices in their community are the best or only ways to behave as Christians, ignoring the fact that Christians over the centuries and across many cultures have found a variety of ways to practice their faith. Visiting a megachurch in Kenya, an underground house church in China, and a mission outpost in Honduras—even if from the same Protestant denomination—will quickly underscore the powerful effects of culture and circumstances. The fact that culture and time can create varied practices and expressions of faith across communities is not a bad thing, and in many ways enhances the overall church, but Christians need to be aware of these influences. Persons in any community of people—including a Christian fellowship—need to take time for a little self-reflection on how the group, community, or culture has adopted ideas or practices that are ultimately bad for us. It's very easy for a church community to gradually adopt practices that lead to excessive individualism, materialism, or even racism without realizing the influence of the wider culture. Author Eric Metaxas provides an extreme example of this influence when he describes how a number of members of the German church gradually conformed to Nazi thinking—in part because of their loyalty to German culture—without noticing the subtle influences that came in small increments.[18] Metaxas also describes how theologian and pastor Dietrich Bonhoeffer was able to resist this influence in part because of

18. Metaxas, *Bonhoeffer*.

his experience with churches outside of Germany, but also due to his complete emersion in Scripture and fellowship with other faithful Christians. So visiting other cultures, groups, or communities can be used as a mirror to examine and critique our own practices and help us to identify how we have been affected—for better or worse.

Final Words on Accountability

Despite these concerns about the negative influences of groups, we would do well to not spend an excessive amount of time trying to disentangle individual responsibility from the responsibility of the group for bad behavior. While there is clearly individual responsibility for bad behavior that we must all recognize, everyday life is often rather complicated. (This complex picture has implications for understanding personality, psychological disorders, and therapy, which we will discuss more in chaps. 14, 15, and 16.)

One reason that we need to be cautious about attributing blame in a given circumstance is that social psychology research shows that we have a strong tendency to underestimate the power of the situation and blame individuals exclusively for their failures. On the other hand, our failures are often attributed to the situation (e.g., "my boss is a jerk," "the train made me late"). Whether this "attribution error" is caused by basic human sinfulness, our cognitive processes, culture, or some other psychological function—or all of these—is somewhat unclear. The truth, of course, is that we do bear the blame for our failures, but so does the group. Why do people become obese? Why do people have messed-up families? Why do individuals have emotional problems? In many of these situations we spend a lot of time dividing up blame, and placing most of it on the individual, when in fact it is the individual in the context of her circumstance. We believe, in most circumstances, that it is more useful to simply focus on doing what needs to be done—individually and collectively—to remedy the problem. This may sound simplistic, but it may also be more fruitful.

Responsible Limited *Groups*?

We hear debates in the church about who should care for the poor, create better families, build a better church, create a better community, and so on. Are these deeds that require individual action or communal responsibility? We believe that God cares little about this question and more about just getting it done; Christians must simply acknowledge that responsibilities are both individual *and* communal.

We also believe that when we study social psychology and the influence that groups have on us, our free will and responsibility are not diminished; they are enhanced. Those who are most oblivious to social influences or think that the social setting has no impact on them are the people who are most limited by their social setting. When we understand the power of these social influences, and when we see the dangers or blessings of being in community, that is when we can most assert our agency in both individual and collective action. Therefore, when we help shape the groups we are in, join with positive groups, and allow ourselves to be shaped positively by a group (being ever mindful of the potential negative influences), great things can be accomplished!

DISCUSSION QUESTIONS

1. Can you think of times when group conformity pressure caused you to do something dreadfully stupid or bad? Can you think of times when social pressure had a very positive influence on your thoughts or actions?

2. Have you experienced times where you had a "coming together of minds" or became like-minded with other individuals? Did you find that the experience drew you closer to those people?

3. If you are part of a church community, can you cite examples of how your church community fosters "being a body"? Can you think of ways your church fosters individualism?

4. How do we manage to form healthy groups and positive, close relationships without forming an in-group/out-group bias?

5. If you have an annoying or bad habit that you would like to change, how could you utilize group influence or community to foster a change?

6. If you feel that a community is influencing you in a very negative way, how can you avoid or change that influence?

13

Faithful Attitude and Action

Social Psychology 2

Chapter Summary: Chapter 12 emphasized the role of others and situations in influencing our behavior and attitudes; this chapter explores the interplay between behavior and attitudes and how each may shape the other. As embodied, responsible limited agents, humans reveal attitudes through behaviors, but behaviors also strongly influence attitudes. Yet the Bible clearly emphasizes the importance of one's heart in determining how a person acts. In this chapter we discuss the interplay of attitude and behavior in the Christian life, in which the Bible claims God is active.

> Therefore, I urge you, brothers and sisters, in view of God's mercy, to offer your bodies as a living sacrifice, holy and pleasing to God—this is your true and proper worship. Do not conform to the pattern of this world, but be transformed by the renewing of your mind. Then you will be able to test and approve what God's will is—his good, pleasing and perfect will.
>
> Romans 12:1–2

Have you ever made a New Year's resolution? If you have, chances are good that you failed to keep your pledge. About half of resolution makers fail within six months of their commitment, and as time goes forward, the percentage of those succeeding only goes down.[1] Of course, failing to live up to a goal or ideal is not limited to New Year's resolutions. Everyone has experienced falling short of a goal, whether it was something general like being a better person or something more specific like eating five servings of vegetables a day. These are instances of behaviors not being consistent with attitudes. Psychologists define an *attitude* as a favorable or unfavorable evaluation of people, objects, ideas—really anything. Attitudes can also be ambivalent. Before we delve into how attitudes work, it makes sense to ask why we even make such evaluations. As Russell Fazio, a leading attitude researcher, has written, "Attitudes simplify our day-to-day existence," and although "relatively thoughtless," they promote behavior that directs us toward what will bring pleasure or away from what will produce pain.[2] Attitudes reflect our nature as meaning seekers (Theme 5) in that they help us make sense of our surroundings and give guidance for what we should do.

Attitudes consist of three components: affect (feelings of liking or disliking), behaviors (tendencies to approach or avoid the thing evaluated), and cognition (thoughts including knowledge and beliefs that reinforce feelings).[3] These are the ABCs of attitude—affect, behaviors, and cognition. When we act, we experience thoughts and feelings, and it makes sense that these would line up so that affect, behavior, and cognition would all point in the same direction: we should *do* what we *feel* and *think* positively about and avoid what we negatively evaluate. Yet many times our thoughts and feelings do not match our behavior.

Looking at the relationship among the components of the ABCs of attitude, we can better see some of the reasons for people falling short of a goal. Consider a goal that people commonly fail to achieve: exercising more. Obviously, a person claiming this goal *feels* that exercising more is positive and *thinks* that exercise is important. Affect and cognition agree: exercise is good. Now "just do it." Likely a person's affect and cognition toward exercise have been favorable for some time (few people think that exercise, in principle, is bad). Yet the feelings and thoughts have not resulted in a change in behavior.

Three Ways Attitudes Diverge from Behavior

Social psychologists point to at least three reasons for this incongruity.[4] First, situations may make it difficult to follow through, as was discussed in chapter

1. Norcross, Mrykalo, and Blagys, "Auld Lang Syne."
2. Fazio, "Attitudes as Object Evaluations," 629.
3. Eagley and Chaiken, "Attitude Structure and Function," 271.
4. Gilovich et al., *Social Psychology*, 238–43.

12. You may lack the time to exercise, have no exercise equipment, or feel social pressure to do something other than exercise (you like to exercise but your significant other does not, and you do not want to complicate that situation). Second, your attitude toward exercise may be positive, but your attitude toward something else may be *more* positive. For example, you may like sitting around watching movies more than you like to exercise, so movies win and exercise loses. Finally, exercising more requires changing habits. *Not* exercising can be a well-practiced, habitual behavior. In addition, those things you already do instead of exercising more—whether that be reading, talking with friends, or staring at a wall—are well practiced, too. Because (as we discussed in chap. 5 on consciousness) we often tend to have little self-awareness of our ways, changing them takes work. It is as if routine behavior has a momentum of its own that needs to be recognized, restrained, and redirected (depending on whether the habit is a good one or a bad one).

In the previous paragraph, we could substitute the words "Christian practice" for "exercise" and draw basically the same conclusions for Christians. In psychology, attitude is often measured through verbal response regarding how strongly something is liked or disliked. This is the same sort of measure that is reported in the Bible. Many passages in Scripture discuss instances of people speaking approvingly or disapprovingly of actions, others, or even God. Yet psychology and Scripture both show that what someone says may not necessarily indicate a person's actual beliefs, and that professed attitudes are not always consistently enacted in behavior. Both Scripture and the history of Christianity clearly show that believers' intentions do not necessarily result in the kind of behaviors one might expect. Let's now examine more fully how situations, the relative strength and consistency of attitudes, and habits influence the relationship between attitudes and behaviors.

Situational Influences

As relational persons (Theme 1), we are influenced by others. We care what people think about us, so what we say often depends on whom we're around. For example, standing up for and doing what you believe in is easier if you are standing with others who believe the same thing. If you believe something else, you may remain silent or moderate the view you express so that it fits or at least is closer to fitting the majority's opinion. So positive talk about exercise comes easily among those who exercise regularly. Similarly, most Christians find it easier to live out their faith among fellow believers than before nonbelievers. An example of this from the Bible is when the apostle Paul called out Peter for behaving like a gentile (people who were not Jewish) by not following Jewish food laws when only gentiles were around. When Jews were present, however, he feared those Jews and followed food laws, even telling gentiles they should do the same.[5] Peter did this despite having been told in a vision from God that such rules were no longer required following Christ's life and death.[6] What people do or say may vary depending on who is listening or watching.

Strength and Consistency of Attitude

An attitude's impact on behavior also varies with a second factor, the relative strength of that attitude.[7] Like the person who believes exercise is good but remains seated, people may claim to love Jesus but not prioritize that belief in a way that significantly influences how they live. God wishes the attitudes and behaviors of his people align with his desires—people should be fully committed to living out God's will. Lack of full commitment to God can be apparent in one's lifestyle. Speaking of the actions of a particular church, in the book of Revelation Jesus says, "I know your deeds, that you are neither cold nor hot. I wish you were either one or the other! So, because you are lukewarm—neither hot nor cold—I am about to spit you out of my mouth."[8]

Attitudes may also vary in relation to behavior when attitudes are not consistent. For example, we may think that following God is a really good idea (positive cognitive appraisal), but actually following God may feel less enjoyable than following our own desires (negative affective appraisal). The A and C of the ABCs of attitude are inconsistent, so the B, or behavior, is likely to vary. When beliefs and behavior do not line up, the result can be hypocrisy. *Hypocrisy* is about not so much what someone *actually* believes but the *difference* between what someone says and does. If a hypocrite's words and deeds differ, how would you know what that person really believes (if you're just asking them to tell you)?

Jesus claimed that the actions of a hypocrite show what that person truly loves (in psychology's terms, which attitude they prioritize). Jesus said a lot about the hypocrisy of Pharisees[9] and other teachers regarding Jewish regulations. Although these groups talked a lot about what a person needed to do to serve God, Jesus said that what these people actually did

5. Gal. 2:11–13.
6. Acts 10:9–16.
7. Fazio, "Attitudes Guide Behavior," 83.
8. Rev. 3:15–16.
9. Pharisees were members of a Jewish group who were experts in the law, emphasizing religious ritual and purity, but were condemned by Jesus for not practicing what they preached.

was often for show—they wore exaggerated signs of their religious devotion on their clothes, basked in seats of honor at special occasions, and loved being recognized as religious leaders.[10] They were "religious" to earn praise, admiration, and (likely) money from others, not because they wanted to align their hearts with God's cause and care for people they purported to serve. The Pharisees' behaviors were indicative of them having inconsistent and conflicting attitudes. While they may have had some desire to serve and glorify God, their greater desire (stronger attitude) was to serve and glorify themselves. As is so easily the case for people, image was more important than substance—hence the hypocrisy. They wanted the impression of religious devotion and being "respectable" that comes from publicly giving physical goods to God. Deeper needs that might be a lot less publicly visible, like caring for an "unimportant" widow in poverty, were left unmet by Pharisees.

If the Pharisees actually had no real interest in serving God, they demonstrated what psychologists today would call moral hypocrisy. This consists of wanting to appear as moral God followers (and reap the praise and admiration that come from acting in such a way) without all the cost of actually being moral (e.g., inconvenience, financial loss).[11] In this case, attitudes would not necessarily be in conflict with behavior; the Pharisees simply wanted to serve themselves. Jesus stabs at the heart of their hypocrisy, saying, "You clean the outside of the cup and dish, but inside they are full of greed and self-indulgence. Blind Pharisee! First clean the inside of the cup and dish, and then the outside also will be clean."[12] The sinful core of serving individual needs and desires was shown in the Pharisees by their actions, regardless of what they said. Jesus described Pharisees as creatures spewing poison: "For the mouth speaks what the heart is full of. A good man brings good things out of the good stored up in him, and an evil man brings evil things out of the evil stored up in him."[13] The outward behavior indicates that their attitude toward self-glorification overruled any attitude toward glorifying God.

Habit

A third factor that influences the relationship between attitudes and behavior is our habits, or well-learned and well-rehearsed behaviors. Habits are apparent in what people consistently do, even if they're not aware that they

10. Matt. 23:5–7.
11. E.g., Batson and Thompson, "Why Don't Moral People Act Morally?," 54.
12. Matt. 23:25b–26.
13. Matt. 12:34b–35. In verse 34, Jesus calls the Pharisees "a brood of vipers."

do it. As we discussed earlier, habits can become automatic and unconscious. If a person's attitude and habitual behavior are not in line, she may not know this if she is not consciously monitoring the habit. Limited self-monitoring means limited agency (Theme 4), which makes change difficult; and habits can be hard to break.[14]

Pharisees and teachers of the law were definitely people of habit. They strongly emphasized the "right" behaviors, like ritual hand washing that would have been done several times a day, every day. Jesus was clear that these regulations could not earn God's favor. Jesus calls the Pharisees and teachers of the law "blind guides," concerned with public displays of righteousness like giving the required 10 percent of their earnings to God but ignoring the heart of God's desires for his people: "justice, mercy and faithfulness."[15] The Pharisees guided Jews in ways that would not bring them toward God, all the while likely blind to their own habitual behavior.

It's natural to ask regarding the Pharisees, Didn't they see their hypocrisy? In Jesus's dealings with the Pharisees, it is possible that he was not just condemning them for their hypocrisy but also hoping to bring about change in their behavior by making them aware of their hypocrisy.

When people are aware that their own behaviors clash with their attitudes, people change either their behaviors or their attitudes to reduce the gap between the two to overcome what psychologists call cognitive dissonance.[16] When what we do does not make sense to ourselves, we find it unpleasant. We are motivated to make sense of ourselves to ourselves—we try to understand the meaning of our own behavior. Imagine someone passing a man holding a sign saying, "Hungry and homeless. Please help." She has concern for poor people but passes him by without helping. How does she justify this difference between her attitude and her action? She may look to her own behavior to justify her attitude ("I can ignore this poor man because I've given money to the church"). Alternatively, she may modify her attitude to justify her behavior ("I'm not giving any money to this man; he should be trying to get a job, not standing on a corner"). Either way, she's making a sensible story of what she did. We, like the Pharisees, may easily explain away our behaviors or simply modify our attitudes to make ourselves less hypocritical. However, when a behavior is habitual and an attitude has been formed or changed without conscious awareness, we may be blissfully unaware of what we do.

14. Wood and Neal, "Habits," 859.
15. Matt. 23:23.
16. Festinger, *Theory of Cognitive Dissonance*, 1–3, said that people find it emotionally unpleasant to experience inconsistency between what they believe and how they act.

The Heart of Behavior and Attitude

The Christian church teaches that Jesus was both fully human and fully God,[17] so Jesus understood that human words and actions do not always go together. As embodied creatures, humans interact with others, creation, and God in physical ways (along with spiritual interactions). Jesus, when alerting his followers as to whom they could trust, said, "Watch out for false prophets. They come to you in sheep's clothing, but inwardly they are ferocious wolves. By their fruit you will recognize them. . . . Every good tree bears good fruit, but a bad tree bears bad fruit."[18] Jesus says that a person's actions (the fruits) give the truer picture of who someone is in their heart—in their core or their gut[19]—while expressed attitudes (words) may mislead. Jesus is saying that in such interactions, people show their heart. What does that mean, relative to attitude?

Jesus points to something deeper than just attitude (simple positive or negative evaluation) as being at the core of persons. Similarly, when the apostle Paul addresses the church in Rome about how to become Christian, he writes, "If you declare with your mouth, 'Jesus is Lord,' and believe in your heart that God raised him from the dead, you will be saved. For it is with your heart that you believe and are justified, and it is with your mouth that you profess your faith and are saved."[20] Paul is talking about speaking aloud a declaration from the center of one's being. Saying "Jesus is Lord" would have been a very big deal in Rome shortly following Jesus's crucifixion. Claiming Christianity in this way amounted to far more than just cheering for the rival team in the home team's stands. Harsh persecution by the Roman government was to be expected for these early Christians; it was that government which carried out Jesus's death sentence and imprisoned Paul on more than one occasion. This was a deep commitment—much deeper than just an "I think exercise is good" attitude because standing up for this belief could result in death!

The Bible states that God is able to see the direct connection between one's heart and external behavior. Unlike psychologists who must use surveys and tests to understand humans, God can read human thoughts.[21] Yet Jesus said, "by their fruit you will recognize them"[22]—what a person believes is shown

17. This is stated in ancient statements of faith, including the Nicene Creed.
18. Matt. 7:15–17.
19. This is an idea laid out by Smith, *Desiring the Kingdom*, 47, in his exposition of human desiring being embodied.
20. Rom. 10:9–10.
21. The psalmist says God knows his thoughts in Ps. 139; Jesus is described as "knowing their thoughts" in Matt. 9:4 and Luke 9:47; and the author of Hebrews writes, "Nothing in all creation is hidden from God's sight," Heb. 4:13.
22. Matt. 7:20.

by actions. The Bible affirms the notion that attitudes are embodied. In this view, attitudes (beliefs) are within a person and are exposed by what a person does. If that is the case—and psychology affirms that attitudes are physically measurable[23]—then the question of what to measure (i.e., what is the appropriate dependent variable) is logical. Present-day psychologists study all sorts of attitudes, from those central to identity (e.g., about race and gender) to more peripheral preferences (e.g., Coke versus Pepsi). Such studies demonstrate that measuring one's preferences as expressed in words may not necessarily represent a person's true beliefs. But if psychologists cannot read minds, how would they know that?

Psychologists have developed effective measures of subtle behaviors that are thought to indicate even unconscious attitudes. These include recording physiological responses like activity in facial muscles when a person is presented with positive and negative items.[24] Such responses can be so subtle that changes in broad facial expression are not noticeable (people did not make an observable frown for negative things, for example), yet slight muscle changes involved in frowning were recorded with electrodes. Even more interestingly, participants in such studies may have no awareness of their physiological response, nor do they necessarily verbally report that they thought the item was negative.[25] In that situation, the person responds without conscious awareness. Other implicit measures also indicate the embodied nature of attitudes. Research on racism, for example, demonstrates that we may physically distance ourselves from things we do not like or respond more slowly or with greater caution toward things we fear, all the while not having conscious awareness of doing such things.[26] In fact, even people who say they're not racist show racist behaviors. The behavior betrays the seemingly unknown attitude. Underlying attitudes can affect our behavior without us knowing it, even if we do not know we have that attitude!

This seems pretty depressing: we believe one thing, but do something else—sometimes without even knowing we're doing that. Obviously, attitude and behavior do go together much of the time, but in instances where they don't, this pattern often reflects the limited agency of humans (Theme 4). Even if people take on a new attitude and give it priority, they often find it difficult to change long-standing behavior, particularly if that behavior is a habit or happens without awareness.

23. E.g., Cacioppo et al., "Electromyographic Activity," 260–68.
24. Ibid.
25. Ibid.
26. See Dovidio et al., "On the Nature of Prejudice," for one of the seminal studies on the relationship between implicit and explicit responses.

Attitude Affects Action, and Vice Versa

It's tempting to think that beliefs are what really drive our behavior (after all, we tend to think of ourselves as being in charge of our own behavior), but psychology has shown that the relationship between attitude and behavior is a two-way street. As David Myers has written, "We are likely not only to think ourselves into a way of acting but also act ourselves into a way of thinking."[27] Behavior clearly affects attitude, as attitude can be changed and formed by what people do. That is, if you're able to get someone to say or do something, she tends to have a more positive appraisal of such behavior afterwards.

For example, role-playing changes attitudes so that what we say becomes what we believe.[28] The more we act in a certain way or say particular things, the more those thoughts and words become part of us. Thinking back on some early teaching experiences, one of us recalls taking on the role of classroom leader and authority figure, not really believing he was either. He role-played being a professor, based on stereotypes he had and models he had experienced from past professors. To begin, it felt unnatural—he acted as he thought he was supposed to act. Frankly, he even felt a little like a fraud whenever he messed up. Soon, however, he became more comfortable in the classroom, coming to believe he really was a professor. Taking on the role of a professor allowed an attitude shift to occur. As Myers writes, "Doing becomes believing."[29] As his actual belief in being a professor became part of his identity, he was then able to modify his behavior from the stilted stereotype of a professor he had when he first started teaching.

The notion of behavior influencing attitude relates to at least two of the biblical characteristics of human nature: our embodiment and our tendency toward meaning seeking (Themes 3 and 5). Physical action changes our thought and our future action, showing that we are not just disembodied minds. This being the case, righteous behavior should positively impact one's attitude toward God, while sinful behavior could make one more distant from God's concerns. Paul writes to Jesus's followers in Rome, "Just as you used to offer yourselves as slaves to impurity and to ever-increasing wickedness, so now offer yourselves as slaves to righteousness leading to holiness."[30] As Myers writes, "Throughout the Old and New Testaments, we are told that full knowledge of

---

27. Myers, *Psychology*, 131. More thorough discussions of this relationship are given in most introductory psychology textbooks, as well as chapters on behavior and attitudes in social-psychology textbooks.

28. Kelman, "Attitudes," 314.

29. Myers, *Psychology*, 556.

30. Rom. 6:19b.

God comes through actively doing the Word. Faith is nurtured by obedience."[31] James K. A. Smith, commenting on our fundamental desires, writes, "Habits are inscribed in our heart through bodily practices and rituals that train the heart, as it were, to desire certain ends."[32] Behaviors that have trained the heart for serving oneself need to be altered to move desires toward worshiping and serving God.

Implications and Applications: An Attitude of Faithful Living

The interactions between attitude and behavior discussed in this chapter show once again the limited agency of human beings. No doubt Ethan from the introduction wanted his life to work out differently than it did. Yet simply setting our mind to do something may not work as we might hope—we do not have the unlimited freedom to do whatever we want, even if we would prefer to believe that is true. Both psychology's findings and the human story told in Scripture show that simply wanting to act in a certain way does not result in us actually acting that way.

In the remainder of this section, we will focus on Christian faith and action. The apostle Paul's letters in the New Testament contain lengthy passages to churches about ways in which Christians fail to live out their claim that Jesus is their Lord, and he gives instruction on how to change those behaviors.[33] Yet Paul himself continued to struggle with sin even after one of the most spectacular conversion experiences recorded (the man was stopped in his tracks and struck blind!).[34] In a broken world, sin will continue (Theme 2) and Christians will struggle to enact their beliefs. Dependence on God and fellow Christians is largely the prescription Paul provides for Christians.

How are Christians to go from saying, "Jesus is Lord," to acting out that belief? It's first important to note that faith is not something people can earn, so it is to some degree different from other kinds of beliefs studied by psychologists. The apostle Paul wrote to the church at Ephesus, "For it is by grace you have been saved, through faith—and this is not from yourselves, it is the gift of God—not by works, so that no one can boast."[35] In addition, when considering how to live faithfully, Christianity makes a unique claim:

31. Myers and Jeeves, *Psychology through the Eyes of Faith*, 195.
32. Smith, *Desiring the Kingdom*, 58.
33. First Corinthians by itself addresses failings that included infighting between believers within the church, varieties of immorality, and abuses of the Lord's Supper.
34. Paul's conversion is in Acts 9; he discusses the struggle with sin in Rom. 7.
35. Eph. 2:8–9.

Christians do not have to do it alone. Paul assures the Roman church that they are controlled not by a sinful core or nature but by "the Spirit, if indeed the Spirit of God lives in you."[36] By contrast, psychology makes no claims about the role of God's Spirit in the lives of people.

It makes sense then that elsewhere in the Bible, Paul, following an encouragement to hold strongly to their faith and follow his instructions for living a life of faith, prays this for Christians: "May our Lord Jesus Christ himself and God our Father, who loved us and by his grace gave us eternal encouragement and good hope, encourage your hearts and strengthen you in every good deed and word."[37] Paul is asking for God to *sanctify* those he is praying for. That is, Paul is praying for Christians to increase in holiness—to "work out your salvation with fear and trembling, for it is God who works in you to will and to act in order to fulfill his good purpose."[38] Again, humans have responsibility for their behavior, but God is with them to uphold and forgive when they fail. As theologian N. T. Wright states, Paul encourages believers to gain virtues, to develop Christian character. In sum, Paul is calling for Christians to have an attitude readjustment that will then result in virtuous behavior.

In order to bring about a change in one's own established behavior (e.g., a new PhD learning to be a professor or a Christian desiring to be more faithful), one first has to become aware of that behavior. For Christians, one of the best antidotes to hypocritical behavior or failing to follow through on beliefs is to return to the Bible for a reality check. How well are beliefs matching behavior? Instructions such as these from John the Evangelist help Christians tie together what they believe about Jesus and what they do: "If we claim to be without sin, we deceive ourselves and the truth is not in us. If we confess our sins, he is faithful and just and will forgive us our sins and purify us from all unrighteousness. If we claim we have not sinned, we make him out to be a liar and his word is not in us."[39] The limited agency of humans is painfully obvious when it comes to sinful behavior and lack of awareness of personal hypocrisy and shortcomings. Because confession follows self-examination of one's thoughts and behaviors, Scripture here is calling God's people to a self-awareness that comes from knowing their actual state and what to do about it.

Changing action can be an important part of growing in faith in God. Theologian Cornelius Plantinga writes, "Anybody who has tried to lose a bad habit . . . knows that good intentions and a few New Year's resolutions

36. Rom. 8:9.
37. 2 Thess. 2:16–17.
38. Phil. 2:12b–13.
39. 1 John 1:8–10.

seldom do the trick. Similarly, to break the power of sin, a Christian needs far more than good feelings and songs about Jesus."[40] People are separated from God by sin. We are meant for a close relationship with God, being his image bearers. Actions can change attitude and can promote similar behavior. Plantinga suggests that for a Christian to do their part in self-change, that person "needs to *attach* to Christ by prayer, sacraments, and listening to the Word of God."[41] Experiencing God and the church is being emphasized here. Psychologists show that attitudes become more potent when they are brought about by actual experience.[42] In order to act on attitudes in the way intended, it may be helpful to practice the act that would go with the attitude, making the action habitual. For example, if you believe reading Scripture is important for your spiritual development, make doing so a habit. A helpful way of doing this is to develop intentional plans for how you will implement your belief by identifying possible situations in which your belief could most easily result in action.[43]

Changing a habit is difficult, requiring self-regulation. Strategies like avoiding cues that prompt old habits can help bring success.[44] For example, if viewing pornography is a struggle for an individual, avoiding places where pornography has been viewed before or setting up an internet filter that blocks websites containing pornography may be beneficial because such actions reduce the prompts for viewing. As relational persons, it is also important to recognize the helpfulness of others in attempts to change. Involvement within a community of believers—the church—or with a study group or accountability partner (someone who will ask you about your success or failure to help you keep your commitment) may be very beneficial.

The Bible shows that physical service and worship by embodied humans can be sanctified by God. Though Christians fail, they are assured of God's forgiveness through his grace. God is at work on behalf of human beings—Christ died to free Christ's followers from the burden and penalty of sin. Humans as responsible limited agents nevertheless should work to overcome sin and its consequences in creation and redirect their desires. Yet in the end, Christians need to recall that salvation is from God, not themselves: "For it is by grace you have been saved, through faith—and this is not from yourselves, it is the gift of God."[45]

40. Plantinga, *Engaging God's World*, 92–93.
41. Ibid., 93.
42. Regan and Fazio, "Consistency," 28–45.
43. Gollwitzer, "Implementation Intentions," 493–503.
44. Wood and Neal, "Habits," 859–60.
45. Eph. 2:8–9.

DISCUSSION QUESTIONS

1. Think of an attitude that you hold that does not prompt you to do a corresponding behavior. Reflect on which of the three reasons for attitudes diverging from behavior may be causing this for you (it may be more than one).

2. Think of a behavior that could positively or negatively influence a Christian attitude. The example can be from your life (something you have done yourself), from someone you know, or hypothetical. Discuss the example and how an attitude would be influenced by the behavior.

3. Identify a specific hypocrisy (or be bold and ask someone else to point one out for you). Reflect on why your behavior goes against your expressed attitude.

4. Some people currently describe themselves as "spiritual but not religious" regarding their faith—that is, they have a favorable affect and cognition toward God, but reject the behavior associated with or expected of organized religion. Why, as meaning seekers, might people be drawn toward this stance? What is it about being an embodied human that may make this stance difficult to maintain?

5. C. S. Lewis wrote in *Mere Christianity*, "Do not waste time bothering whether you 'love' your neighbor; act as if you did."[46] How might loving one another be better thought of as an act than a feeling? How might doing this change one's attitude toward others?

46. Lewis, *Mere Christianity*, 65.

14

The *Real* You!

Personality

Chapter Summary: Theories of personality all have something to say—either implicitly or explicitly—about the themes we have outlined in this book. Given that many of these theories contradict basic biblical assumptions about human beings, does this mean we should reject or abandon all aspects of each theory? Is there a straightforward alternative to these theories that is correctly grounded in a biblical understanding of persons and that is completely compatible with well-established psychological research? This chapter provides a critique of personality theories based on the key themes of this book and provides some direction to Christians grappling with alternatives to the "standard" personality models in psychology.

If it wasn't for the coffee, I'd have no identifiable personality whatsoever.

David Letterman, *Late Show with David Letterman*

In the progress of personality, first comes a declaration of independence, then a recognition of interdependence.

Henry Van Dyke, American author, educator, and clergyman

Just as a body, though one, has many parts, but all its many parts form one body, so it is with Christ.

1 Corinthians 12:12

Here is a riddle: How is personality similar to yet different from hair? It's the same because it comes in many shades; it's different because you can't have more or less of it. Personality is not something that is measured as a quantity—it's measured as a quality. Just as there are many "shades" of personality, there are many shades of theories *about* personality. Because of that fact, most introductory psychology textbooks have a chapter on personality that focuses more on the various "theories of personality" and less about each person's unique set of qualities. While the various views that psychologists have about personality have become more similar over the years—with most psychologists accepting elements of several views—there are still diverse ways that psychologists approach the subject. This diversity comes from the fact that people also differ on their basic views about what defines and distinguishes human beings.

Consider how you might think about this case study presented by Christian psychologist John McDonagh.

> Lucy was referred to me for psychotherapy by her spiritual advisor. The reason for the referral was not clear in Lucy's mind; she was incensed that anyone would tell her that she needed to see a psychologist. It soon became apparent, however, that Lucy was filled with overwhelming rage, and that this rage was ruining her life. In particular, she felt betrayed by nearly every person with whom she was intimate. Most of this rage was being directed against her husband. Lucy believed that it was he, and not she, who "needed to be straightened out," and then her life would be fine.[1]

Why is Lucy this way? Is her anger an inborn trait or has it developed over time? Can she change this characteristic or is she destined to be an angry person all of her life? All theories of personality attempt to explain how and why each person—such as Lucy—is unique compared to any other person, and the extent to which that person's qualities can predict how he or she will act over most of his or her life (i.e., "a person's characteristic pattern of thinking, feeling, and acting"[2]). The explanations for these differences derive primarily from how each theory understands our biology, internal motives, mental operations, and experiences. Of course, all personality theories acknowledge that, as Henry Murray noted, "Every person is in some respects (a) like *all* other persons; (b) like *some* other persons; and (c) like *no* other person,"[3] but the emphasis in personality theory is understandably on the latter two. As psychologist Gordon Allport noted many years ago about personality theorists, "We emphasize the

1. McDonagh, "Working through Resistance," 200.
2. Myers, *Psychology*, 513.
3. Murray quoted in Van Leeuwen, "Personality Theorizing," 174.

fact that the outstanding characteristic of man is his individuality. He is a unique creation of the forces of nature. There was never a person just like him, and there never will be again."[4] This emphasis on individuality and unique qualities is one of the central notions to most theories of personality.

Before evaluating the theories based on this book's biblical themes, we provide a brief summary of the major personality theories here.

Brief Overview of Theories

Roughly in order of their historical development, the major theories about personality include psychoanalytic, behavioristic,[5] trait, humanistic, and cognitive-behavioral approaches.

Psychoanalytic Approach

Sigmund Freud, the primary developer of this approach, emphasized our biological and unconscious instincts for survival—contained within a personality component he called the "id." Humans have additional mental structures called the "ego," which guides conscious and rational thinking, and the "superego," which regulates moral decision making. The relative "strength" of these mental structures, along with early developmental experiences, dictates the growth of unique qualities. The largely unconscious conflicts that occur between these components and our inadequate attempts to resolve them ultimately lead to dysfunctional personalities or psychological disorders. There are more contemporary versions of psychoanalysis within the larger psychodynamic approach to personality; they differ from Freud's view in many ways, but they retain the emphasis on our unconscious motivations and our often "distorted" mental functions. From the psychoanalytic approach, Lucy's anger may be caused by repressed memories or possibly an unchecked id (i.e., underdeveloped ego or superego).

Behavioristic Approach

The behavioristic approach suggests that people have very few unique characteristics at birth, and it de-emphasizes inborn individual differences.

---

4. Allport, *Patterns and Growth in Personality*, 4.
5. Many introductory textbooks in psychology do not include the behaviorist school of thought in the list of personality theories since this approach does not give a great deal of credence to the very notion of having a stable, internally guided personality. However, we include behaviorism here because it does have something to say on the topic of personality, and it is helpful to contrast it with other approaches.

Behaviorism, promoted and popularized by people such as John Watson and B. F. Skinner, emphasizes that our behavior follows very lawful and predictable patterns and that the social environment shapes individual differences. As outlined in chapter 7, behaviorists believe that the situational "associations" we experience, along with the effect of consequences (i.e., rewards and punishments) are what ultimately determine our personality. Over time these tendencies become strong habits that can be very hard to change—at least without extensive and long-term changes in consequences. Watson once suggested that it is easier to "change a zebra's stripes" than a person's personality.[6] A key element to this view is that social and environmental influences determine a person's personality in a passive way because we are simply "response-generating machines." Therefore, Lucy's anger is a product of social consequences that subtly reward her for being angry—such as successfully getting others to do what she wants whenever she is angry with them. Altering her social environment and the rewards and punishments she experiences will eventually lead to changes in her personality.

Trait Approach

The trait approach is less interested in explaining why personality characteristics develop and more interested in simply characterizing the unique traits that we have. Despite this "nontheoretical" approach, its working assumption is that traits are mostly inborn or genetic, or that early child experiences set traits in place for an extended period—perhaps for life. So Lucy was simply born angry; she might manage it, but she will probably always be a somewhat angry individual. By measuring her angry tendencies she might be able to predict or manage her anger better.

Humanistic Approach

Abraham Maslow and Carl Rogers were the primary figures behind the humanistic approach. This approach opposed Freud's more negative view of human nature, as well as the behaviorist emphasis on passively influenced behavior. Humanistic psychologists stressed the importance of conscious choices (i.e., free will) and the basic human goodness within each person. In later years, a good deal of emphasis was placed on individual fulfillment and increased self-esteem as a means to personal growth. In this view, Lucy is not an inherently angry person. Instead, negative messages, lack of acceptance from others, and a lack of self-acceptance lead to these angry tendencies. Only

---

6. Watson, *Corsini Encyclopedia*, 1757.

Lucy can decide to change, and she needs to reach inside herself to find the good person that she really is.

Cognitive-Behavioral Approach

The cognitive movement stresses our reasoning or thinking processes as the primary focus of personality development. Our mental "schemas" or thinking patterns that develop over time (by way of genes, social environment, and patterns of behavior) shape how we think about our environment, how others think about us, and how we think about ourselves. Self-improvement is possible within this view, but it is difficult because these thought patterns become ingrained, so change is difficult on our own. While cognitive psychologists disagree with the somewhat simplistic mechanisms of the behaviorists and are more likely to stress internal mental processes, most still believe that, ultimately, there are external causes for every action (i.e., actions are determined).[7] Perhaps Lucy has developed an "external locus of control"—a thinking pattern that suggests she cannot control her life outcomes, which can lead to a sense of helplessness. Lucy can change if she corrects her thinking patterns; if she does, the anger will go away naturally.

Critiquing Personality Theories

Christians often wonder how to respond to these diverse theories of personality. Do we decide on the basis of research support alone, dismiss them all as potentially dangerous since some elements of these theories seem to contradict elements of Christian thought (see later discussion for details), or pick and choose parts of the approach based on what we do or don't like about the theory? A good starting point in grappling with these questions is to describe the primary strengths and weaknesses of all the theories in relation to the biblical themes concerning human nature. Analyzing all the theories in detail to see how they match each theme would take several more chapters, so we have provided a summary table (see table 1) that shows how each theory does or does not emphasize a particular theme.[8] Obviously this table oversimplifies each view, but it provides a concise way to compare the theories to each other and to the themes. Keep in mind that we are only providing a brief critique of the major personality theories

7. Seligman et al., "Navigating," 123.
8. The first column shown in table 1 is not actually explaining how each theory describes our relationship to God but rather the emphasis each theory places on the human need to understand a deity, or some deeper religious or moral principle.

here; the reader will need to explore these—and many additional theories not mentioned here—in much greater depth to get the full story.

This table summarizes the emphasis that each personality theory places on the human-nature themes developed in this book. Keep in mind that this table provides an abbreviated summary of views, so many subtleties of these theories are lost. The column showing the theories' emphasis on relation to God is mostly focused on how that theory describes our tendency to explain aspects of the world through religious explanations; none of the theories proposes that we have an actual relationship with God.

Table 1

	Relational Persons, relating to			Broken (evil)	Embodied	Responsible Agents (free will)	Meaning Seeking
	God	Others	Creation				
Psycho-analytic Approach[a]	Moderate	Low	Moderate	High	Moderate	Very Low	Moderate
Behavioristic Approach	None	None	High	Neutral	Moderate	None	None
Trait Approach	None	None	High	Neutral	High	None	None
Humanistic Approach	Moderate	Moderate	Low	Low	Low	High	High
Cognitive-Behavioral Approach	Low	Low	Moderate	Neutral	Moderate	Low	Moderate
Emphasis in this book	High	High	High	High	High	Moderate	High

a. The reader should keep in mind that newer psychodynamic theories differ in many ways from psychoanalytic thought—particularly as it pertains to relations with others. However, full discussion of all these differences are beyond the scope of this chapter.

Greatest Strengths

All of these theories certainly must capture some important truths about human nature—or they would not have lasted as long as they have. As table 1 shows, you can find at least some agreement with scriptural themes about human nature within every theory. So we do not believe that Christians should abandon these theories entirely, but should build on their strengths and work to reorient their weaknesses.

Not surprisingly, given the strong materialistic emphasis in psychology, the strongest aspect of personality theories—with the exception of the humanistic approach—is that they emphasize our embodied nature (Theme 3). As we have discussed earlier, the biblical perspective is one that emphasizes our embodied nature and the limitations that come with that existence, so Christians should be willing to embrace this aspect of human nature. In the case of Lucy, we cannot ignore the role that her embodied traits have on her angry tendencies. In the past, some Christians may have favored the humanistic approach precisely because it downplays embodiment (and many Christians have placed less emphasis on this theme, focusing only on the spiritual relationship between God and persons), but we feel that this is actually a shortcoming of the humanistic approach. At the same time, we also need to recognize that other approaches have overemphasized this aspect of our being without proper consideration of our relationality, our brokenness, our responsible agency, and our desire to seek meaning. So there is more going on with Lucy's anger than just an inherited trait, and this also needs to be recognized.

One of the greatest strengths of the humanistic approach is its emphasis on our meaning seeking nature (Theme 5). This approach has long emphasized that humans are motivated by more than a reduction of pain or a need to survive, and that we seek purpose and meaning for our existence. There is also a growing trend within contemporary cognitive-behavioral approaches to emphasize this meaning seeking tendency,[9] so we feel that personality theory is moving in the right direction in this regard, and away from a pure determinist model that strips humans of more complex motives and goals.

A strength of the behavioristic, trait, and cognitive-behavioral approaches is their adherence to scientific investigation. As discussed earlier, Christians need not fear scientific investigation in psychology. The primary reason Christians should value science is that we are charged with caring for creation, and part of that caring is to understand it. Since humans were created as an integral part of that creation, this scientific investigation applies to human activity as well (Theme 1). As Alan Tjeltveit suggests, "In creation, God made a relatively orderly world and gave human beings minds capable of grasping that order fairly well. Because we obtain from psychological science knowledge about human beings, about human problems, and about effective methods to resolve human problems, Christians should pay attention to science."[10] He goes on to say, "Unfortunately, Christian psychologists have done far too little to test empirically therapeutic approaches believed consistent with Christian faith." While Tjeltveit is relating science to therapy, the same applies

---

9. See discussion of recent trends in cognitive science by Smith, *Current Systems in Psychology*, 94.

10. Tjeltveit, "Faith, Psychotherapy, and Christian Counseling," 251.

to personality theory. Too often Christians have been captivated by various elements of personality theories that *appear* consistent with biblical themes but that often have not stood up to scientific scrutiny—and often don't actually match with biblical perspectives. This is particularly true of some elements of humanistic and psychoanalytic approaches that have often not been well supported by contemporary research. For example, psychologists Martin Seligman and colleagues summarize the mixed outcomes for studies on psychoanalytic ideas by suggesting, "Even though recent experimental research has provided increasingly strong and detailed information about the importance of unconscious processes . . . , 100 years of psychoanalytic practice aimed at uncovering repressed childhood conflicts has failed to provide convincing evidence of efficacy."[11]

Several researchers have likewise discredited several claims from humanistic psychologists suggesting that improving self-esteem and self-acceptance will lead to improvements in a variety of problem behaviors.[12] So Christians should be just as careful in embracing ideas that have not been well supported by science as they are in embracing ideas that are incompatible with biblical images of human nature.

Of course, Christians also need to be a prophetic voice within the discipline and speak against the extreme empiricism (i.e., science can discover all truth) and reductionism that has been prevalent in the field. Tjeltveit balances his earlier support for science by suggesting, "Many psychologists claim we know only through science. That reflects a certain understanding of human beings, one not derived from scientific research."[13] In other words, the assumption that we can only understand people by way of scientific research is itself a nonscientific statement and reflects a bias on the part of psychologists to not consider any other sources of knowledge (i.e., Scripture, direct revelation, or guidance by the Holy Spirit).

Greatest Weaknesses

In addition to some weaknesses alluded to above, personality theories often fall short because they have not taken into account key aspects of human nature.

Excessive Individualism

A major concern, in our view, with the psychoanalytic, behavioristic, and trait approaches is that they place so little value on the central theme of being

11. Seligman et al., "Navigating," 123.
12. See Dawes, *House of Cards*, 234–51.
13. Tjeltveit, "Faith, Psychotherapy, and Christian Counseling," 253.

relational persons (Theme 1). Cognitive and humanistic approaches place slightly greater emphasis on interpersonal relationships than do the first three, but even here, the primary focus is on internal and individual psychological processes. As Christian psychologist Paul Vitz suggests, "When [humanistic psychologist] Carl Rogers titles his well-known book *On Becoming a Person,* he is simply wrong. Instead he has written a book on becoming an individual, in particular, an autonomous, self-actualizing, independent individual. An individual is created by separating from others, by breaking, by concentrating psychological energy and effect on the self instead of on God and others."[14]

What are the consequences of this emphasis on the individual at the expense of considering our collective nature? The tendency within personality theory is to misunderstand the way in which our central characteristics are very much the product of reciprocal relationships. This overly individualistic focus may be one of modern psychology's greatest shortcomings. The corrective for this individualism, as Vitz suggests, is a renewed emphasis on a "covenant theory" of personality.

> The central psychological principle here is that personality is developed into its highest form through loving others. It is through *agape:* through serving others—even unto death—that the Christian personality grows and reaches its highest development. The very idea of commitment, of deep caring for another, of being bonded to another, is the exact opposite of so much of today's humanistic psychology. Today nothing must hinder the growth of the ego; nothing—no one—must restrict the autonomy of the individual. Perhaps James Bond of movie fame is the best example of this ideal—a man without any bonds with anyone. He appears to have no mother or father, no true friends; and certainly the whole idea of his relationship with women is to avoid commitment.[15]

Vitz contends that when we enter into covenant with God and others, and then we surrender to God and others, we truly become a flourishing person and have true freedom. The impact of the individualistic nature of personality theory may have led to as many ills as cures for social problems. For example, several contemporary psychologists have suggested that the long-standing emphasis on individual self-fulfillment has led to an "epidemic of narcissism" (e.g., excessive self-love), which in turn leads to more social ills, not fewer.[16]

Of course the other relational aspect of humans that personality theories ignore or distort is our relationship to God. While this may not be within the domain of psychological science, as we have discussed in previous chapters,

---

14. Vitz, "Christian Theory of Personality," 207.
15. Ibid., 205.
16. See Twenge and Campbell, *Narcissism Epidemic,* 9.

missing this fundamental principle means that personality theories will never fully capture what it means to have a healthy personality.

We want the reader to understand that focusing on internal and individual psychological qualities is still a very central part of the discipline of psychology—especially personality theory. The problem is that this emphasis centers primarily on the individual, devoid of substantial consideration of the socially embedded nature of those individuals. One positive note regarding contemporary psychology is that there are a number of studies coming from developmental psychology, social psychology, and even neuropsychology that point to the value of reciprocal and deep relationships providing an increased interest in these issues. This emphasis on relationality has also impacted a growing movement in psychology called positive psychology, which seeks to promote human strengths, including relationship formation.[17]

Determinism

The psychoanalytic,[18] behavioristic, and trait approaches are all strongly deterministic. In psychoanalysis we are determined by our unconscious impulses and past; in behaviorism we are determined by our associations, "contingencies," and our social environment; and in the trait approach we are determined by genetics, biology, and very early experiences that generate our relatively fixed or unchanging personality traits. The cognitive approach places less emphasis on this issue, and some within this approach have recently suggested that we do indeed have freedom of choice; but the majority of cognitive theorists still suggest that we are driven by the past (i.e., determined by experiences).[19] Only the humanistic approach places great value on self-directed and freely chosen behavior.

Again, some Christians may feel that humanistic psychology should be the most favored personality theory because it recognizes our freedom of choice and responsibility. But we want to caution the reader not to ignore the flip side of the coin: our *limited* agency. So perhaps one of the significant failures of humanistic psychology is that it overemphasizes our potential to choose, making it nearly limitless. On the other hand, the shortcoming of the other approaches is their adherence to absolute determinism, which robs human beings of their responsibility and opportunity for change (Theme 4).

On a positive note, there are some voices within the field of psychology that are providing new, welcome ideas regarding agency. In their intriguing

17. Bolt, *Pursuing Human Strengths*, 179–98.
18. Some feel that Freud was actually quite conflicted on this point, but he still gave little room for human choice. See discussion by Morea, *In Search of Personality*, 9–34.
19. Seligman et al., "Navigating," 123.

review article, "Navigating into the Future or Driven by the Past," Seligman and colleagues introduce the notion of "prospection," which is the mental representation of possible futures (i.e., the opposite of retrospection, or reflecting on the past). They feel that prospection is the best way to think about free will, and they speculate that

> viewing behavior as driven by the past was a powerful framework that helped create scientific psychology, but accumulating evidence in a wide range of areas of research suggests a shift in framework, in which navigation into the future is seen as a core organizing principle of animal and human behavior.
>
> . . . The past is not a force that drives [humans and intelligent animals] but a resource from which they selectively extract information about the prospects they face. . . . Prospection casts new light on why subjectivity is part of consciousness, [and] what is "free" and "willing" in "free will."[20]

What Seligman and colleagues are suggesting is that psychoanalytic, behavioristic, and cognitive approaches have so emphasized humans as being driven by the past that this focus has led to a deterministic dogma within psychology. In other words, psychologists have come to believe that we are who we are entirely because of our unchangeable past. It's not that Seligman and colleagues feel the past is irrelevant, but they suggest that our ability to self-consciously (i.e., subjectively) reflect about future possibilities frees humans to consider alternatives and to make choices based on long-term values and goals. We believe this way to understand human action is much more compatible with a limited-agency view found in Scripture. Christianity has a present and future focus, stressing God's work in people's lives toward sanctification (see chap. 10 for a full discussion of our forward-looking tendency called *telos*, or purposeful direction). We also feel that less deterministic perspectives such as Seligman's are very positive developments in the field of personality, and Christians now have the opportunity to help shape psychological thinking away from a purely deterministic view of the person.

Misunderstanding Our Moral Tendencies

Most personality theorists are relatively silent on moral tendencies, or they view humans as neither inherently good nor evil; humans are simply responding to the environment in a way that matches their genetic and mental capabilities. Freud's emphasis on the very self-serving nature of humans is a notable exception. In his view, our basic survival motives—primarily sexual and aggressive urges—are directed toward self-satisfaction without regard to the needs of

20. Ibid., 119.

others. Of course, he felt that the ego and superego could overrule these drives, but our primary motives are still directed toward selfish needs. Both secular and religious authors have noted the parallels between Freud's notion and the idea of sin.[21] In commenting about Freud's position, Richard Webster, in his book *Why Freud Was Wrong: Sin, Science, and Psychoanalysis*, suggests the following:

> In *A Short Account of Psychoanalysis* [Freud] writes that the "impulses . . . subjected to repression are those of selfishness and cruelty, which can be summed up in general as evil, but above all sexual wishful impulses, often of the crudest and most forbidden kind." In a discussion of group psychology, he suggests that the individual tends to lose his repressions when he becomes part of the mass: "The apparently new characteristics he then displays are in fact the manifestations of this unconscious, *in which all that is evil in the human mind is contained as a predisposition*." That Freud sees it as desirable to suppress and control this "evil" part of the mind is made quite clear: "Our mind," he writes, "is no peacefully self-contained unity. It is rather to be compared with a modern State in which a mob, eager for enjoyment and destruction, has to be held down forcibly by a prudent superior class."[22]

While Freud's view may be an important balance to the humanistic emphasis on human goodness (more on that in a moment), and there certainly are parallels to Christian theology, we believe this comparison to the theology of sin is fairly superficial. In Freud's view, this "evil in the human mind" is biologically based, unconscious, confined primarily to the id, and managed by social restraint through the ego and superego—but never ultimately cured. This contrasts significantly with both the biblical picture of our brokenness and possibility for reconciliation with God. Theologians Richard J. Plantinga and colleagues summarize Scripture's depiction of sinfulness this way:

> If *shalom* in the Hebrew Bible refers to the vital flourishing of all things in right relationship with one another, then sin can be described as that which corrupts, distorts, and taints that universal flourishing. Where obedience is called for, disobedience reigns. Where faithfulness to God and other human beings ought to be the norm, faithlessness shatters our lives. Where freedom ought to be used for the benefit of others, the shackles of selfish desires, slothful inaction, and broken relationships tie human beings down.[23]

This view paints sin as affecting the whole of the person—reason, emotions, moral tendencies, and relationships—not just one aspect of personality,

---

21. Morea, *In Search of Personality*, 9–34.
22. Webster, *Why Freud Was Wrong*, 326; emphasis added.
23. Plantinga, Thompson, and Lundberg, *Introduction to Christian Theology*, 195.

as Freud's approach seems to do. Sin is not just a tendency requiring restraint but a pervasive disfigurement of the image of God. Ultimate healing from sin comes in a restoration of shalom and relationship to God by way of the sacrifice of Jesus Christ.

So Christians should be very careful to see that Freud's view seriously misses this basic broken aspect of human nature and that it will ultimately not be successful in fully describing and predicting human personality. (Even Freud's students and ardent followers complained of his overly dark view of human nature, causing later psychoanalytic and psychodynamic theorists to balance Freud's view with additional "positive" motives.) So a biblically grounded personality theory will need to recognize the inherent goodness created in humans from the beginning of time, the corruption that exists, and, by God's grace, the possibility for goodness.

The complete opposite of Freud's dark view is the much more positive view of human potential found within humanistic psychology. While Christians would agree that this human goodness was true in God's original good creation, we cannot ignore the real presence of brokenness. Any approach to understanding the person that ignores the true brokenness of individuals (Theme 2) and the distorted nature of our social being will ultimately fail in fully capturing human behavior at a group or an individual level. In addition, individuals experience brokenness and the effects of sin all around them. And not only our individual nature but also the larger family, social, and economic structures that influence the personality are distorted. Just as individuals can, groups or social structures can have both evil and positive directions and influences, bringing damage or "healing" to individuals.

A Faith-Based Response to Theories of Personality

It's a fairly easy task to point out the "flaws" in each of the common personality theories, but it's another thing to come up with an alternative. If many elements of these theories conflict with a biblical picture of human nature, should we scrap them all and come up with a completely new and uniquely Christian personality theory? Certainly this is a tempting approach, and some Christian psychologists have put forth very interesting theories worthy of our consideration.[24] However, as psychologist Mary Stewart Van Leeuwen has suggested, developing alternative approaches is difficult because personality theories operate at several levels of detail or focus (i.e., from specific individual

24. See Burke, *Man and Mind.*

traits to broad themes of human function), and Christians are also splintered in their theological ideas and "particularities" (i.e., practices, traditions, and emphases).[25] In addition, as we have alluded to at several points in the chapter, Christians don't always get it right either. Sometimes Christians have downplayed our embodiment, been too individualistic, become overly focused on complete freedom of choice (or the opposite), or ignored our relationship to creation. Van Leeuwen argues that "we deceive ourselves if we believe that our social, cultural, and theological backgrounds will make no difference in the way, and the degree to which, we use Scripture as a source of control beliefs for personality theorizing."[26]

At other times, Christian psychologists have been quick to affiliate with one of the major personality theories without properly weighing the underlying perspectives and carefully examining the scientific evidence. As Malcolm Jeeves states in highlighting Van Leeuwen's concerns, "She pointed out the danger of selecting one of several personality theories currently in the psychological marketplace and seeking to baptize it with Christian orthodoxy."[27] Equally dangerous is the temptation to engage in "religious imperialism," as Stanton Jones has cautioned against, where we impose religious dogma that simply overrules all scientific ideas.[28] Rather, Jones calls for a dialogue where Christian psychologists propose tentative models about human personality and behavior that are based on Christian control beliefs but must also be put to the test of scientific scrutiny. He also maintains that Christian models about personality need to be part of a pluralistic discussion (i.e., coming from diverse worldviews) about the model's utility and value for psychological practice.

Therefore, developing a cohesive theory that is biblically grounded, consistent with scientific findings, and has practical value is a very difficult task for Christians engaged in psychology. So in its place, we hope to present a set of contours or "control beliefs" that one could use to guide thinking about contemporary personality theory. While we feel these control beliefs are biblically sound, our goal is to present ideas that could be considered useful within mainstream psychology and not just for Christians alone.

Each Person Is Unique—But We Are Also Related

While we believe each person is unique, we should point out that there are Scripture passages that seem to stress the importance of sameness. These

---

25. Van Leeuwen, "Personality Theorizing," 172.
26. Ibid.
27. Jeeves, *Human Nature at the Millennium*, 153.
28. Jones, "A Constructive Relationship," 195.

passages stress the value of losing one's identity and becoming more like Christ. For example, passages such as Romans 8:29, 1 Corinthians 4:16, and 1 John 3:1–3 suggest that Christians should be like Christ, be conformed to Christ, and even be imitators of the apostle Paul, so one might assume that Christians should be more like one another and more like Christ.

However, Scripture also celebrates individual differences. Passages such as Romans 12 and 1 Corinthians 12 speak about the variety of gifts and the diversity of abilities and roles that each person plays within the body of believers. So while Christ's followers are to conform to Christ's character according to the "fruits of the spirit" (i.e., love, kindness, forgiveness, etc.),[29] Scripture also points to the diversity of qualities and characteristics. This is exemplified further in the diverse personalities of the apostles (i.e., Peter, with strong emotional reactions, and Paul, the thoughtful theologian) that serve the kingdom of God in diverse ways. So, much the way psychologists have noted that each person is in some ways like everyone else and in other ways like no one else, we see this same perspective reflected in Scripture. This balanced view of similarities and differences also points us to the care and respect Christians should show to others who seem very different than themselves, since differences among people are valued in Scripture.

Despite our individual nature, we can never fully understand our individuality apart from the context of relationality. The individual gifts described in the New Testament are always talked about in the context of the unified "body of Christ." As Christian psychologists Mark A. Yarhouse, Richard E. Butman, and Barrett W. McRay suggest, "Costly discipleship and sustained altruism can be nurtured and developed only within healthy communities that know how to balance affirmation with accountability, and the priestly and prophetic witness of the truly committed."[30]

Applying these grand thoughts to the case of Lucy, we can say that she does not need to act like everyone else and that others should respect her individual qualities. She should develop and nurture the characteristics that are unique to her and then seek to utilize them for something (or someone) other than herself. For example, channeling her natural tendency to be angry into constructive action could turn Lucy into an assertive leader who is capable of accomplishing great things. At the same time, she should work to conform herself to the basic qualities and the fruits of the Spirit that Christ exemplified in his life. She can only accomplish this when she immerses herself in a positive community and works hard at building strong

29. See Gal. 5:22–23.
30. Yarhouse, Butman, and McRay, *Modern Psychopathologies*, 306.

relationships with people who accept her but are also willing to hold her accountable.

Personalities Are Stable—But Change Is Possible

Personalities do become relatively stable—meaning that they remain consistent over time—because of the influence of biology, environment, and our own patterns of acting. There is no escaping the fact that some of Lucy's personality traits may be inborn, since research suggests approximately 50 percent of personality "variation" can be "explained" by our biological inheritance.[31] There is also no escaping the fact that environments strongly mold our personalities for better or worse. As Yarhouse and colleagues suggest when discussing personality disorders, "Careful developmental histories of persons struggling with personality disorders suggest that significant others, whether peers or adults, were largely absent or disinterested."[32] They also point out that problem personality traits become harder to change as people get older. But these same authors recognize that Christians simply cannot fall into a deterministic mind-set when thinking about personality. They contend that both research and Scripture hold out hope for change for very difficult personalities, even though that work "can be hard and demanding."[33] The person must desire this change (i.e., express agency), but they also need positive relationships found in mentors, families, supportive communities, or church families.

We Are Broken—But Redeemable

We cannot assume that if Lucy reaches deep into her own mind (as the humanistic psychologists suggest), releases some of her inner conflicts (as psychoanalysis teaches), or places herself into a better environment (as cognitive-behavioral approaches contend) that she will automatically become the type of good person that others would like her to be. Even though these activities may be useful in understanding her own tendencies, recognizing the reality of sin suggests that her rational mind, moral thinking, the seemingly good people around her, and her good intentions can all be subtly twisted by sin. As noted earlier, in addition to our own inner sinful tendencies, we must contend with our broken bodies and brains, and we regularly encounter a broken world. How should Lucy counteract these distortions of God's good world from within and from others? Not by self-exploration alone but by immersing

31. Tellegen et al., "Twins," 1031–39.
32. Yarhouse, Butman, and McRay, *Modern Psychopathologies*, 303.
33. Ibid., 304.

herself in positive communities (for Christians, this likely involves a healthy church community), by conforming her will to the examples set by Christ and other positive role models, and by developing regular practices and habits that develop character (for Christians, a unique Christian character[34]).

Personality Direction Depends on "Meaning"

A Christian approach to personality theory should emphasize that human beings are designed to be more than "satisfaction maximizers" or "pain minimizers" as some behaviorists (and some psychoanalysts) have emphasized. Lucy may be influenced by the physical, mental, internal, and social factors from the past, but she also has the ability to prospect or think about future possibilities. When we imagine future actions, we set priorities based on what we have come to value and what we set our hearts on. As both psychology and Scripture suggest, we are driven to understand the meaning of perceptions and memories, why we do what we do, and our overall purpose. We then direct our behavior based on these purposes and priorities.

Having positive purposes and priorities leads to a healthy personality. As Seligman and colleagues suggest in relation to personality disorders, "There is growing evidence that a strong sense of meaning and purpose . . . is highly protective against psychopathology."[35] So Lucy needs to reflect on the basic values and life goals that she has, what is most valuable and meaningful in her life, and what is her ultimate purpose. This will not make her anger vanish instantly, but it can help her to choose patterns of living that can shape her personality over time.

Summing Up: A Christian Personality Theory?

We have not tried to present a single unified personality theory that can call itself uniquely Christian. The ideas cannot be called uniquely Christian because psychologists from many perspectives could easily find agreement with elements of these control beliefs. We have also tried to avoid a simple eclectic approach common among many contemporary personality theorists—where they pick and choose parts of different theories that fit nicely with their own view without regard to whether they form a cohesive whole. What we have tried to do is put forth basic human nature tendencies that hopefully hang together to develop the beginnings of a cohesive personality theory that might be useful in everyday explanations of behavior.

34. See Wright, *After You Believe.*
35. Seligman et al., "Navigating," 135.

If you are new to the discipline of psychology and have no plans of pursuing a career in this field, you probably are not interested in developing some grand personality theory yourself. However, most people we know are regularly speculating about why people are the way they are. Hopefully we have provided a set of principles that can help you think more about your own personality and the personality of others. So this is certainly not the end of any discussion on what shapes our personality—but only the beginning of your ongoing quest to understand the real you!

DISCUSSION QUESTIONS

1. Are there times you feel the same as everyone else? Are there times you feel very unique and different? Which of these experiences do you prefer?

2. Are there personality traits that you possess that you greatly value? What do you think are the origins of these traits—your parents, your upbringing, your unconscious, your relationships, your own choices?

3. Is it better to simply accept and like yourself just the way you are, or is it important to change who you are?

4. Are there personality traits in yourself or others that you have seen remain the same over a long period of time? Are there personality traits that you have seen change over time?

5. If you take Paul Vitz's "covenant theory" of personality seriously, how would this influence the way you might change your own personality?

6. Have you ever contemplated your long-term life goals—not only career or family goals but also goals for the type of person you would like to be? How might you determine if these goals are right for you?

15

In Search of Normality

Psychological Disorders

Chapter Summary You might think that normality would be a simple concept—perhaps we tend to define it as the way most people are, or you might define it as the way *you* are. Perhaps, as one author has suggested, normal is just a setting on your dryer. This chapter will focus on the difficulty in defining both normality and psychological disorder, and on how God views individuals with such conditions. We will also explore how we can determine whether mental disorders should be considered spiritual, biological, social, or willful problems of living. We use the themes that emphasize that we are embodied, relational persons and responsible limited agents to explore the causes of disorder, as well as how we care for one another when we struggle with disorders.

> In depression you cannot imagine that anyone would really love you, want to be there for you, find you still worthy of friendship and love. Truly darkness seemed my only companion. Of this I was quite convinced.
>
> Kathryn Greene-McCreight,
> *Darkness Is My Only Companion*

> Ah, Lord, my prayers are dead, my affections dead, and my heart is dead. But thou art a living God and I bear myself upon thee.
>
> English preacher William Bridge (1600–1670) quoted by Kathryn Greene-McCreight

The following statements are excerpts from a personal story placed anonymously on a public website called "Mental Health America: Real Lives."

My first marriage was doomed from the start. I knew 3 months into the marriage that it would not last. But being a God-fearing Christian, I stayed in the marriage until my wife betrayed me for another man. I was faithful in my marriage. But during the 12 years I was married I tried to kill myself at least four times.

On the job, my depression cost me promotions as I could not get a handle on my emotions. I would be up and down in my feelings. I could not control them. So I would get passed over for promotions or turn them down because I knew I would fail. The last suicide attempt I had was 3 years ago in April. I was working and wanted to hurt myself really badly. I told a fellow supervisor what I was thinking and was called into the office where I had a confrontation with my managers. They wanted me to get help. I am thankful for that confrontation. It saved my life.

I did not have insurance and the local area had few resources for the uninsured or under insured. I was able to get into a local mental health facility that really changed my thinking. I will never forget my counselor, Kristin.

And then there are those in the Christian community who feel mental illness is a spiritual problem, not a real problem. My wife went to the leaders in my faith and told them how I was and that I was in really bad shape. Not one of them approached or cared to see how I was. They avoided me at all costs. Why? I am not [a] mind reader, but all I can think of is they believed I was spiritually damaged goods in God's view. I was not worthy of being spoken to, prayed with or any other type of help. I was shunned instead of helped.

I still have many ups and downs. I am married to an incredible woman who loves me despite my shortcomings. Mental illness is that—an illness. Help yourself. Help others.[1]

Every person's story of psychological or emotional disorder is unique, but almost all of them share two common features: very personal suffering and disrupted relationships. This particular story describes significant pain, and also the complicating social and personal issues that accompany psychological disorders.

Similarly, Kathryn Greene-McCreight describes how her depression created isolation from others and from God.

I am not necessarily sad when I am depressed. I am not necessarily "down." Sometimes I just have a gnawing, overwhelming sense of grief, with no identifiable cause. I grieve my loved ones as though they were dead and contemplate

1. Anonymous, http://www.mentalhealthamerica.net/reallives/index.cfm/2009/9/4/Learning-to-trust-others-and-forgive-himself.

what their funerals would be like. I feel completely alone; darkness is my only companion.[2]

Greene-McCreight goes on to say,

> In the midst of an impenetrable depression, one is often unable to sense the presence of God at all. Sometimes all one can feel is the complete absence of God, one's utter abandonment by God, the ridiculousness of the very notion of a loving and merciful God. This cuts to the heart of the Christian and challenges everything she believes about the world and about herself. But if one is depressed, one should not expect to feel otherwise.[3]

Greene-McCreight feels that her struggles echo those of Job in the Old Testament who struggled in understanding his own suffering:

> I loathe my very life;
>> Therefore I will give free reign to my complaint
>> and speak out in the bitterness of my soul.
> I say to God: Do not declare me guilty,
>> but tell me what charges you have against me.
> Does it please you to oppress me,
>> to spurn the work of your hands,
>> while you smile on the plans of the wicked? (Job 10:1–3)

Christians have struggled to understand other individuals, or themselves, when they experience personal or psychological difficulties. Historically, persons of faith have placed a great deal of emphasis on our need for personal responsibility and free choice, as well as on the power of God's Spirit to transform our lives. So Christians have often leaned toward explanations that involve a person's spiritual journey—which may account for the reaction of the church in the story at the beginning of the chapter. Due to the increasing influence of medical science, there is also a growing understanding that brain function plays a critical role in various psychological disorders, so Christians also attribute disorders to problems of brain function. If you were to ask many persons of faith about why some individuals become clinically depressed,[4] they typically offer two distinct possibilities: (1) this person likely has some

2. Greene-McCreight, *Darkness Is My Only Companion*, 29.
3. Ibid., 93.
4. A condition where someone experiences at least some of these symptoms for at least two or more weeks: depressed mood, loss of interest or pleasure, weight loss, insomnia, psychomotor agitation, fatigue, feelings of worthlessness, diminished ability to concentrate, recurrent thoughts of death. See American Psychiatric Association, *Diagnostic and Statistical Manual*, 160–61.

form of "chemical imbalance" or (2) the person has made some bad personal choices or has willfully chosen a path that is not entirely virtuous, moral, or faithful, and these choices have ultimately led to this situation. While there is an element of truth in both of these explanations, we believe that the full explanation is far more complicated. This complexity is readily apparent to most people who struggle with psychological disorders and to their family and close friends. Those individuals not only know about the complex causes but also understand the difficulty in changing. People who have never experienced such difficulties may find it hard to understand why someone with these struggles doesn't just "get over it."

What Defines *Disorder*?

Psychological disorders, as defined by the *Diagnostic and Statistical Manual of Mental Disorders* (DSM-V) produced by the American Psychiatric Association, share three key elements: (1) disturbances in behavior, thoughts (cognition), or emotional regulation and (2) significant personal distress or impairment that (3) stems from an internal dysfunction (biological, psychological, or both)—not the typical response to a difficult event (i.e., loss of a job).[5] Although this guide is certainly useful (prior to 1952, there was no system for diagnosing and classifying psychological disorders), it implies a greater understanding of disorders than might actually be the case. The reality is, while we know a lot more about causes and treatments than we did fifty years ago, psychiatrists and psychologists still do not understand all of the specific causes and best treatment options in individual cases. In addition, many controversies and debates remain about this "medical model," in which psychological disorders are described in the same way we might describe physical injuries or diseases. Some of the issues raised have to do with exactly how bad a behavior should be or how long it should continue before it qualifies as a disorder. Other issues raised concern about the fact that a diagnosis can become a crutch to some or a self-fulfilling prophesy to others—because people begin to act in ways that are consistent with their diagnosis.

Persons of faith often have additional questions and concerns. If psychological disorders are simply medical conditions that require a pill, does this imply that all our behavior is determined by our brain function (or dysfunction)? What about issues such as free will and responsibility (Theme 4), relationships with others (Theme 1), meaning (Theme 5), and our relationship to

---

5. American Psychiatric Association, *Diagnostic and Statistical Manual*, 20.

God (Theme 1)? Many people understandably worry that if one adopts this medical model, it eliminates any discussion of these important dimensions of human nature. So it appears that the typical professional description of the nature of psychological disorders is useful but also somewhat oversimplified in the larger scheme of things. The problem comes in trying to understand the true complexity of these conditions and how all these factors interact.

Understanding Psychopathology

To help illustrate the complex influences in psychological disorders, consider a similar but more concrete issue: obesity. When we ask our students to offer explanations about why many North Americans are obese, we often get similar answers to those proposed for psychological disorders: causes such as genetics, physiological characteristics, or some form of willful (or "weak-willed") behavior. However, as the discussion continues, students often begin to offer a much greater variety of explanations. Suggested causes include: (1) emotional issues (e.g., excited, bored, depressed, etc.), (2) increasing affluence and availability of food (e.g., snacks at social events), (3) increased availability of fast-food restaurants, (4) increasing portion sizes at restaurants, (5) decreased activity because of technology (e.g., riding lawn mowers, video games), (6) fewer jobs requiring physical activity, (7) the structure of cities and towns (e.g., fewer sidewalks but more car access) creating longer commutes and less walking, (8) poor diets given to children from an early age, (9) poverty (which is associated with poor nutrition), (10) learned tendencies or habits (e.g., taste preferences learned early in life or a habit of eating snack foods before bed), (11) a sense of hopelessness when diets fail (i.e., called the abstinence-violation effect or sometimes the what-the-heck effect), (12) and a general social acceptance of increasing weight. This long list illustrates a very important point about human behavior: the causes of our behavior are often much more complex than physiology and willful decisions alone.

After identifying all these possible factors, we return students' attention to the possible role of sin, personal weakness, or lack of spiritual growth in the development of obesity. They are then somewhat hard-pressed to see how spiritual factors or one's willful choices could cause obesity. After all, with all these factors pushing North Americans toward obesity, how could we place any blame on individuals for their condition? Even reminding students that the list of seven deadly sins includes gluttony (see Prov. 28:7) doesn't necessarily change their view about obesity being the result of any form of individual sin or weakness. In a sense, they are partly correct to see that the sin of gluttony is often not only an individual responsibility. As we pointed out in chapter 12, on social psychology, there are also sins that occur collectively, so the spiritual condition of a family, a community, or an entire culture may be part of the issue.

These same issues apply to psychological disorders. Christian psychologists Yarhouse and colleagues suggest that we need to consider the whole person in understanding disorders, including the personal and collective impacts of sin. They suggest, "In addition to increased awareness of personal responsibility, an explanatory framework that takes sin seriously will increase our awareness of corporate responsibility. Not only does sin affect individual choices and their consequences, but sin pervades the very structures of society."[6] So obesity and psychological disorders have a lot in common. Like obesity, we believe that physiology and willful choices *do* play a role in psychological disorders, but we also believe that there are mental, social, and cultural forces that mold us, teach us, train us, and in many cases harm us psychologically and physically. Extreme stress brought on by war, broken relationships, an overly materialistic society, abusive parents, rejection or abandonment, and extreme poverty or deprivation all illustrate ways that a sinful and broken world warps the fabric of our experience and can distort our thinking and emotions.

These factors influence us because we are embodied (Theme 3), broken (Theme 2), and relational persons (Theme 1). Comparing psychological disorders to something like obesity also helps us to underscore individual differences because the mix of influences may be different for each person. Some may be strongly influenced by genetics or physiology, others may be more influenced by their situation (e.g., they work at a fast-food restaurant), others may have learned bad habits at a very early age, and some may simply practice gluttony. Specific sins or even sinful tendencies are sometimes obvious in these situations, but more often than not there are no individual sins that one can point to as a single cause. Even when sin is obvious, it doesn't really account for obesity or mental disorders. After all, since "all have sinned and fall short of the glory of God,"[7] why wouldn't every human being suffer from some form of mental illness or have weight control problems? So sinful tendencies are always part of our lives, but the issue of personal sin alone will never help us completely understand disorders. The problem is that, like obesity, the many factors that can influence psychological disorders all interact. In the case of psychological disorders, it's much harder to observe all the influences, and even harder to observe the interaction of these influences.

6. Yarhouse, Butman, and McRay, *Modern Psychopathologies*, 97.
7. Rom. 3:23.

In fact, to use a different analogy, defining psychological disorders and explaining why they exist is like playing golf—it looks simple until you actually try to do it. One of the problems in performing well in the game of golf is that many different variables or conditions can interact—so when you address one issue (e.g., your grip), it can affect something else (e.g., your swing). But with psychological conditions it's even harder to put our finger on an interaction because we can't observe an interaction—even though we can see the results.

We have made progress in understanding some aspects of these complex interactions. For example, the genes we inherit are not the only way we become what we are; these genes have to be "expressed" or "uncovered" before they can influence brain function or behavior. A good deal of contemporary research suggests that our environment (i.e., maternal nurturing, childhood neglect, stress, and other factors) influences whether or not genes associated with depression and other significant disorders are expressed.[8] If those genes were expressed by the wrong environmental conditions, individuals were much more likely to develop symptoms of depression or other disorders. While this research is intriguing, it does not account for all the many other aspects of our being that "come together" to make us what we are, or how those aspects come together.

Interacting Influences and "Disordered Minds"

When it comes to psychological disorders, the ultimate place where this interaction of factors occurs is within our mental life. This leads to a profound and still-controversial notion about the discipline and professional practice of psychology, particularly in relation to psychological disorders. Christian psychologist Don Lindskoog has suggested that the radical notion of psychology is that "in the evolving empirical discipline of psychology, a truly original and unique explanatory language has developed to name and understand an aspect of human experience that has never been named or understood before."[9]

He goes on to suggest that psychology, as a discipline, has captured an aspect of reality that is partially independent of other human fields of knowledge (e.g., biology, chemistry, philosophy, religion)—even though he acknowledges that there is some interdependence for all fields of knowledge (e.g., biology is dependent on chemistry, even though it is also unique). If our mental life has properties that are not explained by other aspects of reality, it implies that our

8. Moffitt, Caspi, and Rutter, "Measured Gene-Environment Interactions," 5–27.
9. Lindskoog, *The Idea of Psychology*, 5.

mental process could be disordered despite healthy brains and relationships. This notion, attributable to Freud and many others, is still a controversial one. To the dismay of many people of faith, it implies that there are aspects of our behavior that are not entirely explained using theological concepts alone. To the dismay of people in biology or medicine, it implies that you cannot reduce human behavior down to purely mechanical forms of scientific analysis.

Even some trained in the disciplines of psychology or psychiatry have questioned this notion. In 1961, psychiatrist Thomas Szasz suggested that mental *illness* is a myth.[10] He argued that an immaterial thing (i.e., the mind) could not be afflicted with illness. He also argued that the development of diagnoses related to mental illness was not a triumph of modern medicine but a way of marginalizing and discriminating against people who deviated from social norms. We believe that Szasz and a few of his followers (including some Christian psychologists) have contributed some important cautions about the way we diagnose mental disorders. However, we also maintain that understanding our mental life directly—in addition to biological issues, spiritual concerns, or social explanations—is central to understanding psychological disorders and that it is very appropriate to speak of "disordered thinking." We also maintain that our mental life, being embodied (not immaterial, as Szasz suggests) is highly dependent on its biological underpinnings, as well as the environment in which we exist. At the same time, our mental life cannot be reduced completely to our biological or spiritual dimensions because it has properties that cannot be explained by these basic qualities alone.

What are the aspects of our mental life that cannot be explained entirely by way of biology, social relationships, or spiritual concepts? Our mental life involves our perceptual ability, learning processes, habits, problem-solving ability, emotional responsiveness, self-awareness, and theorizing about others (i.e., theory of mind)—to name just a few. While we are embodied individuals, and embedded in relationships, we still have a mental life that is greater than the sum of all these many parts. All of our experiences, our brain functions, our choices, and our own mental processes can interact together in a way that can ultimately be dysfunctional or disordered.

Someone with serious clinical depression may have a biological predisposition that lies at the heart of their condition. But they also have had a lifetime of learned habits, ways of thinking and perceiving, memories, positive and negative social relationships, and positive and negative spiritual experiences that can all influence their mood, which in turn can influence other aspects of their lives. They also have had a lifetime of struggling to understand who they

10. See Szasz, *Myth of Mental Illness.*

are and the purpose or meaning of this condition, why life seems so difficult, and why others around them seem to have it so easy.

There are significant implications for this interacting and unifying approach. If we want to understand psychological disorders we will need to do more than study brain scans, engage in talk therapy, explore spiritual growth, or understand broken relationships. We will need to do all these things, but we will also need to understand and deal directly with the mental life of persons in the context of their relationships, personal history, faith perspective, and the fundamental meaning of their existence. Christians who wish to focus exclusively on the spiritual dimension, neuroscientists or behaviorists who want to focus entirely on brain function or environment, or therapists who only focus on the social or family environment fail to appreciate the complex and integrated nature of our psychological functioning. This book's theme of being responsible limited agents (Theme 4) fits nicely with this concept because it suggests that despite our common experiences, we each have an individual thought process that must be understood. However, our additional emphasis on being relational persons (Theme 1) also suggests that we can understand persons only in the context of their relationships—including their relationship to God.

Defining Disorder in the Context of Faith

Understanding something about the causes and the nature of psychological disorders still does not tell us how to distinguish disorders from normal behavior. Is someone who is extremely religious just being devout, or is this an example of some form of psychosis? Is a person diagnosed with a mild form of autism really disordered? Perhaps they are just different—and maybe even superior in many ways (i.e., autistic individuals often have exceptional memory or can be gifted in some artistic or scientific area). If we attach greater value and meaning to possessing exceptional math skills than to having good social skills, then mild autism is a special gift rather than a problem to be diagnosed and "cured." Several hundred years ago, reading was not a very essential skill, but today you are labeled as having a reading disorder if you have difficulty with this ability. Maybe we shouldn't say that individuals have a "reading disorder" but instead that society has a "reading obsession."

Certainly one way that faith impacts this area of psychology is in helping us sort out what society should value and how people should view individuals who struggle with psychological disorders. Faith perspectives have a lot to say about our basic purpose and what our greater purposes in life should be. Certainly there are many psychological disorders where it is clear that the affected individual has little, if any, personal responsibility for the development of her symptoms, that the symptoms and behavior are truly debilitating, and that there is little she can do on her own to overcome this condition. But there are other situations where a person's value system very much influences what we consider normal or normative. So, at a very practical level, we agree with most textbook definitions or descriptions of psychological disorders as being persistent thoughts or actions that are "deviant, distressful, and/ or dysfunctional."[11] However, each of these terms is loaded with all sorts of value judgments. After all, who decides what is deviant, distressful, or dysfunctional?

The answer—like the answer to every question asked in Sunday school—is God. God's intention was to create a harmonious universe where people were not only physically healthy but also emotionally, intellectually, and behaviorally healthy. So there is a normative feature about creation; God had a certain intention about what he wanted his creation to be like.[12] We can also suppose that God did not intend for people to experience uncontrollable anxiety, uncontrollable voices inside their head, overwhelming and unexplained depression, or significant intellectual impairments. Someone who is, or knows someone who is, experiencing mental illness may object to the notion that they are not normative. However, it is important to note that the brokenness of the current world affects all human beings, so none of us should be arrogant in suggesting that others are more broken than us since we all reflect the brokenness of sin, disease, and death.

It is also important to realize that God also desired diversity within his creation. As described in the chapter on personality, Scripture repeatedly stresses the desirable diversity among people. But is a characteristic such as left-handedness a sign of some deviation from the path of normalcy (i.e., God created right-handedness as the norm and any deviation from that is at best an "oddity"), or is this part of the variety God intended? Some Christians have raised similar questions about variations in intellect, personality, and even sexual orientation. These questions are very difficult to answer in our present existence since we don't have direct experience as to what a previously perfect world was like. While more extreme or disturbing examples of abnormal mental functioning are fairly easy to identify as outside of God's intention, other cases are clearly more difficult. So a faith perspective does not by itself answer all the questions about what defines normal or abnormal.

11. Myers, *Psychology*, 606.
12. See Wolters, *Creation Regained*.

What we can say is that any condition, difficulty, or disorder that inhibits us from fulfilling our most basic God-given tasks (e.g., being a responsible parent, sibling, or friend; holding down a job; being a responsible and productive citizen and/or church member; etc.) is at least a *potential* example of a nonnormative situation.

A faith perspective can also help to determine what a healthy mental life and healthy personality look like. Several thinkers in psychology have begun to suggest that clinical psychologists and psychiatrists have placed too much emphasis on unhealthy or disordered personalities and not enough on what a fully functioning human or "flourishing" person would look like. This movement is sometimes referred to as positive psychology, and these psychologists have outlined many personality strengths they believe a person should possess to thrive. Qualities that include wisdom, courage, temperance, transcendence,[13] and many others have been described and studied. We favor this general movement because it helps to guide treatment (i.e., if we want to make you less depressed, what qualities should replace the negative emotions?) and provides a framework for determining what is normative. Persons of faith should enter into this discussion and contribute biblical perspectives as to what constitutes a healthy mental life.

God's View of Disorder

Going a bit deeper into the issue, it's also important to appreciate how God sees human beings in the context of brokenness. God's Son came to this earth to restore the relationship between God and humans by offering himself as payment. But Christ also experienced the range of genuine embodied pain that humans can experience. He felt physical pain,[14] anger,[15] anxiety and deep sorrow,[16] betrayal and abandonment,[17] as well as positive emotional experiences;[18] he knows our pain. But God never promises an easy life, even when we are his children.[19] However, because he has experienced the effects of a broken world that we all know, he does not judge us according to our frailty. Rather, "from everyone who has been given much, much will be demanded; and from the one who has been entrusted with much, much more will be asked"

13. See Bolt, *Pursuing Human Strengths*.
14. Matt. 27:30.
15. Matt. 23:26–28.
16. Matt. 26:37; Luke 22:44.
17. Matt. 26:56.
18. Luke 10:21.
19. Rev. 2:10.

(Luke 12:48). This verse implies that those who have little (e.g., few resources, little emotional regulation, little intellectual capacity, little ability to perceive reality, etc.) will have less expected of them. This puts a new light on how we respond to individuals struggling with psychological or mental disorders. Christians sometimes see individuals who struggle with psychological conditions as damaged goods and not as worthy of God's grace. But we believe that much more will be expected of those who are emotionally and psychologically well balanced, and that special grace is given to those who struggle.

To make this concrete, we know of a woman who struggles with chronic schizophrenia. She has occasional delusions and sometimes hears voices (when not controlled by medication); in many ways she has lived a very debilitated (and nonnormative) life. But this woman is also one of the kindest, most caring persons we know. She is faithful in her church and spiritual life; her prayer life would put most others to shame. She has little to offer the world in terms of productive output, but she outshines most of us in childlike faith. She has been entrusted with very little in life, but we believe that she has far exceeded what many people have accomplished in God's eyes. We also believe that individuals with special needs or psychological disorders are an essential part of our current reality in that they define what others—who have been given much—should do. God will judge those given much by how they have treated those given less (see Matt. 25:40). Christian psychologists Yarhouse and colleagues provide a very eloquent description of how we should respond to those who struggle.

> One of the integrative challenges facing Christian mental health professionals lies in recognizing the common humanity among those with even the most severe expressions of psychopathology. We must stand against a view of those who suffer from problems of psychosis as "other," as it leads to a diminished view of the image of God in them and of our responsibility for the care of the weak and vulnerable.
>
> Christians must cultivate a profound appreciation for the value of being human and of individual human beings (cf. Jones and Butman, 1991, chap. 2). Even in the midst of severe psychosis, the worth and dignity of the afflicted person is in no way diminished; the *imago Dei* may be tainted but is never removed. Given our own humanity, surely we can find some empathy for those who appear to us to be deluded or who have lost touch with reality. Christian philosopher and psychiatrist A. A. Howsepian (1997) argues persuasively that we all have disordered thinking and appetites (desires) to at least some degree. Thus there is room for some humility in this conversation.[20]

20. Yarhouse, Butman, and McRay, *Modern Psychopathologies*, 271.

The Meaning of Suffering

One way for individuals struggling with mental illness to better understand their own condition is to place the symptoms and issues within the context of their lives. Because we are meaning seeking persons (Theme 5), we understand our struggles—and the struggles of others—best if we understand more about the purpose and meaning of our existence. As described in chapter 1, human beings not only react to their environment but also work to understand it and to appreciate an ultimate purpose and significance. When people are struggling with disorders, these disorders can influence and be influenced by a broader understanding of life. So psychological disorders are disorders of meaning in addition to being disorders of brain function, personal failures, personal sins, social/structural sins, or mental dysfunction.

While we would never wish psychological disorders on any individual, there are times when suffering—whether by way of physical, mental, or social pain—can lead individuals to a better place. We know of people who have experienced very difficult and painful emotional and personal struggles, and have come through it as more thoughtful, more empathic, more helpful, and even more spiritual people. This growth only happens when people have social, spiritual, and—in some cases—professional support.

Christian psychologists Yarhouse and colleagues also suggest that individuals struggling with psychological disorders need to reflect on the meaning and significance of their symptoms at two different levels. This reflection on meaning relates first of all to understanding the immediate causes, such as possible biological, social, and personal factors that may contribute to their thinking patterns or symptoms. Such reflection is helpful because it changes a person's perspective from an obsessive focus on the symptoms themselves—an understandable and common tendency—to a focus on root causes. This reframing of the meaning of their symptoms helps to make the symptoms seem more manageable and allows for better distancing from the problems and improved problem solving. In addition, they argue that contemplating a deeper level of meaning related to sin, suffering, and struggle can help individuals cope with their situation and promote healing. They also believe "that a clearly articulated Christian worldview and a congruent and credible Christian lifestyle constitute a form of primary prevention. Reflection on our struggles can help us see what truly matters from the perspective of kingdom values."[21]

21. Ibid., 136.

They are not suggesting that a Christian worldview (or any other worldview) is some magic cure or treatment. They fully appreciate that there are very real biological, mental, interpersonal, and social factors that greatly influence the development of a disorder. However, they are suggesting that psychological disorders can be better understood in the context of broader life issues and that this can contribute to healing or even the prevention of symptoms. As described earlier, psychological disorders—similar to obesity—have complex and interacting factors, and our broader questions about life are an important part of that mix.

Yale graduate and ordained Episcopal priest Kathryn Greene-McCreight (cited earlier) worked to understand the meaning of her severe bipolar depression (i.e., cycling between periods of depression and mania) by writing a book about her experiences. She writes: "This book began, then, as my own agonizing search for the meaning of my mental illness."[22] She struggled with questions such as, "Does God send this suffering? If so, why? And why this particular kind of suffering? Why, if I am a Christian, can I not rejoice? What is happening to my soul?"[23] Even though she was helped tremendously by psychotherapy and medication, she suggests that "while therapists and counselors, psychiatrists and medications abound, I found no one to help me make sense of my pain with regard to my life before the triune God." She knew that she could not completely divorce her experience from her faith: "How could I, as a Christian, indeed as a theologian of the church, understand anything in my life as though it were separate from God? This is clearly impossible. And yet how could I confess my faith in the God who is 'a very present help in trouble' (Psalm 46:1) when I felt entirely abandoned by that God?"[24]

Of course God can relate to us even in our lowest state of mind, but this does not mean that God's care over us eliminates other issues or treatments. As Lewis Smedes, former professor at Fuller Theological Seminary, once wrote about his own struggle with depression: "Then God came back. He broke through my terror and said: 'I will never let you fall. I will always hold you up.'. . . I felt as if I had been lifted from a black pit straight up into joy." But he also adds: "I have not been neurotically depressed since that day, though I must, to be honest, tell you that God also comes to me each morning and offers me a 20-milligram capsule of Prozac. . . . I swallow every capsule with gratitude to God."[25]

22. Greene-McCreight, *Darkness Is My Only Companion*, 12.
23. Ibid.
24. Ibid., 13.
25. Smedes, *My God and I*, 133.

Caring in the Christian Community

We will discuss treatment of psychological disorders more in chapter 16, but we can say at this point that the support of a faith community (e.g., local church, small group, religious college, like-minded friends, etc.) can greatly ease symptoms of psychological disorders or even promote a significant amount of healing. This support requires that persons in those faith communities react in a way that is much more positive than the kind of response described in the opening story. Christian psychologist Warren Brown has written that our humanity, or "soulishness" as he calls it, is defined by our ability to have a relationship with God and others.[26] He also suggests that individuals who lose the ability to have reciprocal relationships (i.e., Alzheimer's patients, individuals with brain injury or disorders) still need to have relationships. In those cases, God can maintain a relationship with them even when they have difficulty responding. Likewise, the community of faith needs to provide a supportive relationship, even if that person is unable to respond in kind. Kathryn Greene-McCreight talks eloquently about how God never left her, even though she could not feel that presence or respond; her husband and many Christian friends did not abandon her but supported her, even when she could not immediately feel their love and support.

> In God's eyes we are not how we feel, we are not what we think, we are not even what we do. We are what God does with us, and what God does with us is to save us from our best yet perverse efforts to separate ourselves from this presence, from his fellowship, communion, sharing.[27]

Conclusions and Applications

So what can we conclude about the value of a faith perspective in trying to understand psychological disorders? Admittedly, persons of faith will still struggle to understand the specific criteria for mental illness—or even what this term means. In addition, biblical insights will not always help us understand all the root causes of psychological disorder for any given individual and people won't always know the best approach for treatment (more on this last point in chap. 16). But to summarize our thoughts on the matter, there are several ways that faith informs understanding of this issue. Faith perspectives can help us to:

26. Brown, "Cognitive Contributions to Soul," 99.
27. Greene-McCreight, *Darkness Is My Only Companion*, 89.

1. See the broader influences on psychological functioning and psychological disorder. We believe that a biblical perspective that sees humans as embodied, relational, spiritual (i.e., in relationship with God), and responsible persons helps to avoid the reductionism that places too much emphasis on one aspect of our being (e.g., brain function, social or cultural factors, spiritual issues alone, etc.).

2. Appreciate that not only do personal sins and failings contribute to disorder, so too can the collective sins of a community or culture. So sin is involved in psychological disorder, but not always because of the personal sins of the individual. The effect of sin is broad and influences our relationships with God, with one another, and with creation. All of these issues influence our mental health.

3. Better understand the defining features of normative (i.e., as God intended) behavior and the types of personal traits that allow people to not only survive but thrive. The value system of faith communities needs to emphasize that part of any person's difficulty is not only to be found within that person but also to be understood according to what their community values (i.e., stress-free living, unbridled happiness, math ability, good social skills, financial success, moral behavior, etc.). We need to evaluate what we collectively value and make sure those values are in line with biblical norms for living (e.g., showing justice, loving mercy, walking humbly, etc., versus the pursuit of wealth, personal success, etc.).

4. Appreciate the value and humanity of each person. We should be able to see the image of God even in the most broken person and be able to respond with the support that only a community of faith can provide. We also need to recognize the unique qualities and gifts that individuals may have even in the face of very debilitating and difficult situations, and first see the person well before we see the disorder within her.

5. Help each person understand the context and meaning of their psychological disorder. A supportive, understanding, and even admonishing community can do much to reduce symptoms and provide a way of working through difficult issues. When persons come to understand the meaning of suffereing—in themselves or others—they experience some healing and are better able to cope with the issues they face.

DISCUSSION QUESTIONS

1. If you or someone you know has experienced some form of psychological disorder or mental illness, how did others respond? Was there acceptance, blame, curiosity, or simply ignoring of the issue? How have you responded to others?

2. If you are part of a Christian community, how would most people in your community explain or account for psychological disorders? Do you mostly agree or disagree with these views? Why? Have your views changed over the course of reading this chapter or book?

3. List some of the ways that sin or brokenness influences mental illness/health. Have you or someone you know experienced some or many of these influences?

4. How do you explain the type of suffering that some people experience with mental illness? Why does God allow people to have these difficulties?

5. If you have experience with mental illness, are there things that others did that made the situation better or worse? What are ways that you can be supportive of others struggling with mental illness? Are there things you should or shouldn't say or do that make it better or worse?

16

"Meaningful" Healing

Therapy

Chapter Summary: There are many attitudes and ideas about the value and nature of psychotherapy. This chapter outlines the ways Christians and others have characterized therapy practice, and it examines various types of helping relationships to consider when needing help. We also attempt to critique common therapy techniques from a biblical worldview and develop foundational concepts that can be used to critique therapy from a Christian perspective.

There are many ways of getting strong, . . . and sometimes talking is the best way.

Former professional tennis player Andre Agassi, Open

My therapist told me the way to achieve true inner peace is to finish what I start. So far today, I have finished 2 bags of M&M's and a chocolate cake. I feel better already.

Humorist Dave Barry

Finally, brothers and sisters, rejoice! Strive for full restoration, encourage one another, be of one mind, live in peace. And the God of love and peace will be with you.

2 Corinthians 13:11

"Mrs. C. was a 39-year-old woman who complained of fear reactions to traffic situations."[1] As described by therapist Joseph Wolpe, Mrs. C. had experienced a traumatic accident and was now extremely anxious while driving or even walking across busy intersections. She would often stay at home for weeks on end to avoid driving. She was also experiencing regular headaches, and her increasing anxiety was beginning to affect her marriage relationship and even her sex life. Wolpe used cognitive-behavioral therapy that included careful assessment of her emotional and marital history, guided imagery, relaxation training, homework assignments to practice her activities, and cognitive activities designed to change her thinking patterns. Seven months of intermittent therapy sessions led to a major reduction of fear, greatly increased driving frequency, and improved sexual and marital relationships with her husband. A nine-year follow-up showed that she remained symptom free.

Results such as these seem impressive—even magical—but after some reflection you may have some questions about the process. Perhaps Mrs. C. would have gotten better on her own after seven months of doing nothing or something equally valuable (and less expensive). Perhaps there are better or even more effective techniques than these (e.g., medication, spiritual healing, sharing with friends). These and many other questions have made people somewhat ambivalent about psychotherapy of any kind.

Attitudes toward Therapy

Have you, or would you, seek psychotherapy if needed? Attitudes in the United States toward mental health treatment have become more favorable over the years. A 2003 survey showed an estimated 41.4 percent reporting that they would "definitely go" for professional help.[2] Of course, this means that a fairly large proportion would still not seek professional help. In fact, the National Institute of Mental Health suggests that even for those individuals with a serious mental health condition, only slightly over half received treatment of any kind.[3] Survey research has identified the most significant factors that cause resistance to mental health services, including cost, personal stigma associated with a mental disorder, cultural beliefs that are resistant or suspicious of therapy,

1. Wolpe, *Practice of Behavior Therapy*, 309.
2. Mojtabai, "Americans' Attitudes," 642–51.
3. National Institute of Mental Health, "Use of Mental Health Services and Treatment among Adults."

and being very religious.[4] Others have more privately questioned the value or effectiveness of therapy. Humorist Dave Barry captured this sentiment when he said most people have "the impression that psychiatrists are just a bunch of bearded voodoo doctors who espouse confusing and wildly contradictory theories that have nothing to do with common sense." To which he replied, "This is totally unfair, many psychiatrists are clean shaven."[5] An only slightly more serious poke at psychotherapy came from a 1950s, tongue-in-cheek definition of therapy from a clinical psychologist who suggested that therapy is "an unidentified technique applied to unspecified problems with unpredictable outcomes. For this technique we recommend rigorous training."[6] His not-so-subtle suggestion is that psychotherapists really don't know what they are doing, but they insist on making the practice look professional.

As the research mentioned above suggests, people who are very religious have been particularly ambivalent about seeking mental health treatment. Despite this tendency, there are certainly differences among Christians about the value of therapy. Many Christians may be favorable to the idea of therapy because they view it as a positive helping profession that brings healing to hurting individuals. Many Christians also feel that Christian faith is valuable but not essential in therapy—as long as the therapy is effective. However, others have questioned psychotherapy on several grounds. Some may feel that psychotherapists operate according to models that are in opposition to Christian faith,[7] and that change only happens through prayer, Scripture reading, spiritual healing, or the support of a church community. Others see value in the insights from psychological theories but feel that therapy is best done by a Christian pastor, spiritual leader, or Christian counselor (i.e., under the direction of a church-related ministry)—not necessarily a person trained and licensed as a professional therapist. Finally, some feel that only well-trained, professionally licensed therapists should treat people—as long as they are devoted to the Christian faith.

One last doubt about professional therapy—and perhaps other forms of helping relationships—comes from Christians who suggest that we should deal with problems on our own or perhaps with God alone. After all, doesn't Scripture suggest that God will not give us more than we can handle? Therefore, we should be able to deal with all difficulty, including psychological disorders, through self-reflection, prayer, and strong faith. One problem with this belief is that it is a misreading of the apostle Paul's statement in 1 Corinthians 10:13:

4. Eisenberg et al., "Stigma and Help Seeking," 522–41.
5. Barry, *Dave Barry's Bad Habits*, 141.
6. Eysenck, *Effects of Psychotherapy*, 698.
7. Farber, *Unholy Madness*.

"God is faithful; he will not let you be tempted beyond what you can bear." This verse is talking about temptation to commit a specific sin, not necessarily about our ability to handle tragedy or difficulty in our lives. Certainly the story of Job in the Old Testament leaves a very different impression of the way tragedy affects persons of faith. In response to the tragedy in his own life, Job says, "I have no peace, no quietness; I have no rest, but only turmoil,"[8] and, "Why did I not perish at birth, and die as I came from the womb?"[9] It appears that even persons of great faith can get "dumped on" with a force that is far more than they can bear—individually. This brings us to the other key fallacy about bearing up in tragedy: it's not something we do alone. As a very old story recounted by Kathryn Greene-McCreight goes, a drowning man refused help from several sources, saying "God will save me." After he drowned, he inquired at the gates of heaven why God had not rescued him. The reply came, "I sent several people to save you, what more did you want?"[10] So not only do we bear God's image collectively, we bear up under tragedy—including the tragedy of mental illness and significant personal traumas—through helping relationships that can include professional psychotherapy. Greene-McCreight concludes her feelings about the role of mental health treatment this way:

> Indeed, Christians sometimes reject therapy *in toto*, claiming that all they need for health, and mental health specifically, is Jesus, and then things will be fine. I had a student once who interpreted her own depression as a preconversion illness that disappeared upon her conversion. Maybe so, but what about those of us who have a vibrant faith and a strong relationship with Jesus and yet are still thrown in the pit? Surely the voice of the psalmist throughout reflects the plight of these mentally ill, as it does the plight of the physically ill, the poor, the outcast. . . . I don't see why God's grace cannot come in the form of a daily dose of antidepressant or in the form of a therapist, even an atheist. That cannot be impossible, surely.[11]

In addition to this wide diversity of views among people of faith (as well as the broader public), there are diverse views among therapists about how therapy should be conducted and what the goals of therapy should be—perhaps the source of Dave Barry's complaint about "wildly contradictory ideas." All of this makes determining the value of therapy and evaluating different therapies from the perspective of faith very difficult, since there are so many views and approaches to consider. While most readers probably do not plan

8. Job 3:26.
9. Job 3:11.
10. Greene-McCreight, *Darkness Is My Only Companion*, 146.
11. Ibid., 145.

on becoming therapists, many of you have or will face questions about when, where, and how to use therapy for psychological problems, so the descriptions and critiques that follow are designed as something of a "consumer guide" to helping and therapy.

Helping Comes in Many Forms

As mentioned earlier, one very simple reason that people are resistant to therapy is that many have experienced great benefit from just sharing their problems with a friend, family member, youth pastor, or someone they trust to have good wisdom. They may have also done some "self-therapy" by going to a movie or eating cake (see the quote from Dave Barry at the opening of the chapter). So a person might ask, why pay for a service when I can get the same thing for free? This is certainly an understandable sentiment, but it may be helpful to point out what is distinct about professional therapy and the benefits and limitations of different types of helping.

Psychotherapy is a specialized helping relationship and is defined by John C. Norcross (and officially adopted by the American Psychological Association[12]) this way:

> Psychotherapy is the informed and intentional application of clinical methods and interpersonal stances *derived from established psychological principles* for the purpose of assisting people to modify their behaviors, cognitions, emotions, and/or other personal characteristics in directions that the *participants deem desirable.*[13]

Note the use of *established psychological principles* that require extensive knowledge and training, making psychotherapy distinct from casual conversations, supportive friendships, prayer, or spiritual counseling. Research over many years has confirmed that licensed professional therapists produce scientifically verifiable benefits to people that are not found in other types of helping relationships.[14]

Does this mean that other forms of helping relationships that don't involve special training are unimportant? Not at all; other helping relationships may also be extremely therapeutic, but for different reasons. Research regularly confirms that strong relationships and social support promote well-being,

12. American Psychological Association, "Recognition of Psychotherapy Effectiveness."
13. Norcross, "An Eclectic Definition of Psychotherapy," 218–20; emphasis added.
14. Smith and Glass, "Psychotherapy Outcome Studies," 752.

reduce or prevent psychological dysfunction, and even reduce the incidence of physical illness.[15] So it appears that sharing with a friend can be extremely helpful. According to Christian therapists Yarhouse and colleagues, this is one area where the church can be at the forefront of prevention and care for those who are hurting.[16] In addition to social support, they argue that the church can be a significant force in reducing other forms of distress such as extreme financial need, poor coping skills, chronic health issues, and other physical needs. These everyday concerns are also strong predictors of future mental health. Pastoral or spiritual counseling, small groups, or informal and formal church organizations that promote supportive and caring relationships can bring about tremendous healing or prevent future problems.

One example of this type of organization is Stephen Ministries. According to their promotional material, "Stephen Ministers are congregation members trained by Stephen Leaders to offer high-quality, one-to-one Christian care to people going through tough times. A Stephen Minister usually provides care to one person at a time, meeting with that person once a week for about an hour."[17] This ministry is not designed to replace psychotherapy, pastoral counseling, or other church ministries. Stephen Ministers are discouraged from giving advice, probing psychological function, or engaging in any other form of therapeutic intervention; the ministry is simply designed to build caring, safe, and confidential relationships.

The benefit provided by these types of informal helping relationships is consistent with the theme of being relational persons (Theme 1). As described in many chapters so far, our need to belong, our need to be in community with others, suggests that when we provide safe places for this community to happen, we can satisfy a basic human need and provide healing for hurting people.

Being responsible limited agents (Theme 4) and broken but redeemable persons (Theme 2) also mean that we need relationships to help hold us accountable. Church families can often provide accountability groups to help us check our own behaviors and remind us of our responsibilities to one another and to God. Church ministries can also remind us of scriptural mandates concerning what God desires of us—always in the context of God's "amazing grace" for fallen people. Certainly there are analogous groups outside the church that can serve similar functions. Families, support groups, and many other informal or formal groups can provide support and accountability, but churches should take a leading role in being healing places for hurting people.

---

15. See Cohen and Wills, "Stress, Social Support, and the Buffering Hypothesis," 310.
16. Yarhouse, Butman, and McRay, *Modern Psychopathologies*, 88–108.
17. Stephen Ministries, "What Is Stephen Ministry?"

Slightly more formal helping relationships may come through pastoral counseling or church-based counseling services. These counselors may or may not be professionally licensed for counseling and may not have all the specialized training described above, but they can provide great benefit. In addition to providing the type of safe relationship building provided by more informal support groups, spiritual or pastoral counseling can also help satisfy our meaning seeking desire (Theme 5). Yarhouse and colleagues have also pointed out that having a strong sense of meaning and purpose is another significant predictor of mental health.[18] They argue that symptoms associated with physical or mental illness need to be understood not only from their biological and psychological basis but also in terms of their ultimate significance and purpose in a person's life. As described in chapter 15, people of faith who have struggled with mental illness or significant personal problems have found great comfort in grappling with the meaning of their suffering or difficulty. Church-based counseling can go a long way in helping people understand a deeper purpose for the difficulties they face and the ultimate reasons for their current situation.

Professional Psychotherapy

Where does this leave us with "professional" psychotherapy? If the church or other groups are capable of supplying many of the basic needs for individuals, is professional, licensed psychotherapy needed? While all these qualities of informal and formal relationships have great value, there are some things that the church, or friends, cannot supply, and that is the specialized knowledge about humans that includes cognition and learning, conscious and unconscious processes, developmental processes that shape personality, the power of social factors to alter our behavior and attitudes, the nature of brain and bodily functions (Theme 3), and many other concepts. In addition, psychotherapists possess specialized knowledge about how to help a person change their thoughts and behaviors. Considering the opening story about Mrs. C., we can assume that most pastors, spiritual healers, or even Stephen Ministers would not have expertise with techniques designed to reduce fear that occurs after a car accident. While social support, improved relationship with God, understanding the overall meaning of her fear, and being held accountable will all help, they will not automatically eliminate the fear itself. As Yarhouse and colleagues confirm:

18. Yarhouse, Butman, and McRay, *Modern Psychopathologies*, 134–43.

It becomes readily apparent to most pastors or Christian workers that medita-
tion on key Scriptures rarely "fixes" serious anxiety struggles, any more than
the regular singing of "Amazing Grace" helps a struggling person feel like she
or he is God's beloved. . . . God's grace, and the truths of Scripture, must be
incarnated (fleshed out) in the context of everyday living.[19]

Likewise, Greene-McCreight suggests that

those Christians who have not faced the ravages of mental illness should not be
quick with advice to those who do suffer. Platitudes such as "Pray harder," "Let
Jesus in," even "Cast your anxiety on him, because he cares for you" (1 Peter
5:7), which of course are all valid pieces of advice in and of themselves, may
only make the depressive person hurt more.[20]

As we discussed earlier, Scripture was not written as a science textbook
or a psychotherapy manual, and it cannot provide specific answers to every
life issue. But we are given minds to learn more about how our minds work,
and we are given the task of using that knowledge to bring healing. Therefore, whatever psychotherapy is, and whatever theories are behind a given
technique, the first order of business is that it be based on sound principles
and well-tested practices. For example, to ensure that the treatment success
for Mrs. C. was not due to the passage of time or client expectations alone,
research needs to compare a nontherapy group to the therapy group under
carefully controlled conditions.

Unfortunately, the history of clinical psychology and psychotherapy has
been riddled with examples of some bad practices and untested ideas. Robyn
Dawes, in his book *The House of Cards*, raises concerns about the state of
affairs in the public mind concerning therapy: "The impression is created
that psychotherapy treatment is all a matter of opinion or conjecture. It isn't,
but many practitioners treat it that way, while the professional associations
support them in doing virtually anything at all that appeals to their 'clinical
intuition,' as if there were no knowledge."[21] He goes on to suggest that a
good amount of research does show that "psychotherapy works. . . . Those
who believe they have problems are encouraged to try it—especially if they
have been unable to change their behavior by simply 'willing' a change."[22] Of
course one should be careful in selecting a therapist; Dawes provides useful—
though slightly unrealistic—advice on this selection by saying, "For myself,

---

19. Ibid., 112.
20. Greene-McCreight, *Darkness Is My Only Companion*, 21.
21. Dawes, *House of Cards*, 9.
22. Ibid., 73.

in choosing a professional psychologist I would want one of the 30 percent of APA members who reads one or more of its scientific journals."[23] In other words, the practice of psychotherapy should be based on well-tested principles and thoroughly studied outcomes.

The same should be true for professional psychotherapy that is conducted by Christians. As mentioned in chapter 14, Christian psychotherapist Alan Tjeltveit suggests that Christian therapists have rarely tested the therapy techniques that they believe are consistent with the principles of Christian faith.[24] This is not to say that these techniques are wrong or ineffective, but that they need to be verified and perhaps refined. We would anticipate that practices that prove effective would also be consistent with biblical views of human nature—but they still should be tested to determine if therapists are applying the concepts correctly. So if professional psychotherapy—whether by a Christian or not—claims that it offers specialized knowledge that goes beyond more informal forms of helping, it needs to demonstrate that this expertise is indeed worth the trouble (and the cost).

Christian Psychotherapy

Are there features that are unique to Christian psychotherapy? First of all, it's hard to precisely define this phrase because there is no one description or technique that could be characterized as uniquely Christian. While having a therapist who is a Christian certainly helps, we feel this is not an absolutely necessary component for therapy to be practiced in a way that is consistent with biblical themes. What is most important (at a minimum) is that the therapy follows techniques and establishes goals that conform to a biblical understanding of persons and that are well tested and shown to be effective.

So what qualities should individuals consider when selecting a therapist or therapy approach? What follows is a list of techniques and characteristics of a therapist or his or her approach that we believe are compatible with well-tested practices and are consistent with the scriptural themes concerning human nature. This is not an exhaustive or detailed list, nor a "therapy for dummies" manual, but a set of basic qualities that should guide Christians when selecting therapies that are most helpful. The reader should consult chapter 14, on personality, for some additional background on the various

23. Ibid., 74.
24. Tjeltveit, "Faith, Psychotherapy, and Christian Counseling," 247–63.

theoretical approaches behind the main psychotherapy approaches. This said, we find techniques and goals that appear most consistent with these themes and which have the most research support to be ones that do the following.

    1. Provide empathy, caring concern, and unconditional acceptance. There is a good amount of research evidence showing that empathy, a sense of trust, and feeling cared for are key elements in the therapeutic process.[25] Even Robyn Dawes—a secular therapist with a preference for a more scientific approach to therapy—summarizes a large body of research by saying, "Much of the success of verbal therapy is influenced by the personal qualities of therapists and how they relate to clients."[26] People who feel trust and some level of basic acceptance are more willing to explore issues and are less resistant to change. "Client-centered" therapy approaches that grew out of humanistic psychology, along with many other approaches—both secular and Christian— have emphasized these aspects of therapy. Behavioral approaches (e.g., behavior modification or behavior analysis) have genuine strengths in other ways and may be the preferred technique in some instances, but they are not as strong in this regard. Of course, this acceptance and care also need to be balanced with accountability—more on this in a moment.

    These qualities of therapy also reflect basic values that are consistent with our being made in the image of God and possessing value simply because God relates to us. We also receive this form of unconditional acceptance from God—through the blood of Christ—so this mirrors what God does for those who seek him.[27] This does not imply that the therapist and client need to be long-term friends, but it does imply that relationship building within the therapy setting should be part of the therapeutic process. While some types of therapies have increasingly stressed these values, more should be done to stress relationship building outside of the therapy session.

    2. Are present and future oriented, rather than focused on the past. The emphasis on past experience may foster a sense of fatalism or determinism because it may be overly focused on being "driven by the past." (See chap. 14 for a full discussion of this issue.) While past experiences and patterns of behavior certainly shape present behavior, and some exploration of past experiences and tendencies is an important part of the initial interview, the primary focus should be on the goals for therapy and how these goals are going to be accomplished. This approach has significant research support. As Martin Seligman and colleagues describe in their summary of this research, one specific example

25. Norcross and Lambert, "Psychotherapy Relationships," 4.

26. Dawes, *House of Cards*, 75.

27. Rom. 5:8: "But God demonstrates his own love for us in this: While we were still sinners, Christ died for us."

of a therapy type utilizing this forward-looking or "intentional" approach was very effective in promoting better self-regulation of emotions and behaviors, and achieved greater success in accomplishing goals.[28] As a result of this type of research, many cognitive-behaviorally oriented therapy approaches have begun to utilize this approach to a greater degree.

Emphasizing future action also seems consistent with being *responsible* limited agents (Theme 4) because it involves consciously considering future alternatives to the present situation and setting priorities based on what is valuable and meaningful to the client.

3. Stress responsibility and accountability. Stressing responsibility and accountability should go together with "unconditional positive regard." One emphasis does not negate the other; parents discipline their children as they also show them unconditional love and acceptance. Accepting a person does not imply that one must approve of their behavior. Stressing accountability is consistent with the idea that we are broken and in need of redemption (Theme 2) and that we are responsible limited agents (Theme 4). As Yarhouse and colleagues suggest:

> Throughout Scripture and Christian theology, people are considered responsible for what they do with what they have been given. These are concepts that have been all but lost in contemporary discussions about psychopathology. . . . In addition to increased awareness of personal responsibility, an explanatory framework that takes sin seriously will increase our awareness of corporate responsibility. Not only does the sin affect individual choices and their consequences . . . , but sin pervades the very structures of society.[29]

Clearly, therapists should recognize and explore the structural and physical evil that exists and that has influenced the present behavior, as many behaviors and thoughts are not at all controllable by the individual seeking therapy. We cannot ignore, however, the reality that individuals—if left to their own devices—will not always select the best action. Many therapists who favor a cognitive-behavioral, client-centered therapy (humanistic), along with some other approaches, do stress this accountability to some degree. However, there is an essential flaw in any approach that assumes that if we look deep within ourselves and shed the constraints of the past, we will automatically choose adaptive, wise, or moral action. The influence of our sinful tendencies means that even what appears to us to be moral, reasonable, or correct can be very self-centered, damaging, or evil.

28. Seligman et al., "Navigating," 135.
29. Yarhouse, Butman, and McRay, *Modern Psychopathologies*, 97.

This emphasis does not imply that therapists need to dictate actions or solutions to clients, any more than clients should dictate entirely what they should do. Recall that the definition of psychotherapy we provided earlier emphasized that therapy should move in directions that the *"participants deem desirable."* Therefore, therapy should be a partnership or joint effort between therapist and client of setting goals consistent with fundamental moral values and exploring useful alternatives. Human self-centered tendencies are reduced when we see things from the perspective of others.

4. Appreciate biological constraints and social context. Every person is not the same (see chaps. 10 and 14). Some people struggle with inborn temperaments or tendencies that are difficult or perhaps impossible to manage individually. A person may have also experienced extremely difficult social or economic environments that make healthy adjustments very difficult. Being embodied individuals (Theme 3) and being responsible *limited* agents (Theme 4) mean that many of the issues a person faces are outside of their direct control. Therapists should be willing to work with psychiatrists, other medical professionals, and social workers in prescribing medication, changing diets or physical habits, or providing other social and environmental changes. As Yarhouse and colleagues have noted:

> We do not believe God will be found in Prozac, or Prozac in God. But when medication is used judiciously and responsibly, it can make all the difference in the world for those who suffer needlessly and those who try to help them. Medication is often a necessary (but not always sufficient) prerequisite for healing and change with the problems of anxiety.[30]

The same principles apply to dealing with the limitations of the physical and social environment that are very evident in other conditions. For example, drug addiction is a good illustration of both the embodied nature of some problems (e.g., continued drug use may cause significant changes in neurological function) and importance of the environment. Successfully treating the physical elements of drug addiction but not considering the social environment surrounding the person may result in a return to drug use once the person returns to their normal situation. Ongoing efforts should be in place to either improve the environment or reduce its negative impact. These constraints do not eliminate responsibility and accountability, but clients should only be held accountable for how they *respond* to their biological or social constraints.

30. Ibid., 139–40.

5. *Are action oriented and (slightly) less insight oriented.* While self-insight is effectively used in cognitive-behavioral, humanistic (client-centered), psychodynamic, and many other types of therapies, an overemphasis on self-insight focuses too much attention on the self. As we discussed in the chapter on personality, Vitz argues convincingly that we should reduce focus on self, not increase it. He states, "This fundamental tendency based on pride creates the pervasive human expression of narcissism, the choice of self-love over love of God and others."[31]

Action-oriented therapies also take advantage of our embodied nature, because (as described in chaps. 3 and 4) engaging in physical action can lead to greater change. Developing positive thoughts and behaviors requires practice, training, and external support. (Anyone taking extensive music training or lessons understands this principle from experience.) Action-oriented therapies are also more present and future oriented (see technique number 2).

6. *Work on establishing purpose and meaningful goals.* As psychologist Martin Seligman and colleagues have suggested, "There is growing evidence that a strong sense of meaning and purpose—which we regard as a paradigm instance of robust future orientation—is highly protective against psychopathology." They go on to describe one study showing that soldiers who had strongly disagreed with the statement "my life has meaning" were much more likely to commit suicide. They also describe therapeutic techniques that focus on "sustainable personal projects" that involve setting goals and contemplating what the client would like to "become or be."[32]

We believe establishing purpose and meaning is consistent with our meaning seeking tendency (Theme 5). But what really distinguishes an approach that is consistent with biblical themes is not only the *process* of setting goals but *which* goals are set. This issue is perhaps far more important than any specific technique in distinguishing a uniquely Christian approach to therapy. There is often little debate among therapists (Christian or secular) that a goal of the therapy is to reduce symptoms of severe depression, or persistent anger, or marital conflict. But what is being put in its place? Here is where a person's worldview and priorities become most evident. Some therapists strive for self-understanding or greater self-esteem. Some encourage greater independence, or taking greater control of one's life, or perhaps pleasing oneself. But are these goals truly consistent with a biblical view? Christian psychologists Mark

31. Vitz, "Christian Theory of Personality," 206.
32. Seligman et al., "Navigating," 135.

Cosgrove and James Mallory outline what they feel are the qualities that define true "mental health."[33] These include:

a. purpose and meaning in life;
b. a realistic self-worth;
c. capacity for self-sacrificing love, empathy, and sensitivity;
d. an accurate view of reality;
e. strong internal standards;
f. the ability to accept what is unchangeable;
g. a sense of freedom to enjoy oneself; and
h. physical, emotional, and intellectual needs in balance.

Christian counselor W. C. McAllister has a similar list describing our basic needs, but he also includes forgiveness, community, and hope.[34] What is striking about these lists is how much the focus is away from the self and toward others. Forgiveness, love, community, and empathy all supersede self-improvement and self-focus.

There are certainly many more issues about psychotherapy that are beyond the scope of this chapter and this book, but we hope that presenting the range and value of various helping relationships, along with contours for professional therapy that are consistent with a biblical view of persons, provides a useful "consumers guide" to helping. We all need help in various ways from time to time, so may we all be open to providing support to others and to accepting the help that God may send our way.

DISCUSSION QUESTIONS

1. If you or someone you know well has experienced psychotherapy, what was their experience like—positive, helpful, challenging, or negative?

2. If you answered yes to question 1 and you are familiar with the way the therapy was conducted, do you think it matched up with the list of qualities that may define Christian psychotherapy? If yes, in what ways? If no, how was it different?

3. Think about various attitudes that Christians have expressed about therapy (that were described early in this chapter). Where

33. See Cosgrove and Mallory, *Mental Health*.
34. McAllister, "Christian Counseling and Human Needs," 55.

would you, your family, or your community (i.e., church, home, school, etc.) fit on that list of attitudes?

4. Some Christians have said that you "only need the Bible" when it comes to tackling personal problems. According to the authors, what are some possible counterarguments for that statement?

5. Are you someone whom others would describe as "a good listener" with whom others share their problems, or can you think of others described in that way? In what ways is that type of support helpful? In what ways is it better, worse, or just different than professional psychotherapy?

6. In being supportive of others, where would difficulties arise in trying to balance accountability and responsibility with relationality, support and care, and empathy?

References

Allport, Gordon G. *Patterns and Growth in Personality*. New York: Holt, Rinehart and Winston, 1961.

American Psychiatric Association. *Diagnostic and Statistical Manual of Mental Disorders: DSM-V*. 5th ed., text revision. Arlington, VA: American Psychiatric Association, 2013.

American Psychological Association, "Recognition of Psychotherapy Effectiveness," http://www.apa.org/about/policy/resolution-psychotherapy.aspx, accessed February 6, 2014.

Anonymous, http://www.mentalhealthamerica.net/reallives/index.cfm/2009/9/4/Learning-to-trust-others-and-forgive-himself, accessed August 30, 2013.

Ashforth, Blake E., and Fred Mael. "Social Identity Theory and the Organization." *Academy of Management Review* 14, no. 1 (1989): 20–39.

Augustine. *Confessions*.

Baer, John, James C. Kaufman, and Roy F. Baumeister, eds. *Are We Free? Psychology and Free Will*. New York: Oxford, 2008.

Bakke, O. M. *When Children Became People: The Birth of Childhood in Early Christianity*. Translated by Brian McNeil. Minneapolis: Fortress Press, 2005.

Bandura, Albert, Dorthea Ross, and Sheila A. Ross. "Transmission of Aggression through Imitation of Aggressive Models." *Journal of Abnormal and Social Psychology* 63 (1961): 575–82.

Bargh, John A. "Free Will is Un-Natural." In *Are We Free?*, edited by John Baer, James C. Kaufman, and Roy F. Baumeister, 128–54. New York: Oxford University Press, 2008.

Bargh, John A., and Tanya L. Chartrand. "The Unbearable Automaticity of Being." *American Psychologist* 54 (July 1999): 462–79.

Barrett, Justin L. *Born Believers: The Science of Children's Religious Belief*. New York: Free Press, 2012.

———. "Cognitive Science of Religion: What Is It and Why Is It?" *Religion Compass* 1, no. 6 (November 2007), 768–86.

———. *Cognitive Science, Religion, and Theology: From Human Minds to Divine Minds*. West Conshohocken, PA: Templeton Press, 2011.

Barry, Dave. *Dave Barry's Bad Habits: A 100% Fact-Free Book*. New York: Henry Holt and Company, 1993.

———. "Dave Barry Quotes." Goodquotes.com. http://www.goodquotes.com/quote/dave-barry/i-would-not-know-how-i-am-supposed-to, accessed August 1, 2013.

Bartlett, Frederic C. *Remembering*. Cambridge: Cambridge University Press, 1932.

Bastardi, Anthony, Eric L. Uhlmann, and Lee Ross. "Wishful Thinking: Belief, Desire, and the Motivated Evaluation of Scientific

Evidence." *Psychological Science* 22 (2011): 731–32. doi:10.1177/09567976711406447.

Batson, C. Daniel, and Elizabeth R. Thompson. "Why Don't Moral People Act Morally? Motivational Considerations." *Current Directions in Psychological Science* 10, no. 2 (2001): 54–57.

Baumeister, Roy F. *The Cultural Animal: Human Nature, Meaning, and Social Life.* New York: Oxford University Press, 2005.

———. "Free Will in Scientific Psychology." *Perspectives on Psychological Science* 3 (2008): 14–19.

Baumeister, Roy F., Ellen Bratslavsky, Mark Muraven, and Dianne M. Tice. "Ego Depletion: Is the Active Self a Limited Resource?" *Journal of Personality and Social Psychology* 74 (1998): 1252–65.

Baumeister, Roy F., and Mark R. Leary. "The Need to Belong: Desire for Interpersonal Attachments as a Fundamental Human Motivation." *Psychological Bulletin* 117, no. 3 (1995): 497–529.

Benson, Herbert, et al. "Study of the Therapeutic Effects of Intercessory Prayer (STEP) in Cardiac Bypass Patients: A Multicenter Randomized Trial of Uncertainty and Certainty of Receiving Intercessory Prayer." *American Heart Journal* 151, no. 4 (2006): 934–42.

Bering, Jesse. *The Belief Instinct.* New York: Norton, 2011.

Bloom, Harold. *The American Religion: The Emergence of the Post-Christian Nation.* New York: Simon & Schuster, 1992.

Bloom, Paul. *Descartes' Baby: How the Science of Child Development Explains What Makes Us Human.* New York: Basic Books, 2004.

———. "Is God an Accident?" *Atlantic* 296, no. 3 (2005): 105–12.

———. "Religion Is Natural." *Developmental Science* 10 (2004): 147–51.

Bodies Revealed. Premier Exhibitions. http://www.bodiesrevealed.com/, accessed August 1, 2013.

Bolt, Martin. *Pursuing Human Strengths: A Positive Psychology Guide.* New York: Worth Publishers, 2004.

Bolt, Martin, and David G. Myers. *The Human Connection: How People Change People.* Downers Grove, IL: InterVarsity, 1984.

Bonhoeffer, Dietrich. *Life Together: The Classic Exploration of Christian Community.* San Francisco: HarperOne, 1978.

Bower, Gordon H., Michael C. Clark, Alan M. Lesgold, and David Winzenz. "Hierarchical Retrieval Schemes in Recall of Categorical Word Lists." *Journal of Verbal Learning and Verbal Behavior* 8 (1969): 323–43.

Bowlby, John. *Attachment and Loss.* Vol. 1, *Attachment.* New York: Basic Books, 1969.

———. "Attachment and Loss: Retrospect and Prospect." *American Journal of Orthopsychiatry* 52, no. 4 (1982): 664–78.

Boyle, Gregory. *Tattoos on the Heart: The Power of Boundless Compassion.* New York: Free Press, 2010.

Bradley, Raymond Trevor. "Values, Agency, and the Theory of Quantum Vacuum Interaction." In *Brain and Values: Is a Biological Science of Values Possible?*, edited by Karl H. Pribram, 471–504. Mahwah, NJ: Erlbaum, 1998.

Brakke, David. *The Gnostics: Myth, Ritual, and Diversity in Early Christianity.* Cambridge: Harvard University Press, 2010.

Brown, Warren S. "Cognitive Contributions to Soul." In *Whatever Happened to the Soul? Scientific and Theological Portraits of Human Nature*, edited by Warren S. Brown, Nancey Murphy, and H. Newton Malony, 99–125. Minneapolis: Fortress Press, 1998.

———. "Conclusion: Reconciling Scientific and Biblical Portraits of Human Nature." In *Whatever Happened to the Soul? Scientific and Theological Portraits of Human Nature*, edited by Warren S. Brown, Nancey Murphy, and N. Newton Malony, 213–22. Minneapolis: Fortress Press, 1998.

Brown, Warren S., Nancey Murphy, and H. Newton Malony, eds. *Whatever Happened to the Soul? Scientific and Theological Portraits of Human Nature.* Minneapolis: Fortress Press, 1998.

Buehlman, Kim T., John Gottman, and Lynn F. Katz. "How a Couple Views Their Past Predicts Their Future: Predicting Divorce from an Oral History Interview." *Journal of Family Psychology* 5 (1992): 295–318. doi:10.1037/0893-3200.5.3–4.295.

Bufford, Rodger K. *The Human Reflex: Behavioral Psychology in Biblical Perspective.* San Francisco: Harper & Row, 1981.

Burke, Thomas J., ed. *Man and Mind: A Christian Theory of Personality*. Hillsdale, MI: Hillsdale College Press, 1987.

Burr, David. "Vision: In the Blink of an Eye." *Current Biology* 15 (2005): 554–56.

Bussema, Ken. "Perspectives on Developmental Psychology." *Pro Rege* 22 (September 1993): 1–8.

Cacioppo, John T., Richard E. Petty, Mary E. Losch, and Hai Sook Kim. "Electromyographic Activity over Facial Muscle Regions Can Differentiate the Valence and Intensity of Affective Reactions." *Journal of Personality and Social Psychology* 50 (1986): 260–68. doi:10.1037/0022–3514.50.2.260.

Calvin, John. *Commentaries on the First Book of Moses, Called Genesis*. Translated from the original Latin and compared with the French edition by John King. Grand Rapids: Eerdmans, 1948.

Carter, John D., and Bruce Narramore. *The Integration of Psychology and Theology: An Introduction*. Grand Rapids: Zondervan, 1979.

Catholic Church. *Catechism of the Catholic Church*. 2nd ed. Vatican City: Libreria Editrice Vaticana, 2000.

———. *Reconciliation and Penance*. Washington, DC: Office of Publishing and Promotion Services, United States Catholic Conference, 1984.

Christensen, Larry B., Burke R. Johnson, and Lisa A. Turner. *Research Methods, Design, and Analysis*. 11th ed. Boston: Allyn & Bacon, 2011.

Ciccarelli, Saundra K., and J. Noland White. *Psychology: An Exploration*. 2nd ed. Boston: Pearson Education, 2013.

Cohen, Sheldon, and Thomas A. Wills. "Stress, Social Support, and the Buffering Hypothesis." *Psychological Bulletin* 98, no. 2 (1985): 310.

Conway, Martin A. "Memory and the Self." *Journal of Memory and Language* 53 (2005): 594–628.

Cooper, John W. "The Body-Soul Question." *Pro Rege* 20 (1991): 1–12.

———. *Body, Soul, and Life Everlasting*. Grand Rapids: Eerdmans, 1998.

Cosgrove, Mark P. *The Essence of Human Nature*. Grand Rapids: Zondervan, 1977.

Cosgrove, Mark P., and James D. Mallory. *Mental Health: A Christian Approach*. Grand Rapids: Zondervan, 1977.

Crick, Francis. *The Astonishing Hypothesis: The Scientific Search for the Soul*. New York: Touchstone, 1994.

Crowley, Michael J., Jia Wu, Erika R. McCarty, Daryn H. David, Christopher A. Bailey, and Linda C. Mayes. "Exclusion and Microrejection: Event-Related Potential Response Predicts Mitigated Distress." *Neuroreport* 20, no. 17 (2009): 1518–22.

Damasio, Antonio R. *Descartes' Error: Emotion, Reason, and the Human Brain*. New York: Putnam's Sons, 1994.

———. *The Feeling of What Happens: Body and Emotions in the Making of Consciousness*. Orlando, FL: Harcourt, 1999.

Dawes, Robyn M. *House of Cards: Psychology and Psychotherapy Built on Myth*. New York: Free Press, 1994.

Dawson, Michael E., and Paul Reardon. "Effects of Facilitory and Inhibitory Sets on GSR Conditioning and Extinction." *Journal of Experimental Psychology* 82, no. 3 (1969): 462.

Dement, William C. *The Promise of Sleep*. New York: Delacorte Press, 1999.

Deregowski, Jan B. "Pictorial Perception and Culture." *Scientific American* 227 (1972): 82–88.

Derryberry, Douglas, and Mary K. Rothbart. "Arousal, Affect, and Attention as Components of Temperament." *Journal of Personality and Social Psychology* 55 (1988): 958–66.

Dijksterhuis, Ap, and Henk Aarts. "Goals, Attention and (Un)Consciousness." *Annual Review of Psychology* 61 (2010): 467–90.

Dovidio, John F., Kerry Kawakami, Craig Johnson, Brenda Johnson, and Adaiah Howard. "On the Nature of Prejudice: Automatic and Controlled Processes." *Journal of Experimental Social Psychology* 33 (1997): 510–40.

Durmer, Jeffrey S., and David F. Dinges. "Neurocognitive Consequences of Sleep Deprivation." *Seminars in Neurology* 25 (2005): 117–29.

Eagley, Alice H., and Shelly Chaiken. "Attitude Structure and Function." In *The Handbook of Social Psychology*. 4th ed. 2 vols. Edited by Daniel T. Gilbert, Susan T. Fiske, and Gardner Lindzey, 1:269–322. Boston: McGraw-Hill, 1988.

Eisenberg, Daniel, Marilyn F. Downs, Ezra Golberstein, and Kara Zivin. "Stigma and Help Seeking for Mental Health among College Students." *Medical Care Research and Review* 66, no. 5 (2009): 522–41.

Erikson, Erik. *Identity: Youth and Crisis.* New York: Norton, 1968.

———. "Reflections on the Last Stage—And the First." *Psychoanalytic Study of the Child* 39 (1984): 155–65.

Evans, C. Stephen. "The Concept of the Self as the Key to Integration." *Journal of Psychology and Christianity* 3 (1984): 4–11.

———. "Separable Souls: Dualism Selfhood, and the Possibility of Life after Death." *Christian Scholar's Review* 34:3 (2005): 327–40.

Evans, Jonathan St. B. T., and Keith E. Stanovich. "Dual-Process Theories of Higher Cognition: Advancing the Debate." *Perspectives on Psychological Science* 8, no. 3 (May 2013): 223–41.

Eysenck, Hans Jurgen. *The Effects of Psychotherapy.* New York: International Science Press, 1966.

Farber, Seth. *Unholy Madness: The Church's Surrender to Psychiatry.* Downers Grove, IL: InterVarsity, 1999.

Farnsworth, Kirk E. *Whole-Hearted Integration: Harmonizing Psychology and Christianity through Word and Deed.* Grand Rapids: Baker, 1985.

Faw, Harold. *Sharing Our Stories: Understanding Memory and Building Faith.* Belleville, ON: Essence Publishing, 2007.

Fazio, Russell H. "Multiple Processes by which Attitudes Guide Behavior: The MODE Model as an Integrative Framework." In *Advances in Experimental Social Psychology,* vol. 23, edited by M. P. Zanna, 75–109. San Diego: Academic Press, 1990.

———. "On the Automatic Activation of Associated Evaluations: An Overview." *Cognition and Emotion* 15 (2001): 115–41.

———. "Attitudes as Object Evaluations of Varying Strength." *Social Cognition* 25, no. 5 (2007): 603–37.

Fazio, Russell H., David M. Sanbonmatsu, Martha C. Powell, and Frank R. Kardes. "On the Automatic Activation of Attitudes." *Journal of Personality and Social Psychology* 50 (1986): 229–38.

Festinger, Leon. *A Theory of Cognitive Dissonance.* Stanford, CA: Stanford University Press, 1957.

Forgas, Joseph P. "Don't Worry, Be Sad! On the Cognitive, Motivational, and Interpersonal Benefits of Negative Mood." *Current Directions in Psychological Science* 22 (2013): 225–32.

Foster, Richard J. *Celebration of Discipline.* Rev. ed. San Francisco: Harper & Row, 1988.

Fowler, James W. *Becoming Adult, Becoming Christian.* Rev. ed. San Francisco: Jossey-Bass, 2000.

Freud, Sigmund. *The Complete Introductory Lectures on Psychoanalysis.* Translated and edited by James Strachey. New York: Norton, 1966.

Gazzaniga, Michael S. *Who's in Charge? Free Will and the Science of the Brain.* New York: HarperCollins, 2011.

Gelman, Susan A. *The Essential Child: Origins of Essentialism in Everyday Thought.* Oxford: Oxford University Press, 2003.

Gilbert, Daniel. *Stumbling on Happiness.* New York: Alfred A. Knopf, 2006.

Giles, K. *Understanding the Christian Faith.* Canberra: Acorn Press, 1982.

Gilovich, Thomas, Dacher Keltner, Serena Chen, and Richard E. Nisbett. *Social Psychology.* 3rd ed. New York: Norton. 2013.

Gollwitzer, Peter M. "Implementation Intentions: Strong Effects of Simple Plans." *American Psychologist* 54 (1999): 493–503.

Gopnik, Alison. *The Philosophical Baby.* New York: Farrar, Strauss and Giroux, 2009.

Gopnik, Alison, Andrew N. Meltzoff, and Patricia K. Kuhl. *The Scientist in the Crib.* New York: William Morrow and Company, 1999.

Gottman, John M., and Robert W. Levenson. "The Timing of Divorce: Predicting When a Couple Will Divorce over a 14-year Period." *Journal of Marriage and Family* 62 (2000): 737–45. doi:10.1111/j.1741–3737 .2000.00737.x.

Graesser, Arthur C., Murray Singer, and Tom Trabasso. "Constructing Inferences during Narrative Text Comprehension." *Psychological Review* 101 (1994): 371–95.

Grandin, Temple, and Margaret Scariano. *Emergence: Labeled Autistic*. Novato, CA: Arena Press, 1986.

Greene-McCreight, Kathryn. *Darkness Is My Only Companion: A Christian Response to Mental Illness*. Grand Rapids: Brazos, 2006.

Hall, E. L. "What Are Bodies For? An Integrative Examination of Embodiment." *Christian Scholar's Review* 39, no. 2 (2010): 165.

Hamlin, J. Kiley. "Moral Judgment and Action in Preverbal Infants and Toddlers: Evidence for an Innate Moral Core." *Current Directions in Psychological Science* 22, no. 3 (2013): 186–93.

Hampson, Sarah E. "Mechanisms by Which Childhood Personality Traits Influence Adult Well-Being." *Current Directions in Psychological Science* 17, no. 4 (2008): 264–68.

Harlow, Harry F., and Robert R. Zimmerman. "Affectional Responses in the Infant Monkey." *Science* 130 (1959): 421–32.

Harrison, Yvonne, and James A. Horne. "The Impact of Sleep Deprivation on Decision Making: A Review." *Journal of Experimental Psychology: Applied* 6 (2000): 236–49.

Hastorf, Albert H., and Hadley Cantril. "They Saw a Game: A Case Study." *The Journal of Abnormal and Social Psychology* 49, no. 1 (1954): 129.

Hefner, Philip. "Imago Dei: The Possibility and Necessity of the Human Person." In *The Human Person in Science and Theology*, edited by N. H. Gregersen, W. B. Drees, and U. Görman, 73–94. Grand Rapids: Eerdmans, 2000.

Hennessey, Beth A., and Theresa M. Amabile. "Creativity." *Annual Review of Psychology* 61 (2010): 569–98.

Hodges, Bert E. "Perception, Relativity, and Knowing and Doing the Truth." In *Psychology and the Christian Faith: An Introductory Reader*, edited by Stanton L. Jones, 51–77. Grand Rapids: Baker, 1986.

Hoekema, Anthony A. *Created in God's Image*. Grand Rapids: Eerdmans, 1986.

Hofman, Wilhelm, and Lotte Van Dillen. "Desire: The New Hot Spot in Self-Control Research." *Current Directions in Psychological Science* 21, no. 5 (2012): 317–22.

Hofman, Wilhelm, Kathleen D. Vohs, and Roy F. Baumeister. "What People Desire,

Feel Conflicted About, and Try to Resist in Everyday Life." *Psychological Science* 23, no. 6 (June 2012): 582–88.

Holmes, Arthur. *All Truth Is God's Truth*. Grand Rapids: Eerdmans, 1977.

Hong, David S., Signe Bray, Brian W. Haas, Fumiko Hoeft, and Allan L. Reiss. "Aberrant Neurocognitive Processing of Fear in Young Girls with Turner Syndrome." *Social Cognitive and Affective Neuroscience*, November 21, 2012, http://scan.oxfordjournals.org/content/early/2013/05/29/scan.nss133.full.

Howell, Russell, and James Bradley. *Mathematics through the Eyes of Faith*. New York: HarperOne, 2012.

Hull, Jay G. "A Self-Awareness Model of the Causes and Effects of Alcohol Consumption." *Journal of Abnormal Psychology* 90, no. 6 (1981): 586–600.

Hulse, Stewart H., H. Fowler, and W. K. Honig. *Cognitive Processes in Animal Behavior*. Hillsdale, NJ: Erlbaum, 1978.

Hyman, Stephen F., and Robert C. Malenka. "Addiction and the Brain: The Neurobiology of Compulsion and Its Persistence." *Nature Reviews Neuroscience* 2, no. 10 (2001): 695–703.

Idleman, Kyle. *Gods at War: Defeating the Idols That Battle for Your Heart*. Grand Rapids: Zondervan, 2013.

Itti, Laurent, and Christof Koch. "Computational Modelling of Visual Attention." *Nature Reviews Neuroscience* 2, no. 3 (2001): 194–203.

James, William. *Psychology*. New York: Henry Holt, 1890.

Jeeves, Malcolm A. *Human Nature at the Millennium: Reflections on the Integration of Psychology and Christianity*. Grand Rapids: Baker, 1997.

Jenny, Timothy P. "Sanctification." In *Eerdmans Dictionary of the Bible*, edited by David Noel Freedman, Allen C. Myers, and Astrid B. Beck, 1165–66. Grand Rapids: Eerdmans, 2000.

Johnson, Eric L., ed. *Psychology and Christianity: Five Views*. Downers Grove, IL: InterVarsity, 2010.

Jones, Stanton L. "A Constructive Relationship for Religion with the Science and Profession of Psychology: Perhaps the Boldest

Model Yet." *American Psychologist* 49, no. 3 (1994): 184-99.

Kahneman, Daniel. *Thinking, Fast and Slow.* New York: Farrar, Straus and Giroux, 2011.

Kandel, Eric R., Irving Kupfermann, and Susan Iverson. "Learning and Memory." In *Principles of Neural Science*, edited by Eric R. Kandel, James H. Schwartz, and Thomas M. Jessel, 1227–46. New York: McGraw-Hill, 2000.

Kanwisher, Nancy, and Paul Downing. "Separating the Wheat from the Chaff." *Science* 282 (1998): 57–58.

Kaufman, Joan, and Edward Zigler. "The Intergenerational Transmission of Abuse Is Overstated." In *Current Controversies on Family Violence*, edited by Richard J. Gelles and Donileen R. Loseke, 209–21. Thousand Oaks, CA: Sage Publications, 1993.

Kawakami, Kerry, John F. Dovidio, Jasper Moll, Sander Hermsen, and Abby Russin. "Just Say No (to Stereotyping): Effects of Training in the Negation of Stereotypic Associations on Stereotype Activation." *Journal of Personality and Social Psychology* 78, no. 5 (2000): 871–88.

Kaye, Kenneth. *The Mental and Social Life of Babies.* Chicago: University of Chicago Press, 1982.

Keleman, Deborah. "Are Children 'Intuitive Theists'? Reasoning about Purpose and Design in Nature." *Psychological Science* 15 (2004): 295–301.

Kelman, Herbert C. "Attitudes Are Alive and Well and Gainfully Employed in the Sphere of Action." *American Psychologist* 29, no. 5 (1974): 310–24.

Kerkhoff, G. A. "Inter-Individual Differences in the Human Circadian System: A Review." *Biological Psychology* 20 (1985): 83–112.

Kihlstrom, John F. "Consciousness and Me-ness." In *Scientific Approaches to Consciousness*, edited by Jonathan D. Cohen and Jonathan W. Schooler, 451–68. Mahwah, NJ: Erlbaum, 1997.

Kirkpatrick, Lee A. "God as a Substitute Attachment Figure: A Longitudinal Study of Adult Attachment Style and Religious Change in College Students." *Personality and Social Psychology Bulletin* 24 (1998): 961–73.

Kohlberg, Lawrence. "Stage and Sequence: The Cognitive-Developmental Approach to Socialization." In *Handbook of Socialization Theory and Research*, edited by David A. Goslin, 347–480. Chicago: Rand McNally, 1969.

Kroger, Jane. *Identity Development: Adolescence through Adulthood.* 2nd ed. Thousand Oaks, CA: Sage Publications, 2007.

Kuhl, Patricia K. "Language, Mind, and Brain. Experience Alters Perception." In *The New Cognitive Neurosciences*, edited by Michael S. Gazzaniga, 99–115. Cambridge: MIT Press, 2000.

Kuhn, Thomas S. *The Structure of Scientific Revolutions.* Chicago: University of Chicago Press, 1962.

Kuyper, Abraham. *The Work of the Holy Spirit.* Translated by Henri de Vries. New York: Funk & Wagnalls, 1900.

La Greca, Annette M., and Nadja Lopez. "Social Anxiety among Adolescents: Linkages with Peer Relations and Friendships." *Journal of Abnormal Child Psychology* 26, no. 2 (1998): 83–94.

Laureys, Steven. "Eyes Open, Brain Shut." *Scientific American* 4 (2007): 32–37.

Lavie, Nilli. "Distracted and Confused? Selective Attention under Load." *Trends in Cognitive Sciences* 9 (2005): 75–82.

L'Engle, Madeleine. *And It Was Good.* Wheaton: Harold Shaw Publishers, 1983.

Lepper, Mark R., David Greene, and Richard E. Nisbett. "Undermining Children's Intrinsic Interest with Extrinsic Reward: A Test of the 'Overjustification' Hypothesis." *Journal of Personality and Social Psychology* 28, no. 1 (1973): 129–37.

Leslie, Alan M., and Stephanie Keeble. "Do Six-Month-Old Infants Perceive Causality?" *Cognition* 25 (1987): 265–88.

Lett, Heather S., James A. Blumenthal, Michael A. Babyak, Timothy J. Strauman, Clive Robins, and Andrew Sherwood. "Social Support and Coronary Heart Disease: Epidemiologic Evidence and Implications for Treatment." *Psychosomatic Medicine* 67, no. 6 (2005): 869–78.

Lewis, C. S. *Mere Christianity.* New York: Macmillan, 1952.

Libet, Benjamin. "Unconscious Cerebral Initiative and the Role of Conscious Will in Voluntary Action." *Behavioral and Brain Sciences* 8 (1985): 529–66.

Libet, Benjamin, Curtis A. Gleason, Elwood W. Wright, and Dennis K. Pearl. "Time of Conscious Intention to Act in Relation to Onset of Cerebral Activation (Readiness-Potential)." *Brain* 106 (1983): 623–42.

Lindskoog, Donald. *The Idea of Psychology: Reclaiming the Discipline's Identity.* Washington, DC: Howard University Press, 1998.

Locke, John. *Some Thoughts concerning Education.* Edited by R. H. Quick. 1690. Reprint, Cambridge: Cambridge University Press, 1892.

Loftus, Elizabeth F., and G. R. Loftus. "On the Permanence of Stored Information in the Human Brain." *American Psychologist* 35 (1980): 409–20.

MacKay, D. M. *Behind the Eye.* Oxford: Blackwell, 1991.

MacLeod, Colin M. "Half a Century of Research on the Stroop Effect: An Integrative Review." *Psychological Bulletin* 109 (1991): 163–203.

Madole, Kelly L., and Lisa M. Oakes. "Making Sense of Infant Categorization: Stable Processes and Changing Representations." *Developmental Review* 19 (1999): 263–96.

Markman, Arthur B., and Eric Dietrich. "Extending the Classical View of Representation." *TRENDS in Cognitive Neuroscience* 4 (2000): 470–75. doi:10.1016/S1364-6613(00)01559-X.

Martin, Rod A. *The Psychology of Humor: An Integrative Approach.* London: Elsevier Academic Press, 2006.

Maslow, Abraham H. *Motivation and Personality.* 2nd ed. New York: Harper & Row, 1970.

Mason, Mason F., Michael I. Norton, John D. Van Horn, Daniel M. Wegner, Scott T. Grafton, and Neil C. Macrae. "Wandering Minds: The Default Network and Stimulus-Independent Thought." *Science* 315 (2007): 393–95.

McAllister, Edward W. C. "Christian Counseling and Human Needs." In *Christian Counseling and Psychotherapy*, edited by David G. Benner, 53–56. Grand Rapids: Baker, 1987.

McDonagh, John. "Working through Resistance by Prayer and the Gift of Knowledge." In *Christian Counseling and Psychotherapy*, edited by David G. Benner, 200–203. Grand Rapids: Baker, 1987.

McLean, Kate C. "Late Adolescent Identity Development: Narrative Meaning Making and Memory Telling." *Developmental Psychology* 41, no. 4 (2004): 683–91.

McLemore, Clinton W., and David W. Brokaw. "Psychotherapy as a Spiritual Enterprise." In *Psychology and the Christian Faith*, edited by Stanton L. Jones, 178–95. Grand Rapids: Baker, 1986.

McNamara, Timothy P. *Semantic Priming: Perspectives from Memory and Word Recognition.* New York: Psychology Press, 2005.

Metaxas, Eric. *Bonhoeffer: Pastor, Martyr, Prophet, Spy.* Nashville: Thomas Nelson, 2010.

Middleton, J. Richard. *The Liberating Image: The Imago Dei in Genesis 1.* Grand Rapids: Brazos, 2005.

Milgram, Stanley. "Behavioral Study of Obedience." *Journal of Abnormal and Social Psychology* 67, no. 4 (1963): 371–78.

Miller, William R., and Harold D. Delaney, eds. *Judeo-Christian Perspectives on Psychology: Human Nature, Motivation, and Change.* Washington, DC: American Psychological Association, 2005.

Moffitt, Terrie E., Avshalom Caspi, and Michael Rutter. "Measured Gene-Environment Interactions in Psychopathology Concepts, Research Strategies, and Implications for Research, Intervention, and Public Understanding of Genetics." *Perspectives on Psychological Science* 1, no. 1 (2006): 5–27.

Mojtabai, Ramin. "Americans' Attitudes toward Mental Health Treatment Seeking: 1990–2003." *Psychiatric Services* 58, no. 5 (2007): 642–51.

Monahan, Jennifer L., Sheila T. Murphy, and Robert B. Zajonc. "Subliminal Mere Exposure: Specific, General, and Diffuse Effects." *Psychological Science* 11 (2000): 462–66.

Moon, Christine, Robin Panneton Cooper, and William P. Fifer. "Two-Day-Olds Prefer Their Native Language." *Infant Behavior and Development* 16 (1993): 495–500.

Morea, Peter. *In Search of Personality.* London: SCM Press, 1997.

Moxley, Roy A. "Skinner: From Determinism to Random Variation." *Behavior and Philosophy* 25, no. 1 (1997): 3–28.

Muraven, Mark, and Roy F. Baumeister. "Self-Regulation and Depletion of Limited Resources: Does Self-Control Resemble a

Muscle?" *Psychological Bulletin* 126 (2000): 247–59.

Muraven, Mark, Roy F. Baumeister, and Diane M. Tice. "Longitudinal Improvement of Self-Regulation through Practice: Building Self-Control Strength through Repeated Exercise." *Journal of Social Psychology* 139 (1999): 446–57.

Myers, David G. "A Levels-of-Explanation View." In *Psychology and Christianity: Five Views*, edited by Eric L. Johnson, 49–78. Downers Grove, IL: InterVarsity, 2010.

———. *Psychology*. 9th ed. New York: Worth, 2010.

———. *Psychology*. 10th ed. New York: Worth, 2013.

Myers, David G., and Malcolm A. Jeeves. *Psychology through the Eyes of Faith*. Revised and updated edition. San Francisco: Harper SanFrancisco, 2003.

Myers, David G., and Helmut Lamm. "The Group Polarization Phenomenon." *Psychological Bulletin* 83, no. 4 (1976): 602.

National Institute of Mental Health. "Use of Mental Health Services and Treatment among Adults." http://www.nimh.nih.gov/ statistics/ 3USE_MT_ADULT.shtml, accessed August 5, 2013.

Neisser, Ulric. *Cognitive Psychology*. New York: Appleton, 1967.

Nisbett, Richard E., Kaiping Peng, Incheol Choi, and Ara Norenzayan. "Culture and Systems of Thought: Holistic versus Analytic Cognition." *Psychological Review* 108, no. 2, (2001): 291–310. doi:10 .1037/0033–295X.108.2.291.

Norcross, John C. "An Eclectic Definition of Psychotherapy." In *What Is Psychotherapy? Contemporary Perspectives*, edited by J. K. Zeig and W. M. Munion, 218–20. San Francisco: Jossey-Bass, 1990.

Norcross, John C., and Michael J. Lambert. "Psychotherapy Relationships That Work II." *Psychotherapy* 48, no. 1 (2011): 4.

Norcross, John C., Marci S. Mrykalo, and Matthew D. Blagys. "Auld Lang Syne: Success Predictors, Change Processes, and Self-reported Outcomes of New Year's Resolvers and Nonresolvers." *Journal of Clinical Psychology* 58 (2010): 397–405.

Oakes, Lisa M. "Using Habituation of Looking Time to Assess Mental Processes in Infancy." *Journal of Cognition and Development* 11, no. 3 (2011): 255–68.

Ochsner, Kevin N., Silvia A. Bunge, James J. Gross, and John D. Gabrieli. "Rethinking Feelings: An fMRI Study of the Cognitive Regulation of Emotion." *Journal of Cognitive Neuroscience* 14 (2002): 1215–29.

Ogden, Jenni A. *Fractured Minds: A Case-Study Approach to Clinical Neuropsychology*. Oxford: Oxford University Press, 1996.

O'Hara, Ross E., Frederick X. Gibbons, Meg Gerrard, Zhigang Li, and James D. Sargent. "Greater Exposure to Sexual Content in Popular Movies Predicts Earlier Sexual Debut and Increased Sexual Risk Taking." *Psychological Science* 24 (2012): 984–93.

Österlund, M. K., E. Keller, and Y. L. Hurd. "The Human Forebrain Has Discrete Estrogen Receptor α Messenger RNA Expression: High Levels in the Amygdaloid Complex." *Neuroscience* 95, no. 2 (1999): 333–42.

Otten, Sabine, and Gordon B. Moskowitz. "Evidence for Implicit Evaluative In-Group Bias: Affect-Biased Spontaneous Trait Inference in a Minimal Group Paradigm." *Journal of Experimental Social Psychology* 36, no. 1 (2000): 77–89.

Paul, Marla. "Your Memory Is Like the Telephone Game." Northwestern University News (website), September 19, 2012, http:// www.northwestern.edu/newscenter/stories /2012/09/your-memory-is-like-the-tele phone-game.html.

Pearson, Birger A. *Ancient Gnosticism: Traditions and Literature*. Minneapolis: Fortress Press, 2007.

Penton-Voak, I. S., D. I. Perrett, D. L. Castles, T. Kobayashi, D. M. Burt, L. K. Murry, and R. Minamisawa. "Menstrual Cycle Alters Face Preference." *Nature* 399 (1999): 741–42.

Pinker, Steven. *The Blank Slate: The Modern Denial of Human Nature*. New York: Penguin, 2003.

———. "The Brain: The Mystery of Consciousness." *Time*, January 29, 2007, http://www.time.com/time/printout/0,8816 ,1580394,00.html, accessed August 1, 2013.

———. "How to Think about the Mind." *Newsweek*, September 27, 2004, http://pinker.wjh .harvard.edu/articles/media/2004_09_27 _newsweek.html, accessed August 1, 2013.

Plantinga, Cornelius Jr. *Engaging God's World.* Grand Rapids: Eerdmans, 2002.

———. *Not the Way It's Supposed to Be: A Breviary on Sin.* Grand Rapids: Eerdmans, 1995.

Plantinga, Richard J., Thomas R. Thompson, and Matthew D. Lundberg. *An Introduction to Christian Theology.* Cambridge: Cambridge University Press, 2010.

Regan, Dennis T., and Russell Fazio. "On the Consistency between Attitudes and Behavior: Look to the Method of Attitude Formation." *Journal of Experimental Social Psychology* 13 (1977): 28–45.

Riek, Blake M., and Eric W. Mania. "The Antecedents and Consequences of Interpersonal Forgiveness: A Meta-Analytic Review." *Personal Relationships* 19 (2012): 304–25. doi:10.1111/j.1475–6811.2011.01363.x.

Rizzolatti, Giacomo, and Laila Craighero. "The Mirror-Neuron System." *Annual Review of Neuroscience* 27, no. 1 (2004): 169–92.

Roberts, Leanne, Irshad Ahmed, Steve Hall, and Andrew Davison. "Intercessory Prayer for the Alleviation of Ill Health." *Cochrane Database of Systematic Reviews* 2, no. CD000368 (2009). doi:10.1002/14651858 .CD000368.pub3.

Roberts, Robert C. "Parameters of a Christian Psychology." In *Limning the Psyche*, edited by Robert C. Roberts and Mark R. Talbot, 74–101. Grand Rapids: Eerdmans, 1997.

Roese, Neal J., and Kathleen D. Vohs. "Hindsight Bias." *Perspectives on Psychological Science* 7 (2012): 411–26. doi:10.1177/174 5691612454303.

Rogers, Carl. "Notes on Rollo May." *Journal of Humanistic Psychology* 22 (Summer 1982): 8–9.

———. *On Becoming a Person: A Therapist's View of Psychotherapy.* Boston: Houghton Mifflin, 1961.

———. *A Way of Being.* Boston: Houghton Mifflin, 1980.

Rothbart, Mary K. *Becoming Who We Are.* New York: Guilford Press, 2011.

Rousseau, Jean-Jacques. *Emile.* Translated by William H. Payne. New York: D. Appleton and Company, 1892.

Sacks, Oliver. *An Anthropologist on Mars: Seven Paradoxical Tales.* New York: Vintage Books, 1995.

Sagi, Abraham, and Martin L. Hoffman. "Empathic Distress in the Newborn." *Developmental Psychology* 12 (1976): 175–76.

Santrock, John W. *Life-Span Development.* 13th ed. New York: McGraw-Hill, 2011.

Schacter, Daniel L. "Adaptive Constructive Processes and the Future of Memory." *American Psychologist* 67 (2012): 603–13. doi:10.1037/a0029869.

Schacter, Daniel L., Daniel T. Gilbert, and Daniel M. Wegner. *Psychology.* 2nd ed. New York: Worth, 2011.

Schaffer, H. Rudolph. *Social Development.* Cambridge, MA: Blackwell, 1996.

Schore, Allan N. "The Experience-Dependent Maturation of an Evaluative System in the Cortex." In *Brain and Values: Is a Biological Science of Values Possible?*, edited K. H. Pribram, 337–58. Mahwah, NJ: Erlbaum, 1998.

Seligman, Martin E. P. *Authentic Happiness: Using the New Positive Psychology to Realize Your Potential for Lasting Fulfillment.* New York: Free Press, 2002.

Seligman, Martin E. P., Peter Railton, Roy F. Baumeister, and Chandra Sripada. "Navigating into the Future or Driven by the Past." *Perspectives on Psychological Science* 8, no. 2 (2013): 119–41.

Shotter, John. "Getting in Touch: The Metamethodology of a Postmodern Science of Mental Life." *The Humanistic Psychologist* 18, no. 1 (1990): 7–22.

Simons, Daniel J., and Christopher F. Chabris. "Gorillas in Our Midst: Sustained Inattentional Blindness for Dynamic Events." *Perception* 28 (1999): 1059–74.

Simons, Daniel J., and Daniel T. Levin. "Change Blindness." *Trends in Cognitive Sciences* 1 (1997): 261–67.

Skinner, B. F. *Beyond Freedom and Dignity.* New York: Knopf, 1971.

———. "Why I Am Not a Cognitive Psychologist." *Behaviorism* 5, no. 2 (1977): 1–10.

Smallwood, Jonathan, and Jonathan W. Schooler. "The Restless Mind." *Psychological Bulletin* 132 (2006): 946–58.

Smedes, Lewis B. *My God and I: A Spiritual Memoir.* Grand Rapids: Eerdmans, 2003.

Smith, Edward E., and Stephen M. Kosslin. *Cognitive Psychology.* Upper Saddle River, NJ: Pearson Prentice Hall, 2007.

Smith, James K. A. *Desiring the Kingdom.* Grand Rapids: Baker Academic, 2009.

———. *Imagining the Kingdom.* Grand Rapids: Baker Academic, 2013.

Smith, Mary L., and Gene V. Glass. "Meta-Analysis of Psychotherapy Outcome Studies." *American Psychologist* 32, no. 9 (1977): 752.

Smith, Noel W. *Current Systems in Psychology: History, Theory, Research, and Applications.* Belmont, CA: Wadsworth, 2001.

Sroufe, L. Alan. "Attachment and Development: A Prospective, Longitudinal Study from Birth to Adulthood." *Attachment and Human Development* 7, no. 4 (2005): 349–67.

Stanovich, Keith E. *How to Think Straight about Psychology.* 10th ed. Boston: Allyn & Bacon, 2013.

Stanovich, Keith E., and Richard F. West. "Individual Differences in Reasoning: Implications for the Rationality Debate?" *Behavioral and Brain Sciences* 23, no. 5 (October 2000): 645–65.

Steele, Claude M., and Joshua Aronson. "Stereotype Threat and the Intellectual Test Performance of Africa Americans." *Journal of Personality and Social Psychology* 69, no. 5 (1995): 797–811.

Stephen Ministries, "What Is Stephen Ministry?" http://www.stephenministries.org/stephenministry/default.cfm/917, accessed September 3, 2013.

Stroop, J. Ridley. "Studies of Interference in Serial Verbal Reactions." *Journal of Experimental Psychology* 18 (1935): 643–62.

Struthers, William M. *Wired for Intimacy: How Pornography Hijacks the Male Brain.* Downers Grove, IL: InterVarsity, 2009.

Stump, James B. "Non-Reductive Physicalism—A Dissenting Voice." *Christian Scholar's Review* 36:1 (2006): 63–76.

Szasz, Thomas S. *The Myth of Mental Illness: Foundations of a Theory of Personal Conduct.* New York: HarperCollins, 2011.

Tellegen, Auke, David T. Lykken, Thomas J. Bouchard, Kimerly J. Wilcox, Nancy L. Segal, and Stephen Rich. "Personality Similarity in Twins Reared Apart and Together." *Journal of Personality and Social Psychology* 54, no. 6 (1988): 1031–39.

Thomas, Manoj J., and Vicki Morwitz. "Penny Wise and Pound Foolish: The Left-Digit Effect in Price Cognition." *Journal of Consumer Research* 32 (2005): 54–64.

Tjeltveit, Alan C. "Faith, Psychotherapy, and Christian Counseling," In *Science and the Soul: Christian Faith and Psychological Research,* edited by Scott W. VanderStoep, 247–63. Lanham, MD: University Press of America, 2003.

Torrance, Alan J. "What Is a Person?" In *From Cells to Souls—and Beyond: Changing Portraits of Human Nature,* edited by Malcolm A. Jeeves, 199–222. Grand Rapids: Eerdmans, 2004.

Travis, Carol. *Anger, the Misunderstood Emotion.* New York: Simon and Schuster, 1982.

Tulving, Endel. "Episodic and Semantic Memory." In *Organization of Memory,* edited by Endel Tulving and Wayne Donaldson, 381–403. New York: Academic Press, 1972.

Twenge, Jean M., and W. Keith Campbell. *The Narcissism Epidemic: Living in the Age of Entitlement.* New York: Free Press, 2009.

Valenza, Eloisa, Francesca Simion, Viola Macchi Cassia, and Carlo Ulmità. "Face Preference at Birth." *Journal of Experimental Psychology: Human Perception and Performance* 22 (1996): 892–903.

VanderStoep, Scott W. "Psychological Research Methods and Christian Belief." In *Science and the Soul: Christian Faith and Psychological Research,* edited by Scott W. VanderStoep, 97–110. Lanham, MA: University Press of America, 2003.

Van Leeuwen, Mary Stewart. "Personality Theorizing within a Christian World View." In *Man and Mind: A Christian Theory of Personality,* edited by Thomas J. Burke, 171–98. Hillsdale, MI: Hillsdale College Press, 1987.

Vitz, Paul C. "A Christian Theory of Personality: Covenant Theory." In *Man and Mind: A Christian Theory of Personality,* edited by Thomas J. Burke, 199–202. Hillsdale, MI: Hillsdale College Press, 1987.

Volf, Miroslav. *After Our Likeness: The Church as the Image of the Trinity.* Grand Rapids: Eerdmans, 1998.

Warneken, Felix, and Michael Tomasello. "Varieties of Altruism in Children and Chimpanzees." *Trends in Cognitive Sciences* 13, no. 9 (2009): 397–402.

Watson, John B. *Behaviorism*. Rev. ed. Chicago: University of Chicago Press, 1930.

———. *The Corsini Encyclopedia of Psychology and Behavioral Science*. Vol. 4. New York: Wiley, 2002.

Weaver, Glenn D. "Embodied Spirituality: Experiences of Identity and Spiritual Suffering among Persons with Alzheimer's Dementia." In *From Cells to Souls—and Beyond*, edited by Malcolm A. Jeeves, 77–101. Grand Rapids: Eerdmans, 2004.

Webster, Richard. *Why Freud Was Wrong: Sin, Science, and Psychoanalysis*. New York: Basic Books, 1995.

Wegner, Daniel M. "Who Is the Controller of Controlled Processes?" In *The New Unconscious*, edited by Ran R. Hassin, James S. Uleman, and John A. Bargh, 19–36. Oxford: Oxford University Press, 2005.

Whitaker, R. C., and W. H. Dietz. "Role of the Prenatal Environment in the Development of Obesity." *The Journal of Pediatrics* 132, no. 5 (1998): 768–76.

Wilson, Timothy D. *Strangers to Ourselves: Discovering the Adaptive Unconscious*. Cambridge, MA: Harvard University Press, 2002.

Wolpe, Joseph. *The Practice of Behavior Therapy*. 3rd ed. New York: Pergamon Press, 1982.

Wolters, Albert M. *Creation Regained: Biblical Basics for a Reformational Worldview*. Grand Rapids: Eerdmans, 2005.

Wolterstorff, Nicholas. *Reason within the Bounds of Religion*. 2nd ed. Grand Rapids: Eerdmans, 1984.

Wood, Wendy, and David T. Neal, "A New Look at Habits and the Habit-Goal Interface." *Psychological Review* 114, no. 4 (2007): 843–63.

Worthington, Everett L. *Coming to Peace with Psychology*. Downers Grove, IL: InterVarsity, 2010.

Wright, James L. "The Mortal Soul in Ancient Israel and Pauline Christianity: Ramifications for Modern Medicine." *Journal of Religion and Health* 50, no. 2 (2011): 447–71.

Wright, N. T. *After You Believe: Why Christian Character Matters*. New York: HarperOne, 2010.

———. *The Lord and His Prayer*. Grand Rapids: Eerdmans, 1996.

———. "Mind, Spirit, Soul and Body: All for One and One for All—Reflections on Paul's Anthropology in His Complex Contexts." Paper presented at the Society of Christian Philosophers Regional Meeting, Fordham University, Bronx, New York, March 18–19, 2011.

Yannaras, Christos. *The Freedom of Morality*. Translated by Elizabeth Briere. Crestwood, NY: St. Vladimir's Seminary Press, 1984.

Yarhouse, Mark A., Richard E. Butman, and Barrett W. McRay. *The Modern Psychopathologies: A Comprehensive Christian Appraisal*. Downers Grove, IL: InterVarsity, 2005.

Zeskind, Philip S., Laura Klein, and Timothy R. Marshall. "Adults' Perceptions of Experimental Modifications of Durations of Pauses and Expiratory Sounds in Infant Crying." *Developmental Psychology* 28, no. 6 (1992): 1153–62.

Index